BOBBY FISCHER
and his
PREDECESSORS
in the
World Chess Championship

BOBBY FISCHER
and his
PREDECESSORS
in the
World Chess Championship

☆

MAX EUWE

LONDON: G. BELL & SONS LTD

Copyright © 1976 by
G. Bell and Sons, Ltd
York House, Portugal Street
London, WC2A 2HL

ISBN 0 7135 1955 X

Printed in Great Britain by
The Camelot Press Ltd, Southampton

CONTENTS

ACKNOWLEDGMENTS

I am very grateful to Mr Steve Wygle of Columbus, Ohio, for his careful reading of the entire manuscript, for his checking of the accuracy of the scores of the games, and for his valuable suggestions on the organization of the material. I wish to thank my friend and collaborator, Dr Walter Meiden, of the Ohio State University, for his suggestions on presentation and style.

M. Euwe

PREFACE

Fischer's amazing results have staggered the entire chess world. Has Caïssa ever had such a hero? Such a sequence of brilliant successes has seldom occurred in chess history. Between the interzonal tournament in Palma de Mallorca in 1970 and the famous world championship in Reykjavik in 1972, chess fans have witnessed an uninterrupted series of glorious feats by a single player, and the question has arisen: 'Is not Fischer the greatest chess player of all time?'

That question has induced me to write this book.

On a numerical basis, comparisons between contemporary performances and those of long ago are hardly possible, although in the Introduction to this work such an attempt has been made, based on the highly respected and universally accepted rating methods developed by Professor Elo.

However, the question certainly cannot be answered in this way alone. Therefore, I have tried to illustrate certain aspects of Fischer's style and compare them with similar aspects of play of the three most recently deceased world champions. Such comparisons can never be complete. The repertory of favourite openings is changing all the time, the strength of top players varies at different times, and consequently the resistance which the respective world champions had to overcome has not always been the same.

Still, I hope that in this book I give an impression of the strength of certain previous world champions in relation to Fischer's capacities.

It is not possible yet to make any serious comparisons between Fischer and Karpov, who inherited his title in 1975. The writing of this book was in any case nearing completion at the time Karpov assumed the throne.

Comparisons may be possible if and when Fischer resumes tournament play, or when Karpov has been champion sufficiently long for a proper estimate of his true stature to be made.

For these reasons no mention of Karpov is made in this book.

The games of world champions are universally known and, for the most part, thoroughly analysed, usually by more than one master. So the main task was to select and present the games I considered most characteristic of the style of Fischer and his predecessors. Only in a few cases have I been able to mention the names of the original author of a given analysis. In general, the analyses by different masters are similar, and it is often impossible to know who first published a given analysis.

BIBLIOGRAPHY

In the preparation of this book, I have consulted the following works:

Dr S. Tarrasch, *Die moderne Schachpartie*
Weltgeschichte des Schachs, Band 11: Lasker
Weltgeschichte des Schachs, Band 14: Capablanca
Dr M. Euwe and Lod. Prins, *Het Schaakfenomeen Capablanca*
Dr A. Alekhine, *My Best Games of Chess 1924–1937*
A. Kotov, *Schachmatnije rasledie A. Aljěchin*
Dr A. Alekhine and Dr M. Euwe, *Aljěchin–Euwe 1935*
R. G. Wade and K. J. O'Connell, *The Games of Robert Fischer*
R. Fischer, *My Sixty Memorable Games*
H. Kramer and S. H. Postma, *Das Schachphänomen Robert Fischer*
R. Byrne, *Both Sides of the Chessboard*
Dr M. Euwe and J. Timman, *De tweekamp Spasski–Fischer 1972*
Dr M. Euwe and Dr W. Meiden, *Master vs. Master*

INTRODUCTION

One often hears the question: 'Is Fischer the best chess player of all time?' This question is asked because it is natural to wish to compare Fischer with those great players of the past whom he never could have met over the chess board. Any comparisons of Fischer with the present-day grandmasters he has frequently played would certainly be in his favour, not only by reason of the results but also because of the quality of these games.

In this present work we confine our comparison to former world champions. It is much more interesting to compare Fischer with Lasker, Capablanca and Alekhine than with some of the living ex-world champions who have played with Fischer over the board. Although we devote a chapter to such games, we thus deal mainly with those ex-world champions with whom Fischer had no chance to play.

A possible comparison between Botvinnik and Fischer has to be considered more closely. It is a pity that Fischer and Botvinnik met only once over the board. Botvinnik had already retired from practical chess by the time Fischer had reached his full strength. There are arguments for making a comparison of Botvinnik and Fischer in the same way as of the deceased world champions and Fischer, but I prefer to be consistent and restrict the application of the indirect method of comparison only to Capablanca, Alekhine and Lasker. If we made a special case for Botvinnik, why not for Smyslov, who certainly played with Fischer only after he had passed his zenith? And what about Petrosian?

There can never be an absolute comparison between the relative strengths of Fischer and his deceased predecessors, because chess has so many different elements: a player may excel in some while remaining weak in others. We distinguish between various abilities such as combinative power, strategic skill, consistency in handling a given position, all-round capability and so on. All previous champions have excelled in some particular aspect. For instance, Capablanca was a great strategist in the middle game and end game. This does not mean that he was not good at combinative play, but that strategy and positional play were his special fields. A question we might pose would be: 'Who is the greatest positional

player of all time—Capablanca or Fischer?' Similarly we might ask:
'Who is the greatest combinative player of all time—Alekhine or
Fischer?' And 'Who is the greatest all-round player of all time—
Lasker or Fischer?'

I have not included Steinitz in this review, for I number him
among the scientific players. Steinitz handled the game according to
principles which he had logically deduced from the rules valid for
attack and defence in general. I do not think that it makes sense to
compare Steinitz and Fischer in this respect. In the first place
Fischer is a practical player, and he would never—as Steinitz did—
put up with a difficult position for the sole purpose of proving the
correctness of his theory.

Another player left out of consideration is Paul Morphy, the
greatest star of all time, who lived and played before the establish-
ment of the world championship. The most brilliant of Morphy's
games are characterized by the exploitation of the clear misconcep-
tions of his opponents. Clear, seen with our eyes, but Morphy's
great contribution lay in the fact that he discovered these as mis-
conceptions and in this way became the teacher of all later genera-
tions.

It can be seen that it is impossible to say whether Fischer is the
greatest champion of all time. One would have to sum up all factors
and evaluate them in order to reach a comparison and a valid
conclusion, yet these factors are not quantifiable. We can only
quantify results, and these are just what are lacking when comparing
Fischer with his non-living predecessors.

Recently, a method has been developed which enables us to rate
any player, living or dead, according to the results of the games and
which makes possible a comparison of any player with any other
—a feat which, up to now, appeared impossible. I have in
mind the rating system invented and expanded during the past
ten years by Arpad Elo, professor of physics at the University of
Milwaukee.

Many attempts have been made to measure the performances of
chess players in such a way that we can compare the strength of any
two players, irrespective of whether they have participated in the
same contests and even of whether they have ever met at all. The
most important system is Professor Elo's, which has been adopted
by the World Chess Federation.

A rating system seeks to evaluate performances on some scale so
that players may be listed in the probable order of their strength.
Professor Elo has developed his system by statistical method, based
on the normal distribution of performances. This means that the
theory starts from the assumption that the strength of a player is a

variable physical quantity. A player has good days and bad days, good tournaments and bad tournaments. On the average he performs at a certain level. Deviations from this level are normally distributed, just as is the case when you throw dice or study the behaviour of natural processes.

From this basic assumption, using the mathematical theory of probabilities, we derive the basic rule for the rating system: that there is a relationship between the probable performance of two opponents and the difference in their ratings. For example, if player A has a rating which is 100 more than the rating of player B, there is a probability of 64% that he can beat his opponent. (For simplicity's sake the theory only works with wins and losses, a draw being counted as half a win.)

The rating scale thus developed is arbitrary in that the absolute values of the ratings are not important, though the differences between successive ratings are important; the relationship between the strength of two players is defined by the difference between their ratings. The scale can just as well start with, say, Karpov = 1000 or Fischer = 2000. However, as soon as we have established the rating of one player, the ratings of all the others, which are based on their performances, will follow from it in a strictly mathematical way. The variations in the performances of a player will tend to be normal in the long run.

Professor Elo has chosen his scale in such a way that the majority of the international grandmasters have ratings between 2500 and 2700 and the international masters from 2300 to 2500. To give an impression of the ratings we list the position of the 20 leading players on 1 May 1974:

Fischer 2780	Hübner 2615
Karpov 2700	Geller 2610
Korchnoi 2670	Ljubojevic 2605
Spassky 2650	Smyslov 2600
Portisch 2645	Hort 2600
Petrosian 2640	Smejkal 2600
Tal 2635	Kuzmin 2600
Larsen 2630	Byrne 2595
Kavalek 2625	Gligoric 2585
Mecking 2615	Savon 2575

Below is an example, from the Palma de Mallorca tournament, 1969, of the way the Elo system has worked in the past. The original ratings (Ro) are taken from the International rating list issued in the spring of 1969.

Contestant	Old Rating R_0	Game Score W	Expected Score W_e	Difference $W - W_e$	New Rating R_n
Larsen	2630	12·0	10·8	1·2	2640
Petrosian	2650	11·5	11·2	0·3	2650
Hort	2590	10·5	10·2	0·3	2590
Korchnoi	2670	10·5	11·7	−1·2	2660
Spassky	2690	10·0	12·0	−2·0	2670
Del Corral	2420	9·5	5·9	3·6	2460
Mecking	2530	9·0	8·5	0·5	2540
Panno	2530	9·0	8·5	0·5	2540
Najdorf	2590	8·5	9·7	−1·2	2580
Parma	2530	8·5	8·5	0	2530
Szabo	2490	8·0	7·5	0·5	2500
Unzicker	2560	8·0	9·0	−1·0	2550
Pomar	2490	7·5	7·5	0	2490
Bobotsov	2500	6·5	7·8	−1·3	2490
Damjanovic	2440	6·5	6·5	0	2440
Penrose	2500	6·5	7·8	−1·3	2490
Toran	2390	6·0	5·3	0·7	2400
Medina	2380	5·0	5·1	−0·1	2380

The expected scores are rounded to the nearest tenth, and the new ratings to the nearest 10 points (today the scores are rounded to the nearest five points). The meaning of the first two columns is evident. The third column gives the score which would be expected on the basis of the ratings given in the first column. In the fourth column one can see whether the players have performed better or worse than expected.

The fifth column is calculated by adding 10 times the figure in the fourth column to the old rating. The number 10, which we call the numerical coefficient (K), is somewhat arbitrary. The value for the coefficient is dependent on the number of games used for the calculation of the rating. In other words, if player A's rating of 2500 is based on performances in, say, 100 games, this rating has greater reliability than the 2500 rating of player B obtained in 30 games. B's rating should be liable to greater fluctuation than the rating of A.

According to Professor Elo's research, the minimum value for K should be 10 and the maximum about 40. The calculation in the example is based on K = 10, which is fully justified in view of the nature of the participants.

If Del Corral's old rating were based on a small number of

games (say 30), then $K = 40$ would be justified, and his new rating would be $2420 + (40 \times 3\cdot6) = 2564$, rounded to 2560.

So much for Elo's theory as applied to the strength of the present-day players. However, one can go back into the past, since we have tournament tables of practically all events of the last 100 years. Professor Elo has indeed projected his work into the past, and so we can arrive at some really surprising discoveries.

Steinitz started in 1860 with a rating of 2440, and in 1880 he reached his culminating point at 2640. After that his curve gradually decreased to 2610 in 1890 and to 2530 in 1900, the year of his death.

The next world champion, Lasker, started with 2570 in 1888 and went up to 2720 in 1905. Until 1918 his rating remained about 2700, and then it went down, at first slowly and then more rapidly, to 2540 in 1941, the year of his death.

Capablanca started with 2660 in 1906, and his rating went up to 2730 in 1920. Afterwards, it went down to 2630 in 1935, and after that began a slow descent to 2610 in 1940 (Capablanca died in 1942).

Alekhine started with 2520 in 1911 and went up to 2690 in 1930. After 1935 he gradually went down to 2630 in 1945. He died in 1946.

Euwe started in 1922 with 2450 and climbed to 2650 by 1935. He went down slowly to 2600 in 1947, and after that to 2530 in 1974.

Botvinnik started with a rating of 2540 in 1927. He rose to 2730 in 1945 and then went down to 2630 in 1963. Botvinnik's score has not changed much since; in the rating list of 1973 he still stood at 2630.

Smyslov started in 1936 with 2490. He climbed to 2700 in 1953 and then went down to 2610 in 1963. His most recent rating is 2600.

Tal's performances are too variable to give a reliable figure. According to Professor Elo's calculations, his rating in the 1960s was a little over 2600, with jumps in both directions. His most recent rating is 2635.

Petrosian started with 2420 in 1944 and rose to 2690 in 1964. After that his score went down a little and, as one can see from the list, his score is now 2640.

As for Spassky, Professor Elo made no retrospective analysis, so we must restrict ourselves to the following figures: 1970—2680; 1971—2690; 1972—2660; 1973—2655; 1974—2650.

Finally, Fischer's ratings for the same years are: 1970—2720; 1971—2760; 1972—2785; 1973—2780; 1974—2780.

Fischer deserves his high rating by reason of his superb performances in tournaments and in the Candidates' Matches.

It is clear that Fischer's present rating is the highest of all time. We have, of course, no idea of the duration of Fischer's great superiority. Apart from the maximum rating achieved, the duration should also count, and we do not know yet whether Fischer's high rating will be the same ten or twenty years from now, as was the case with Lasker. This still leaves unanswered our question: Who is the best chess player of all time? We should be careful when drawing our conclusions from the figures given for the past. Not all chess events have been evaluated; the accent has been put on the matches, and the figures are rather rough approximations, obtained with inexact methods such as extrapolation.

If we cannot measure the player's absolute strength based on the results of games won and lost, we can still compare Fischer's skill with that of his predecessors and eventually stress the points where Fischer excels or falls behind.

We shall now compare Fischer and the deceased world champions, in the order Capablanca, Alekhine and Lasker; Fischer has most in common with Capablanca, and least with Lasker.

CHAPTER I

CAPABLANCA AND FISCHER

1. GENERAL

To compare two top players of a completely different nature is a difficult task because top players are talented in all fields. Although we may make a comparison with regard to any given quality, such as endgame skill or combinative powers, any attempt at a total comparison must be incomplete.

Capablanca is generally praised as the strategist *par excellence*, the positional player who is able to convert even the smallest advantage into a win. He did this with such ease, such conviction and such accuracy that in the first years of his chess career Capablanca was compared to a chess machine. If we pass in review the multi-faceted series of his games, it appears that positional skill was only one of the high qualities of the Cuban world champion. It is not difficult to present dozens of games in which Capablanca, as an attacking player, mated his opponent on KR2, the most vulnerable square of the K-wing.

Was Capablanca a combinative player too? First we must ask: What do we mean by a combination? Is it just the calculation of a series of successive moves, or a series of branched continuations leading to a certain goal? Both are important, and each one belongs to Capablanca's field. He could calculate long series of moves with astonishing exactitude, and he could also, considering the combination as a whole, carry out strategic combinations, mating combinations, or whatever other specific combinations there might be. The latter kind, the goal-aimed combinations, contain in general a great number of variations, far too many to master, but Capablanca's great intuition filled the gaps where the human mind had to fail. Thus he practically excluded the element of chance which seems so attractive to certain types of players. Fischer, still more than Capablanca, tries to figure out the slightest details in the combination, thus providing a firm foundation for his intuition, which he, too, certainly has.

Capablanca showed a special virtuosity in his treatment of practically closed positions in which to-and-fro manœuvring plays a great part. The treatment of these positions is particularly difficult because on each move one has to calculate in detail the consequences of a breakthrough here or there. Capablanca, who possessed exceptional qualities in the field of exact calculation, usually overwhelmed his opponent in this type of position. It is noteworthy that Fischer, who can also calculate deeply and exactly, very seldom gets into these closed positions. Therefore it is impossible to compare the two world champions in this respect.

Capablanca was certainly not an artist in the field of the openings. In general, his build-up of the position was sound with both White and Black. With the White pieces he often managed to get a small advantage, and with Black he strove for equality. He therefore often got into positions with a drawish character, which might have led to quick draws in other hands. Capablanca, however, succeeded in breathing new life into such apparently dull positions, and it then often happened that his opponent failed.

Capablanca's undistinguished performances in the field of the openings are sometimes explained by his laziness and love of ease. However, another explanation seems to be more correct: at the time when Capa's career started, a serious study of openings had not yet been made; the general opinion was that one could play anything if it was not contrary to the logic and sound principles of chess. Capablanca relied on his genius, and he was right to do so, at any rate in the first part of his successful chess career. In the thirties, however, he met with much more difficult problems in the openings, and it sometimes happened that he was caught in opening traps.

The opening plays quite another role for Fischer, for whom this phase is the first step to victory. The World Champion is unrivalled as an expert on the openings. He plays over every game or article he can get hold of and continually studies opening variations on his pocket chess set. It very seldom happens that Fischer finds himself in a difficult or unfavourable position after the opening. As a rule, Fischer has the better of it in the first phase, and it occurs from time to time that he is able to demolish his opponent quickly with a prepared variation. Thanks also to the gain in time which he attains in the opening, Fischer is seldom short of time. It is very rare that he has to fight against the clock, as so many other top players must do. For that matter, Capablanca, at least in his boom period, had no more trouble with the clock than Fischer. Playing loosely, he produced one blow after the other. Later, when he approached the age of fifty, one could see quite a different Capa at work, anxiously looking at the clock, his head deep in his hands. The years of lightheartedness and geniality were over. Therefore Capablanca's games from the thirties should not be taken as material for comparison. For the same purposes Fischer's first appearances in the international chess arena, his games played before 1960, should be considered of only limited importance.

Capablanca certainly had fighting spirit, but his attempts to win were based not on the characteristics of the position but on his self-confidence. He would be able to find better moves than his opponents, and in this way a hopeless draw would be converted almost automatically into a position offering numerous possibilities.

Fischer's fighting spirit is inborn. His unlimited ambition enables him to develop his full force under all circumstances. Through that spirit he has been able to beat strong opponents by a score of six to nothing and to win tournaments with a lead of three points or more.

In general, Capablanca used his energy more economically and attained what we could call exaggerated results only if there was something special at stake. So, for example, in 1919 he beat Kostic with five to nothing and no draws, just to prove to the chess world that he, Capablanca, and no one else, was the real opponent for the world champion, Lasker. Furthermore, he won the double round-robin master tournament at New York (1927) $2\frac{1}{2}$ points ahead of Alekhine to make clear his superiority over his contemporaries just before he had to play his rival in the world championship match which ended so sadly for Capablanca.

During his period as world champion Capablanca showed less fighting spirit than before. A considerable percentage of his games ended in draws consisting of about 20 moves, sometimes fewer. This happened especially in those games played at the end of a tournament, when the situation could not change very much.

In this respect Fischer has given a far better example to the chess world. His motto is, 'No quick draws; fight to the bitter end!' Fischer's approach means a real breakthrough at the grandmaster level and will save chess for years from the continually returning threat of the so-called 'death by draw'.

In making a fair comparison between Capablanca's and Fischer's capacities, we shall have to restrict ourselves mainly to their ability in the fields of positional play and endings. Fischer's skill in the field of the openings, attacks and combinations will be mentioned only incidentally, but will be shown to their full advantage in other chapters.

Capablanca and Fischer are both matchless in the exploitation of small advantages. They succeed in gradually improving a somewhat better position, and finally they attain the victory. They reach the same results, and yet there is a difference in method. The way in which Capablanca gains the victory seems to be very simple, while Fischer in many cases wins with inventive manœuvring which rightly arouses great admiration.

B

It has never happened that both Capablanca and Fischer found themselves faced with the same technical problems. If so, we could have seen how Capa handled the problem, and how Fischer did. However, even if that had happened nothing could have resulted from such a comparison. If there had only been one way to win, both would certainly have found it. The difference lies in what happened before they got to such a critical position. Capablanca and Fischer both aim for positions which are in harmony with their temperament, and therefore the experiment just suggested is unrealistic.

2. MODEL ENDGAME PERFORMANCE BY CAPABLANCA

We shall restrict a detailed discussion to the most important and most characteristic parts of the game.

Game 1   White: J. R. Capablanca   Havana 1913
                  Black: A. Kupchik   Four Knights' Game

1. P—K4	P—K4	4. B—N5	B—N5
2. N—KB3	N—QB3	5. 0—0	0—0
3. N—B3	N—B3	6. B × N	

One of the characteristics of Capablanca's play: he simplifies in the opening in order to attain a small advantage.

| 6. ... | NP × B | 8. N—Q3 | B × N |
| 7. N × P | Q—K1 | 9. QP × B | Q × P |

Material is equal, but White stands a little better.

10. R—K1	Q—KR5	14. P × B	Q—KN5
11. Q—B3	B—R3	15. B × N	Q × Q
12. B—B4	QR—B1	16. P × Q	P × B
13. B—K5	B × N		

White has a small advantage: Black's RPs are both vulnerable and besides his BPs are doubled. White also has weak Pawns, it is true, but since White is a little better developed he can press and attack first. His weaknesses will play a role only in the final phase of the game, the 'catch as catch can' phase.

17. R—K4   KR—K1   18. QR—K1

In these endgames of four Rooks one must never allow a hostile R to penetrate along the seventh rank. Therefore 18. R—QR4 would not be good on account of 18 ... R—K7

18. ...	R—K3	21. K—K2	K—K2
19. QR—K3	QR—K1	22. R—QR4	
20. K—B1	K—B1		

Only now can White start his attacking manœuvres.

22. ...   R—QR1   23. R—R5   P—Q4

Preventing White's R—K4 (and R—QR4) at a given moment

24. QP—B4   K—Q3   25. P—B5ch

Closes the position without, however, limiting White's possibilities on the Q-wing, as we shall see later. It is noteworthy that Capablanca often makes use of the opportunity to block the pawns, which he does to limit his opponent's possibilities.

| 25. ... | K—Q2 | 27. R × R | P × R |
| 26. P—Q4 | P—B4 | | |

After 27. ... K × R things would have been easier: 28. R—R6, K—Q2; 29. K—K3 and 30. K—B4.

28. P—B4   K—B1   29. K—Q2   K—N2

This frees the Rook, which could now penetrate into the hostile position.

30. R—R3   R—KN1   31. R—R3

The real struggle has started. Black is at the parting of the ways: defence or counterattack.

31. ...   R—N2?

In general, in Rook endings the counterattack is preferable. Probably Black had expected he could hold out by a passive attitude. It is doubtful whether White would have won this ending if Black had chosen the right continuation. Below are some possibilities.

31. ... R—N8; 32. R × P, R—N8 (better than 32. ... R—QR8; 33. R—R3, R × P; 34. R—N3ch, K—B1; 35. P—R4); 33. P—KR4 (33. K—B3, R—KB8; 34. R—R6, R × P; 35. R × P. R × BP leads to a drawn position), 33. ... R × Pch; 34. K—K3, R × RP; 35. K—B3 (in order to go to KN2, thus preventing the Black Rook from coming behind White's KRP) 35. ... P—R4; 36. P—R5, P—R5.

(1) 37. P—R6

    (a) 37 ... P—R6?; 38. R × Pch, K × R; 39. P—R7 and wins

    (b) 37. ... R—R8; 38. K—N2, R—QN8 (parries the threat
        39. R × Pch); 39. R—N7, P—R6
        40. P—R7 (40. R—N3, P—R7 and White can certainly not
        win)
        40. ... P—R7; 41. P—R8 = Q, P—R8 = Q
        Again: White is not better off than Black.

(2) 37. R—N7

    (a) 37. ... R—R6ch?; 38. K—N2, R—N6; 39. P—R6, P—R6;
        40. P—R7, P—R7; 41. P—R8 = Q, P—R8 = Q; 42. Q—Q8,
        Q—R4; 43. R—N8 wins

    (b) 37. ... R—R8!; 38. K—N2, R—QN8; 39. R—N3, R—N6;
        40. P—R6, R × Rch; 41. P × R, P—R6; 42. P—R7, P—R7;
        43. P—R8 = Q, P—R8 = Q; 44. Q—K5. The Queen ending is
        a little better for White but not won.

32. K—K2   K—R3

Now 32. ... R—N8 would have lost, because the White King has gained a tempo.

| **33. R—R6** | **R—K2** | | **35. P—KR4**   (see diagram) |
| **34. K—Q3** | **K—N2** | | |

This is the beginning of the systematic way to the win. White now plans: R—R5, R—N5, P—R5, P—R6 and R—N7

| **35. ...** | **K—B1** | **37. R—N5** | **R—B2** |
| **36. R—R5** | **K—Q2** | **38. K—B3** | |

The Black King is too near for White to carry out the plan mentioned, e.g. 38. P—R5, K—K2; 39. P—R6, R—B3; 40. R—N7ch, R—B2.

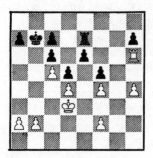

(Position after White's 35th move)
With the text White intends to force the Black King back to the Queenside:

38. ... K—B1
Black cannot permit the White King to walk to his QR6

39. K—N4 R—B3
Black is ready to answer 40. P—R5 by 40. ... R—R3. This means that White's primary plan is out of the question. White soon comes up with a new concept.

40. K—R5 K—N2   **41. P—R4**
Advance of the Q-side Pawns

41. ... P—QR3   **42. P—R5**
This move was necessary anyhow.

42. ... R—R3   **44. P—N5 RP × P**
43. P—N4 R—B3   **45. P × P**

The threat is now: 46. R—N7 and 47. P—N6. If Black plays 45. ... R—B2 White wins easily: 46. P—R6, R—B3 (forced);

47. R—N7, P × P; 48. K × P, R × P; 49. P—B6ch, K—N1; 50. R—
N8ch, K—R2; 51. R—QB8, etc.

It should further be remarked that 45. ... P × P; 46. K × P,
P—B3ch does not facilitate Black's play, since the seventh rank is
freed for the White Rook.

45. ...   R—B1

In order to drive back the White King.

46. R—N7   R—QR1ch   47. K—N4   P × P

White threatened 48. P—N6.

48. K × P   R—R7   50. R × RP
49. P—B6ch   K—N1

50. R—N8ch, K—R2; 51. R—QB8 would not work on account of
51. ... R—N7ch; 52. K—B5, R—B7ch; 53. K—N5, R—N7ch;
54. K—R4, K—N3, etc.

50. ...   R—N7ch   52. K—N4   R × P
51. K—R5   R—R7ch   53. R—K7   R × P

If 53. ... R—KR7 then 54. R × KP, R × P; 55. K—B5, etc. If
Black had not given the check on his 51st move then the White King
would be placed on R5 and White would have won (after 53. ...
R—KR7) by 54. R × KP, R × P; 55. R—K8ch, K—R2; 56. R—QB8.

54. P—R6   R × Pch   55. K—N5   R—Q8

or 55. ... R—R5; 56. P—R7 (threatening 57. R—K8ch); 56. ...
K—R2; 57. R × Pch, etc.

56. P—R7   R—N8ch

Black's last try.

57. K—B5	**R—B8ch**	**63. R × R**	**K—N3**
58. K—Q4	**R—Q8ch**	**64. K × P**	**K × P**
59. K—K5	**R—K8ch**	**65. K × P**	**K—B4**
60. K—B6	**R—KR8**	**66. K—K5**	**P—B3**
61. R—K8ch	**K—R2**	**67. R—R6**	**K—N4**
62. P—R8Q	**R × Q**	**68. K—Q4**	Black resigns.

3. MODEL ENDGAME BY FISCHER

Game 2   *White:* R. Fischer   Sicilian Defence
                  Black: M. Taimanov

1. P—K4	**P—QB4**	**4. N × P**	**Q—B2**
2. N—KB3	**N—QB3**	**5. N—QB3**	**P—K3**
3. P—Q4	**P × P**		

This system is known as the Taimanov variation, one of the main points of which is to bring the Black KB into the open field rather than hiding it on K2 behind the QP.

6. P—KN3   P—QR3

Necessary: after 6. ... N—B3; 7. KN—N5, Q—N1; 8. B—KB4 Black is in trouble.

7. B—N2	N—B3	9. Q × N	B—B4
8. 0—0	N × N		

In accordance with the aim of this variation the KB is brought out.

10. B—B4!

A well-known riposte. The openings theory states that after 10. ... B × Q; 11. B × Q, B × N; 12. P × B, P—Q4; 13. P × P, N × P; 14. B—K5, White is a little better off.

10. ...   P—Q3   11. Q—Q2   P—R3

This move is important to prevent B—N5 in one of the next few moves.

12. Q—RQ1   P—K4

Forced.

13. B—K3   B—KN5   14. B × B

After 14. P—B3, B × Bch; 15. Q × B, B—K3 Black has a solid position; his only weak spot (Q3) can easily be defended.

14. ...	P × B	16. P—B4	R—Q1
15. P—B3	B—K3		

Or 16. ... 0—0; 17. Q—Q6, Q—RB1; 18. P—B5 with some positional advantages for White.

17. N—Q5	B × N	19. KR—K1	
18. P × B	P—K5		

Boleslavsky gives a pretty variation. After 19. P—Q6, Q—N3!; 20. KR—K1, 0—0; 21. B × P, P—B5ch; 22. K—B1, N × B; 23. R × N, Q—B3; 24. Q—Q5, R × P! and Black equalizes.

19. ...	R × P	23. Q × Qch	K × Q
20. R × Pch	K—Q1	24. R—K5	P—QN3
21. Q—K2	R × Rch	25. B—B1	
22. Q × Rch	Q—Q2		

White forces Black's Queenside Pawns to go to Black squares in order to get an open route for his king (Q3—QB4—QN5), which later in the game appears to be decisive.

25. ...   P—QR4

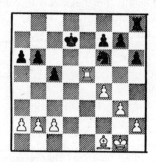

Black's position is vulnerable, which appears most clearly from the fact that the text is forced, e.g. 25. ... R—R1 would cost a Pawn after 26. B—B4 (26. ... N—N5; 27. R—K2).

26. B—B4	**R—B1**	**28. K—B3**	**N—Q2**
27. K—N2	**K—Q3**		

The Knight would be best posted at QB2 or Q3, but for the moment Black cannot reach this square since 28. ... N—K1 is refuted by 29. B × P!.

29. R—K3	**N—N1**	**30. R—Q3ch**	**K—B2**

After 30. ... K—K2; 31. B—N5! the Black Knight is locked in, which could lead to a quick catastrophe: 31. ... R—Q1?; 32. R × R, K × R; 34. K—K4, N—Q2; 35. B × N, K × B; 36. K—Q5, with an easy win for White.

31. P—B3

To take away the Q5 square from the Knight.

31. ...	**N—B3**	**33. P—QR4**	
32. R—K3	**K—Q3**		

To fix the line of march (already mentioned) for the White King.

33. ...	**N—K2**	**34. P—R3**	**N—B3**

Black's great handicap is that his N cannot reach the Q3 square without allowing the White R to enter via the seventh rank. E.g. 34. ... N—B1; 35. P—R4 and then:

(1) 35. ... K—B2; 36. P—N3, N—Q3; 37. R—K7ch.

   (a) 37. ... K—B3; 38. B—Q3. Black is even more helpless than before.

   (b) 37. ... K—Q1; 38. R—R7, N × B; 39. P × N, P—N3; 40. P—B5 and White can go into a won Pawn ending at any time.

(2) 35. . . . K—Q2; 36. B—N5ch, K—B2; 37. P—KN4, R—Q1;
   38. B—K8, N—Q3?; 39. R—K7ch and 40. B × P.
Still, 34. . . . N—B1 might have offered better opportunities for a
draw.

35. P—R4   P—R4

This leads almost automatically to the Pawn structure that will arise
later: all the Pawns on the wrong colour (the colour of the hostile
Bishop). On the other hand, Black could not allow White's P—R5,
which paralyses Black's Kingside and would afford White a second
line of march to Black's interior position.

36. R—Q3ch   K—B2   37. R—Q5   P—B4

37. . . . P—N3 would have given White more problems. However, it
was difficult to see how White could proceed at all. What is White
aiming at? We shall soon see.

38. R—Q2   R—B3   41. B—N5   R—Q3
39. R—K2   K—Q2   42. K—K2
40. R—K3   P—N3

This is the starting-point of a closer examination. From the ending
R + B against R + N three types of simplified endings can arise:
1 Pawn ending after the exchange of Rooks, Bishop and Knight.
2 Rook ending after the exchange of Bishop against Knight.
3 Bishop *vs* Knight ending after the exchange of Rooks.

1 PAWN ENDING

We presume a hypothetical continuation (from the diagram):
42. . . . K—B2; 43. R—Q3, R × R?; 44. K × R, K—Q3?; 45. B × N,
K × B; 46. K—B4.
   This ending is a win for White: 46. . . . . K—B2; 47. K—N5,
K—N2; 48. P—B4, K—B2; 49. K—R6, K—B3; 50. K—R7,

K—B7; 51. P—N3! (the deciding tempo), 51. . . . K—B3; 52. K—N8, etc.

This means that if the White K can come to his B4 square when the Black K is on his B3, White wins the Pawn ending. However, if the Black K can reach his Q4 square in time, the result is a draw.

In his 43rd move Black should have played 43. . . . K—Q2; 44. R × Rch, K × R; 45. K—Q3, N—K2, thus avoiding the hopeless pawn ending.

2 ROOK ENDING

After 42. . . . K—B2 (from the diagram); 43. B × N, K × B; 44. R—K7, White's prospects look favourable; Black has nothing better than to move his R on the third rank. However, there is no win: 44. . . . R—B3; 45. R—KN7, R—K3ch; 46. K—Q3, R—Q3ch; 47. K—B4, R—K3; 48. P—QN4?, BP × P; 49. P × P, P × P; 50. K × P, R—K5ch and 51. . . . R—K6ch. White can only lose this ending.

Conclusion: in the Rook ending there are very few prospects for White.

3 BISHOP VS KNIGHT

If instead of White's last move before the diagram (42. K—K2) White had played 42. R—Q3, he could have forced the Bishop *vs* Knight ending. However, after 42. . . . R × Rch; 43. B × R, N—Q1!; 44. B—B4, K—K2; 45. B—Q5 (to prevent the manœuvre N—N2—Q3); 45. . . . K—Q3; 46. B—N8, K—K2 (now 46. . . . N—N2; 47. B—B7 would cost a Pawn); 47. K—K3, N—N2; 48. K—Q3, N—Q3.

Nothing further can be done: the White King cannot penetrate, and even if White should succeed in carrying through P—QN4, Black is not forced to exchange. The Black Pawns maintain their places on QR4 and QB4, and nothing can happen.

White's problem is clearly: how to exchange Rooks without allowing the Black Knight to come to Q3. The continuation shows White's solution. (From the diagram)

42. . . . K—Q1   43. R—Q3!

It makes a great difference that in this case the King can take back and the Bishop can keep control over the line QN5—K8.

43. . . . K—B2

The same principle. After the exchange of Rooks, Black wants to have his King near the battlefield.

44. R × R   K × R   45. K—Q3

45. B × N, K × B; 46. K—Q3, K—Q4 leads to a draw. White is forced to drive back the Black K by 47. P—B4ch, and then everything is blocked.

45. ...   N—K2

White threatened to win by 46. B × N, K × N; 47. K—B4, as shown previously. Black could not play 45. ... N—Q1, because this would immediately cost a Pawn after 46. B—K8.

46. B—K8   K—Q4   48. K—B4   K—B3
47. B—B7ch   K—Q3   49. B—K8ch

The bishop is very powerful: it ties the Black N to its place, and it supports the march of the White K by continuing to drive away the Black K.

49. ...   K—N2   50. K—N5

It looks as if White has already attained his goal: the Black N cannot move and so the Black K is compelled to give free way to his White counterpart.

50. ...   N—B1!

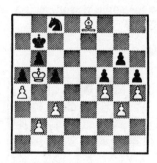

Threatens 51. ... N—Q3 mate.

51. B—B6ch   K—B2

51. ... K—R2 is also answered by 52. B—Q5, N—K2; 53. B—B3 and the N must move, after which the White K can penetrate via B6. If Black plays 52. ... N—Q3ch (instead of 52. ... N—K2) then 53. K—B6, N—K5; 54. B—B7 leads to a variation which is discussed in the comment on the next move.

52. B—Q5   N—K2

Interesting is 52. ... N—Q3ch; 53. K—R6, N—K5; 54. B—B7, N × NP; 55. B × P, K—B3; 56. B—K8ch, K—B2; 57. K—N5 and then

(1) 57. ... N—K7; 58. B×P, N×P; 59. B—B7, N—R6; 60.
     P—R5, N—N4; 61. B—N8, P—B5; 62. K—B4, P—B6;
     63. K—Q3 and wins
(2) 57. ... K—Q1; 58. B—B6, K—B2; 59. B—B3 and Black is
     in zugzwang. He must either give up his KRP or lose all his
     Queenside Pawns.

53. B—B7   K—N2   54. B—N3
The beginning of a new series of manœuvres.

54. ...   K—R2   56. B—B3ch   K—B2
55. B—Q1   K—N2   57. K—R6
This immobilizes the Black King. Now the N has to move, and this
enables the B to enter the hostile position once more.

57. ...   N—N1   58. B—Q5   N—K2
58. ... N—B3; 59. B—B7, N—K5; 60. B×P, N×P; 61. B—K8,
K—Q1; 62. B—B6, K—B2; 63. B—B3 has about the same consequences as the variations given under Black's 52nd move.

59. B—B4   N—B3   60. B—B7   N—K2
Repetition of moves for some reason such as time trouble, uncer-
tainty, or psychology.

61. B—K8   K—Q1

Seemingly White has attained nothing (62. B—B7, K—B2), but the
dénouement is near.

62. B×P!   N×B   63. K×NP
White has two Pawns for his piece and at least one more to come.
The following series of moves had to be calculated very accurately.
One tempo more or less can make the difference between victory and
defeat.

63. ...   **K—Q2**   **65. P—QN4**
64. K × BP   **N—K2**

White's K stays in its place to prevent the Black N from quickly attacking White's KNP (square Q4 is inaccessible for the Black N).

65. ...   **P × P**   **68. P—N5**   **N—K5ch**
66. P × P   **N—B1**   **69. K—N6**   **K—B1**
67. P—R5   **N—Q3**

If 69. ... N × P then 70. P—R6, and the Pawn cannot be stopped.

70. K—B6   **K—N1**

Or 70. ... N × P; 71. P—R6, K—N1 (White threatened 72. P—R7); 72. P—N6, N—K7; 73. P—R7ch, K—R1; 74. P—N7ch, K × RP; 75. K—B7, etc.

71. P—N6   Black resigns

There could have followed: 71. ... N—B6; 72. P—R6, K—R8; 73. P—R7 (not 73. K—B7 on account of 73. ... N—Q4ch). Now, however, Black is again in zugzwang. He has to play 73. ... N—R5; 74. P—N7ch (74. K—B7?, N × P; 75, K × N stalemate) 74. ... K × P; 75. K—B7 and wins.

Anyone who has studied these two games will notice a remarkable difference. It was not easy to find the win in either of the games, but the manner in which Capablanca gained the victory was clear and simple. Fischer's path to victory consisted of a system of complicated manœuvres, difficult to understand and still more difficult to find. Certainly Capablanca's task was not the same as Fischer's, but as has been noted, the positions into which one lands depend on one's style.

Capablanca's play gives the impression of simplicity, not only in this but in practically all his endings. One is even inclined to think that chess is easy, and that everyone could play like Capablanca. However, there is a great gap between understanding what to do and doing it yourself.

The same ease which we have seen in the Capablanca–Kupchik game and which is characteristic of the Cuban champion can be witnessed below under the title 'Top performances'.

Fischer too is recognizable in his top games, which really are exquisite examples of how to exploit positional advantage. Capablanca and Fischer are both experts in strategy, but they differ in the manner in which they obtain the advantage. Fischer owes this mostly to his superior theoretical knowledge, and Capablanca to his fine manœuvring, adorned here and there with sharp little combinations.

4. TOP PERFORMANCES BY CAPABLANCA

Game 3 White: F. J. Marshall   23rd (last) Match Game, New York
   Black: J. R. Capablanca   1909
                                              Queen's Gambit, Tarrasch
                                                              Variation

**1. P—Q4, P—Q4; 2. P—QB4, P—K3; 3. N—QB3, P—QB4;
4. P × QP, KP × P; 5. N—B3, N—QB3; 6. P—KN3, B—K3; 7.
B—N2, B—K2; 8. 0—0, N—B3; 9. B—N5, N—K5.**
Capablanca had a preference for simplifying manœuvres in the
opening, especially when he had Black.

**10. B × B, Q × B; 11. N—K5, N × QP; 12. N × N, P × N; 13. P—
K3, N—B6ch; 14. N × N, P × N; 15. Q × P, 0—0.**

The situation is now clear: White has one Pawn more on the Kingside, Black on the Queenside. It is well known that the majority on
the Queenside weighs heavier unless the opponent has possibilities
to start an attack by advancing his Kingside Pawns. Evidently this is
not the case here. The Black K-wing does not offer any targets and
the White pieces are few in number, and also badly placed for a
Kingside attack. Black, then, possesses a clear positional advantage
with the majority of Pawns on the Queenside. Capablanca exploits this
advantage in a marvellous and instructive way.

16. KR—B1(?)
It is easy to see that 16. Q × NP does not solve White's problem.
After 16. ... Q × Q; 17. B × Q, Q—RN1; 18. B—B3, R × P,
Black has two advantages: a powerful passed Pawn and the seventh
rank for his R. Given that chances for a Kingside attack were not very
great, White should at least have tried to build an attack by moves
such as P—K4, Q—K3, P—B4—B5, P—K5, etc. As White actually
plays, he goes down without counter chances.

16. ...   QR—N1   18. R—B3(?)
17. Q—K4   Q—B2

Perhaps 18. P—QR4 would have been a little better in order to exchange one of the Queenside Pawns. After 18. ... P—B5; 19. P—R5, P—N4; 20. P × P *e.p.*, P × P White's QR would have been more active than in the text.

18. ...   P—QN4

The pawn majority starts rolling.

19. P—QR3   P—B5   20. B—B3(?)

Faulty judgment. The Q-file is more important than the QB-file. It will appear later that along the Q-file a Black R will deal the deciding blow. Therefore, correct would have been 20. R—Q1, KR—Q1; 21. R(3)—B1. Black could have continued by P—QR4 and P—N5, but he would certainly have met with greater difficulties. It is noteworthy that 20. P—N3 would be answered by 20. ... Q—R4; 21. P—QN4, and Black has a strong, protected passed pawn.

20. ...   KR—Q1   22. B × R   R—Q1
21. R—Q1   R × Rch

Takes possession of the Q-file.

23. B—B3

With 23. B—B2, P—N3 White does not attain anything, and his R would be in a very cramped position.

23. ...   P—N3

Before the Black R leaves the first rank, Black has to open a flight square for his King: 23. ... R—Q7 would lead to nothing after 24. Q—R8ch (24. R—B2 is good too). Moreover, the text contains a hidden threat: 24. ... B—Q4; 25. Q—N4, P—KR4 gaining material.

24. Q—B6   Q—K4

Exchange of Queens would have given White a tempo. Black now threatens to win a Pawn by 25. ... R—Q7.

25. Q—K4

White has nothing better: 25. R—B2 would be answered by 25. ... B—B4 and then 26. R—K2 fails against 26. ... R—Q8ch; 27. K—N2, B—Q6. Further, 26. P—K4 (instead of 26. R—K2) fails against 26. ... B—R6 and 27. ... Q—Q5!

25. ...   Q × Q   26. B × Q   R—Q8ch

Keeps the White K as far as possible from the Queenside. If the K could have come to his K2, things would not have been so easy for Black.

It is clear that 26. ... R—Q7; 27. R—B2 would have produced no immediate result. Exchange of Rooks would have considerably improved White's chances to draw.

27. K—N2 P—QR4
Continuation of the advance. White has no counters whatsoever.

28. R—B2 P—N5   **30. B—B3 R—QN8**
29. P × P P × P

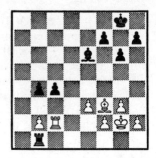

The decision draws nearer. Black threatens. 31. ... P—N6; 32. R—Q2, R—QB8; 33. B—K4, P—B4; or 33. B—Q1, P—B6 as in the game.

31. B—K2 P—N6
This is possible because 32. R—B3, R × P; 33. B × P is refuted by 33. ... R—B7!.

32. R—Q2 R—QB8
With the deadly threat of 33. ... R—B7.

33. B—Q1
White has nothing better.

33. ... P—B6
Wins a piece for two Pawns.

34. P × P P—N7   **35. R × P R × B**
Quite a new situation has been created: Bishop *vs* two Pawns. This advantage sometimes contains many difficulties for the stronger side but here the win is relatively easy because Black's pieces are very well placed. Capablanca shows how to make the best use of his superior position.

36. R—B2 B—B4!
A simple manœuvre to drive the White R from his best place, behind the passed Pawn.

37. R—N2   R—QB8
All very simple. The White QBP is no longer dangerous.

38. R—N3   B—K5ch   39. K—R3
Forced: 39. P—B3, R—B7ch would cost a Pawn.

39. ...   R—B7   40. P—KB4   P—R4!
Leads to the gain of a Pawn which makes White's position quite hopeless.

41. P—N4
Black threatened 41. ... B—B4ch; 42. K—R4?, R × Pch; 43. K—N5, K—N2 and mate will soon follow.

41. ...   P × Pch   43. R—N4   P—B4ch
42. K × P   R × RP
Leads to the win of another Pawn.

44. K—N3   R—K7   46. K—R4
45. R—B4   R × Pch
With 46. K—R2, R—B6 Black captures the KBP. After the text the White K gets into a mating net.

46. ...   K—N2   48. R—Q7   B—N7!
47. R—B7ch   K—B3
Threatens mate (49. ... R—R6)

49. R—Q6ch   K—N2
White resigns. He cannot stop the mate after 50. ... R—R6ch; 51. K—N5, R—R4 mate.

Game 4   *White:* J. R. Capablanca   Berlin 1928
            Black: A. Rubinstein   Queen's Gambit Reversed

1. P—Q4, P—Q4; 2. N—KB3, P—QB4; 3. P × P, P—K3; 4. P—K4, B × P; 5. P × P, P × P; 6. B—N5ch, N—QB3; 7. 0—0, KN—K2; 8. QN—Q2, 0—0; 9. N—N3, B—N3; 10. R—K1, B—N5; 11. B—Q3 (threatens 12. B × Pch), **11. ... N—N3; 12. P—KR3, B × N; 13. Q × B, QN—K4; 14. Q—B5, N × B; 15. Q × N, P—Q5** (15. ... Q—B3 would be preferable); **16. B—Q2, Q—B3; 17. R—K4, QR—Q1; 18. QR—K1** (threatens 19. B—N4, winning the exchange), **18. ... Q—B3; 19. P—N3, KR—K1; 20. B—R5** (simplification to make the defence of Black's QP more difficult for him), **20. ... R × R; 21. Q × R, N—B1; 22. Q × Q, P × Q; 23. R—K7, R—Q4** (preferable is 23. ... P—Q6); **24. B × B, P × B**

c

White has a considerable advantage; however, perfect technique is needed to exploit this advantage and convert it into a win. White has a Rook on the seventh rank which enables him to attack the Black Pawns from the rear. This type of attack must be carried out very carefully, otherwise it will prove barren.

It is remarkable that if at this stage Black had had his KNP on N3 he could easily have held the game. Such details may sometimes decide the battle.

25. R—N7
Pawn hunting has started.

25. ... N—Q2   26. R—B7
The order of moves is most important in this phase of the ending. If White had played 25. R—B7 first, then things would have been quite different after 25. ... R—Q3; 26. R—N7, N—Q2; 27. N—Q2, P—QN4; 28. N—K4, P—Q6!; 29. P × P, R × P; 30. N—B5, R—Q8ch; 31. K—N2, N—B1, when Black has good chances to draw.

26. ... R—Q3
26. ... P—QB4; 27. R—B8ch, N—B1; 28. R—N8, R—Q3; 29. N—Q2 leads with transposition of moves to the game.

27. R—B8ch
It is most important to give this check before Black has opened a gap.

27. ... N—B1
Now the Black N is not only passive but also vulnerable.

28. N—Q2 P—QB4
It seems odd that Rubinstein does not take the opportunity to simplify the game by 28. ... P—Q6; 29. P × P, R × P. However, there would follow: 30. N—B4, P—QN4; 31. N—K5, R—Q7; 32. N × QBP, P—N3 (32. ... R × NP?; 33. N—K7ch); 33. P—QN4!, R × RP; 34. R—N8 and White must win—although perhaps not so easily.

Rubinstein, who is a great expert in the field of endings, has an escape in mind which might have eluded the attention of players less capable than Capablanca (compare the next diagram).

29. N—B4   R—K3   31. K—N2   P—KN4
30. R—N8   R—K8ch

It is necessary to create the gap immediately. After 31. .... R—QR8; 32. N × P, it would have been too late (32. .... P—N3; 33. N—Q7).

32. P—QR4!

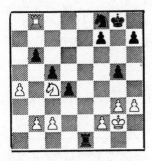

Black had hoped for the obvious 32. N × P, K—N2, and now it is difficult for White to defend his QBP, whose loss would give Black a dangerous advanced passed Pawn. Certainly White already has a passed Pawn himself, but mutual threats often lead to simplification and drawn positions; e.g. 33. P—QR4, R—QB1; 34. P—R5, N—K3; and now 35. P—R6? would cost a Pawn after 35. .... R—QR8 (36. R—QR8, N—B2). White must find something else, such as 36. N—Q7. After 36. .... R × P; 37. P—R6, P—Q6; 38. P—R7, P—Q7; 39. P—R8 = Q, P—Q8 = Q, Black has at least a draw.

With the text Capablanca follows a much safer way to assure himself of the win. Consider (from the previous diagram):

(1)   32. .... R—QB8; 33. N—R3!, P—B5; 34. R × P, P—Q6; 35. P × P, P × P; 36. R—Q6, R—Q8; 37. P—R5, N—K3; 38. P—R6, N—B2; 39. P—R7, K—N2; 40. R—Q7, N—R8; 41. R—Q8, P—Q7; 42. K—B3, R—QB8; 43. R × P, R—B2; 44. N—N5, R—N2; 45. R—Q8, etc.

(2)   32. .... R—K7; 33. N × P (now 33. N—R3 would have been bad on account of 33. .... P—Q6; 34. P × P, R × QNP), 33. .... K—N2 (White threatened 34. N—Q7); 34. P—R5, R × QBP; 35. P—R6, P—Q6 (35. .... N—K3; 36. P—R7, N—B2; 37. R—B8, etc.); 36. P—R7, P—Q7; 37. P—R8 = Q, P—Q8 = Q; 38. R × N and White wins, since 38. .... R × Pch; 39. K × R does not lead to perpetual check.

(3) 32. ... K—N2; 33. R×P, N—K3 (33. ... R—K7 or
      33. ... R—QB8; 34. N—R3, etc.); 34. P—R5, N—B2;
      35. P—R6. White has no difficulties, since 35. ... R—QR8
      is answered by 36. N—R3.

32. ...   R—QR8   33. N × P K—N2
Necessary in view of 34. N—Q7.

34. R—B8 N—K3   35. N—Q7
White gives up his QRP in exchange for Black's QBP.

35. ...   R × P   36. N × P R—N5
36. ... N × N; 37. R × N would not have given drawing chances
either and 36. ... R—B5? was impossible on account of 37. N ×
Nch.

37. N—Q3

After 37. N × Nch?, P × N; 38. R—B7ch, K—B3; 39. P—N3,
P—Q6! Black would reach a drawn position.

White has now consolidated his advantage and a new phase starts.
White has a plus Pawn for which Black has no compensation
whatsoever. On the contrary, Black still has weaknesses in his Pawn
position which White will now try to exploit. This does not seem very
easy because of the strong central position of the Black N. However,
Capablanca manages the job in the simplest way.

37. ...   R—N4   39. P—QN4! P—R4
38. K—B3 P—R3
This move contains a resourceful threat: 40. ... P—N5ch; 41. P × P,
N—N4ch; 42. K—B4, N—K3ch; 43. K—B3, K—N4ch and the
White K has to withdraw: 44. K—N2 (or K—K2), P × P; 45.
R—B4 (as in the game), 45. ... N—B6, and a fresh struggle starts.

40. P—N4
Parries the threat.

40. ...	P × Pch	42. R—B4!	K—B2
41. P × P	P—B3	43. N—B5!	

White's 39th, 42nd and 43rd moves make up a fine manœuvre which leads to the capture of Black's QP.

43. ... N—Q1

43. ... N × N; 44. P × N, R—N2; 45. P—B6, R—QB2; 46. K—K4 would have been just as hopeless.

44. N—N3

Not 44. R × P, N—B3, with the recapture of one Pawn.

Black resigns. Even Rubinstein could not give Capablanca a handicap of two Pawns.

The way in which Capablanca has transformed his positional into material advantage is exemplary, taking into account the fact that he had to be continually on his guard all the time against the opponent's clever attempts to lead the play into the paths of drawn endings.

Game 5   *White:* Ed. Lasker   New York 1915
                 Black: J. R. Capablanca   Manhattan Variation
                                              (of the Queen's Gambit)

1. P—Q4, P—Q4; 2. N—KB3, N—KB3; 3. P—B4, P—K3; 4. N—B3, QN—Q2; 5. B—N5, B—N5; 6. P—K3, P—B4; 7. B—Q3, Q—R4; 8. Q—N3, N—K5; 9. 0—0, N × B; 10. N × N, P × QP; 11. N—N5, (11. P(3) × P would cost a piece after 11. ... P × P; 12. ... B × N and 13. ... Q × N), **11. ... N—B4; 12. Q—B2, N × B; 13. Q × N, P—QR3** (13. ... P × KP to keep the plus Pawn would have been risky; the open KB file may become strong). **14. N × QP, P × P; 15. Q × P, B—Q2; 16. N—N3, Q × N; 17. Q × B, B—B3** (White is already in trouble); **18. P—K4, P—QR4!; 19. Q—Q2** (if 19. Q—B4 then 19. ... B—N4 and if 19. Q—Q4 then 19. ... R—Q1) **19. ... Q × Q; 20. N × Q, 0—0—0!**

Black has a small advantage: his B is better than the White N. Capablanca, through skilful play, will show that the B is not only better but much better.

21. N—B4

To avoid the loss of a Pawn, White must compensate himself with Black's QRP. This is just what Capablanca is playing for: on his QR5 the N will be locked in by the Black B. Another possibility consisted of: 21. KR—Q1, R—Q5; 22. N—N3 (not 22. P—B3,? KR—Q1), 22. ... R × P; 23. N × P, B—Q4 with about the same consequences as in the game.

21. ...   B × P   23. P—B3
22. KR—B1   K—N1

White had to make a difficult choice. After an immediate 23. N × P Black could play either 23. ... R—Q7; 24. N—B4, R—K7; 25. N—Q6, B—N3; 26. P—QN3, R—Q1 or 23. ... B—Q4; 24. P—QN3, (24. N—B4, B × N; 25. R × B, R—Q7), 24. ... R—QB1 as in the game but with one tempo less, which does not mean much.

23. ...   B—Q4   24. N × P   R—QB1!

Both to exchange Rooks and to keep the N imprisoned. How can the N be freed? There are two ways of escape: via QN3 or via QB4 (after the preparatory P—QN3). Both lead to a weakening of the White pawn structure, which in a pure Pawn ending would be fatal. That is why Black tries to get rid of the Rooks as soon as possible.

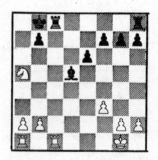

25. P—QN3

White chooses the exit via QB4, which seems to be less harmful.

25. ... R × Rch	27. R × Rch
26. R × R R—QB1	

Not 27. N—B4 because of 27. ... P—QN4

27. ... K × R	29. K—K3 K—N3
28. K—B2 K—B2	

Just in time. If the White K had already been on Q3, the ending would have resulted in a draw, since White after his N—B4, B × N could have recaptured with the K, i.e. without weakening his Pawn structure.

30. N—B4ch   B × N   31. P × B

The Pawn ending is completely lost for White.

31. ...   K—B4   32. K—Q3   P—K4

Advance of the Pawns on the majority wing.

33. P—N4   P—B3   34. P—KR4   P—KN3

34. ... P—R3? would have been a bad error: after 35. P—R5 the White King marches in via K4—B5—N6.

35. K—K4

Very surprising. After 35. ... K × P; 36. P—N5!, P × P; 37. P × P, White is also lost, but 'less convincingly'. There follows: 37. ... K—N5; 38. K × P, K—R6 and now

(1)   39. K—B6, K × P; 40. K—N7, P—N4; 41. K × RP, P—N5 and Black queens first.

(2)   39. K—Q6, K × P; 40. K—B5, K—N6 etc.

35. ...   K—Q3

Safety first: 36. P—N5 would now be answered by 36. ... P—B4ch.

36. P—B4

More instructive would have been 36. K—Q3, P—B4; 37. P × P,

P × P; 38. P—R5, P—R3; 39. K—B3, K—B4; 40. P—R3, P—K5, etc.

36.	**. . .**	**P × P**	**39. K—K4**	**P—QN4**
37.	**K × P**	**K—B4**	**40. P—R3**	**K—N6**
38.	**P—R5**	**K × P**		

Resigns.

A fine performance by Capablanca, although relatively simple. But that is simply characteristic of his style.

5. FISCHER'S TOP PERFORMANCES

As already stated, we are restricting the comparison between Capablanca and Fischer mainly to performances in endgames and in strategy. They both excel in inventiveness and accuracy. If there is a difference, it stems from the manner in which they build up a given game. Capablanca strives for a solid position, from which he searches possibilities to steer the game into his most desired direction. Fischer is armed from head to toe with opening tricks and innovations, which makes things easier for him.

Game 6   *White:* R. Fischer   Leipzig 1960
        Black: Dr M. Euwe   Caro-Kann, Panov Variation

1. P—K4, P—QB3; 2. P—Q4, P—Q4; 3. P × P, P × P; 4 P— QB4, N—KB3; 5. N—QB3, N—B3; 6. N—B3, B—N5; 7. P × P, KN × P; 8. Q—N3, B × N; 9. P × B, P—K3 (9. . . . N—N3 is probably better) **10. Q × P, N × P; 11. B—N5ch, N × B; 12. Q— B6ch, K—K2; 13. Q × QN, N × N?; 14. P × N, Q—Q2.**

Here the book variation ends with the statement: 'Black has at least equality'. However, Fischer had analysed this position thoroughly and had come to the conclusion that White's position is far superior. Fischer succeeds in proving this in a convincing way.

15. R—QN1!
This is the key move, originally suggested by grandmaster P. Benkö and gratefully adopted by Fischer. The idea is clear: make the completion of Black's development as difficult as possible. In a few moves it will appear that Black can accomplish this only at the cost of one Pawn. In most variations the victim will be Black's QRP, which is the more dangerous, since White then will have at his disposal a passed Pawn.

15. ... R—Q1
Black hopes to hold out on his second rank but this will be at the expense of his development. Fischer recommends as preferable 15. ... Q × Q; 16. R × Q, K—Q3; 17. R—N7, P—B3; 18. K—K2, K—B3; 19. R—KB7, P—QR4; 20. B—K3, and Black is not as badly off as in the game, although in this variation too the loss of a Pawn soon cannot be avoided.

16. B—K3 Q × Q   18. K—K2
17. R × Q R—Q2
White need not hurry. He can capture Black's QRP at any time. This is one of the strong points of Fischer's style: postpone the capturing of material until the time is ripe for it. 18. R—R5 would have given Black sufficient counterplay. After 18. ... P—N3 19. R × P, R × R; 20. B × R, B—N2

18. ... P—B3
Or 18. ... P—N3; 19. B—B5ch, K—K1 (forced); 20. R—N8ch, R—Q1; 21. R × Rch, K × R; 22. B × P and White's superiority has increased.

19. R—Q1!
Very clever. White exchanges Black's only active piece.

19. ...   R × R   21. R—N8
20. K × R K—Q2
Again that marvellous self-restraint. Black's QRP will not run away. After the text White threatens 22. B—B5.

21. ... K—B3
21. ... P—N4; 22. B—B5, B—N2; 23. R—N7ch, K—B3; 24. R × B, K × B; 25. R × QRP, R—Q1ch would give Black some drawing

chances. White, however, plays the better 22. B×P, which after
22. ... K—B3 may lead to the same position as in the game.

22. B×P   P—N4

Black must free his game in some way or other.

23. P—QR4   B—N2   24. R—N6ch

Exchange of rooks would diminish White's winning chances.

24. ... K—Q4	27. R—N5ch K—B3
25. R—N7 B—B1	28. R—N6ch K—Q4
26. R—N8 B—N2	

This is the same position as four moves earlier. We can see this kind
of repetition (one time!) in many of Fischer's games. Its purpose is
first to give the opponent the possibility of making a wrong choice,
second to show the opponent that he is completely at Fischer's
mercy, and third (though seldom) to gain time.

29. P—R5!

The directness of White's strategy is remarkable. His QRP must do
the job and it does so in the most efficient way. Some variations:

(1) 29. ... R—QB1; 30. P—R6
  (a) 30. ... R×P; 31. R—N7, B—B1; 32. B—K3, R—R6;
    33. P—R7 and 34. R—N8.
  (b) 30. ... B—B1; 31. R—N7.
    (i) 31. ... R—R1; 32. R×P, K—B3; 33. R—KB7, B—Q3
      (33. ... P—B4; 34. B—Q4); 34. B—K3, R×P; 35. R×
      P. White's plus Pawns must decide.
    (ii) 31. ... P—R4; 32. B—Q4, P—K4; 33. P—R7, etc.
    (iii) 31. ... B—B4?; 32. R—N5 and wins.
  (c) 30. ... R—QR1; 31. R—N7, B—B1; 32. R×P leads to (i)
(2) 29. ... R—QR1; 30. R—N7, B—B1; 31. R×P, B—B4;
  32. B—N6! and wins
(3) 29. ... P—B4 see the game.

29. ... P—B4   **30. B—N8! R—QB1**

Black could have held his own longer by 30. ... B—K4. After 31. R—N5ch, K—B5; 32. R × B (32. B × B?, R—Q1ch); 32. ... R × B; 33. R × KP, K × P; 34. R—K5, P—B5; 35. R × P, R—N8ch; 36. K—K2, R—QR8; 37. R—KB5, White's task is not so easy.

It is clear that after 30. ... B × P, White's RP advances irresistibly: 31. P—R6, B—Q5; 32. P—R7

31. P—R6 R × P   **32. R—N5ch**

32. R—N7 would not have changed the situation after 32. ... B—B3 (32. ... B—Q5; 33. R—Q7ch leads to the continuation of the game).

32. ... K—B5(?)

Better 32. ... K—B3; 33. R—R5, B—Q5, after which 34. B—K5? leads only to a draw on account of 34. ... R—B4. If White, however, plays 34. K—K2, then 34. ... R—N6 (34. ... R—B4; 35. R—R2); 35. P—R7, R—N7ch; 36. K—Q3, B × P; 37. B × B and White still has some obstacles to overcome.

33. R—N7

33. R—R5 would have made things more difficult.

33. ...   **B—Q5**   **35. R × Rch K × R**
34. R—B7ch K—Q6   **36. B—K5!**

36. P—R7, B × P; 37. B × B would have won too, but with much more difficulty.

Black resigns: White's QRP will queen.

Game 7   *White:* R. Fischer   7th Match Game, Buenos Aires 1791
        Black: T. Petrosian   Sicilian Defence

1. P—K4, P—QB4; 2. N—KB3, P—K3; 3. P—Q4, P × P; 4. N × P, P—QR3; 5. B—Q3, N—QB3; 6. N × N, NP × N; 7. 0—0, P—Q4; 8. P—QB4 (Unless Black plays P—Q5 in one of his next moves, this move must lead to a weakening of Black's Pawn position), **8. ... N—B3; 9. BP × P, BP × P; 10. P × P, P × P** (or 10. ... N × P; 11. B—K4, B—K2; 12. N—B3, B—N2; 13. Q—R4ch with advantage to White) **11. N—B3, B—K2; 12. Q—R4ch, Q—Q2** (12. ... B—Q2; 13. Q—B2 is favourable for White since 13. ... 0—0; 14. B—N5 would win a pawn: Black's KRP or QP) **13. R—K1!** (13. B—N5, P × B; 14. Q × R, 0—0 would give Black attacking chances) **13. ... Q × Q; 14. N × Q, B—K3**

White has an important positional advantage. Black's QRP is weak and Black's QP is isolated. Moreover, White has the Pawn majority on the Queenside. Still, it is not so easy to exploit these advantages against a sublime defender like Petrosian.

15. B—K3   0—0   16. B—B5!
Eliminates the Black KB from the Black squares. This enables White to exercise more pressure on Black's QRP and on Black's Q.

16. ...   KR—K1

17. B × B   R × B   18. P—QN4!
Again a strong move which practically prevents Black from playing P—QR4 on account of the answer P—N5, which would give White a strong passed Pawn. 18. N—B5 would not have been effective after the obvious answer; 18. ... P—QR4. Now, however, the threat 19. N—B5 is acute.

18. ...   K—B1
Protects the KR so that the QB can move freely.

19. N—B5   B—B1   20. P—B3
Prevents the jump of the Black N to his K5 permanently.

20. ...   KR—R2(?)
Black wishes to bring his B to Q2 and therefore needs to protect his QRP once more. However, he could have put up more resistance by bringing his N via K1 to B2.

The text eases White's problem. Fischer seems to have a special capacity for creating positions in which his opponents—even the strongest—often go wrong.

It appears to be a great handicap for Black that from now on his N is doomed to stay on KB3.

21. R—K5
Ties the N to its place.

21. ...   B—Q2
This was the intention of Black's previous move.

22. N × Bch!
It looks illogical to exchange a strong N for a weak B, but White has judged the consequences very accurately.

22. ...   R × N   23. R—QB1

Threatening 24. B × QRP, R × B; 25. R—B8ch and mate.

23. ...   R—Q3
This gives the important second rank to the White R but what else could Black do? 23. ... N—K1 is not satisfactory: 24. R—B6 and now 24. ... N—B2; 25. B—B5 would cost material. The move 23. ... P—QR4 could be answered by 24. P—N5 (always strong) but also by 24. P × P since Black cannot retake: 24. ... R × P; 25. R—B8ch.

24. R—B7
White gratefully makes the most of his chances and is already threatening 25. KR—K7 with immediate decision.

24. ...   N—Q2
Drives the R back and prevents the doubling along the second row.

25. R—K2   P—N3
A flight square for the K and the elimination of the 'half-threat' B × KP.

26. K—B2
The K will try to reach the strong square Q4.

26. ...   P—KR4
Black is already in a kind of zugzwang. His pieces can hardly move: his N has to prevent the doubling of the Rooks, his K must control the K2 square. Black's QR could play 27. ... R—N1 after which

both 28. P—QR3 and 28. B × P are good (28. ... R × B; 29. R × N
or 28. ... R × P; 29. B—B8). That is why Black prefers to play his
Pawns; 26. ... P—N4? is refuted by 27. B—B5.

27. P—B4 P—R5
To prevent the White K from entering into Black's position via
N3 and R4.

28. K—B3 P—B4
A further weakening, necessary to prevent 29. K—N4.

29. K—K3 P—Q5ch
Again forced: Black cannot permit the White K to go to his strong
square Q4.

30. K—Q2 N—N3

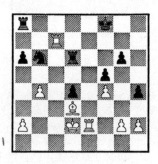

Black ventures the flight to liberty and White now makes short work
of him. Black could have tried 30. ... K—B2, after which White
continues 31. R—K5!, K—B3; 32. R—R5 if necessary followed by
33. P—N5 and Black's QRP falls.

31. KR—K7
White has attained his main goal, doubling of Rooks on the seventh.
As a consequence of this, signs of mate will soon appear.

31. ... N—Q4   32. R—B7ch K—K1
After 32. ... K—N1; 33. R—KN7ch the other Rook will also be
able to escape from the N-threat by check. On the other hand, the K
in the middle is more exposed to mating possibilities.

33. R—QN7 N × NP
33. ... N × BP also leads to mate or heavy material loss: 34. B—
B4, P—N4; 35. R—N7, R—B3; 36. R—KN8ch, R—KB1; 37. B—
N7ch, etc. Or 34. ... N—Q4; 35. R—KR7, etc.

34. B—B4

Black resigns; he can no longer prevent the mate.

The ending is played by Fischer with perfect precision. It is remarkable how he continually exercises increasing pressure, until the opponent is 'beaten to a pulp' and throws in the towel.

6. SPECIAL CAPACITIES OF CAPABLANCA: MANŒUVRING AND 'PETITES COMBINAISONS'

How does a World Champion play for a win? There are several possibilities. Alekhine laid the basis for a win in the opening and his successors followed more or less this policy. The openings were carefully studied and the outcome of this part of the game determined to a certain extent the World Champion's further attitude towards that game.

Steinitz tried to overcome his opponents by a strict application of his strategical theories. Lasker did about the same thing, but he also had a very sharp eye for tactical possibilities.

Capablanca had no special preference for openings, nor did he have an absolute belief in Steinitz' theories, but he did have a sound conception of chess and an unbelievably strong imagination which enabled him to see a long series of moves ahead, even in the quietest or dullest positions. If he failed to overwhelm his opponents in the attack (which occurred more often than one might think) then he outwitted them in the exact calculation of variations which sometimes contained a tricky turn, which Capablanca used to call 'une petite combinaison'. Those little combinations presented themselves in many games after lengthy manœuvring in positions considered by most of his contemporaries as completely equal and dead but by Capablanca as promising starting points for a consistent exploitation of a small positional advantage.

We shall discuss three of Capablanca's masterpieces in this field.

Game 8 White: B. Kostic   4th Match Game, Havana 1919
       Black: J. R. Capablanca   Queen's Pawn Opening

1. P—Q4, N—KB3; 2. N—KB3, P—K3; 3. B—N5, P—B4; 4. P—K3, N—B3; 5. P—B3, Q—N3; 6. Q—N3, P—Q4. (Nothing special has happened in the opening: Black has a sound position, and need not fear an early surprise. This was, in general, what Capablanca aimed at in the first phase of the game.) **7. QN—Q2, B—Q2; 8. B—K2, P × P** (simplification which can be seen often in Capablanca's treatment of the opening) **9. KP × P, B—Q3; 10. 0—0, P—KR3** (it is remarkable that Capablanca does not fear the doubling of his Pawns on the Kingside) **11. B—R4, N—KR4** (in order to follow with 12. ... P—N4; 13. B—N3, N × B, thus obtaining the two Bishops, although it is dubious whether this means anything in the closed state. But at any rate things begin to happen in this colourless position). **12. Q × Q, P × Q** (Capablanca in general did not mind the isolated double Pawn in positions like this. The compensation for which he is striving will become clear after the 20th move) **13. KR—K1** (White had also to take into consideration 13. ... N—B5 which move can be now answered by 14. B—B1). **13. ... P—KN4; 14. B—N3, N × B; 15. RP × N, P—B3** (Capablanca had no fear of a weakness in his Pawn position as long as he could see that it could be defended easily and satisfactorily.) **16. P—KN4, K—B2; 17. N—R2, N—R4; 18. KN—B1, P—N4; 19. P—R3, N—B5; 20. N × N** (practically forced); **20. ... NP × N.**

Black's position is only a little superior but the main thing is that there is something to play for: White's weak QNP. How should it be attacked? Capablanca will soon show you.

21. N—K3   R—R3   22. P—KN3   R—N3
Very simple.

23. R—R2
Here the R is in a sense better placed than at QN1. This will become clear in a few moves.

23. ...   R—R1   25. K—N2   R(4)—N4
24. B—B3   R—R4
How simple chess is; the weak Pawn is attacked for the second time. However, it can easily be defended.

26. R—K2
If White's Rook had gone to QN1 (23rd move) instead of R2, then 26. ... B × RP would have been possible now.

26. ... B—K1   27. R—Q2   K—N2

White could now have parried new attacks on his QNP by 28. N—Q1 (which he could have done before and will do later) but he rightly does not like this move for two reasons: first the N is an obstacle for the communication between the White pieces, and second the N at its central post (K3) is able to prevent all kinds of Pawn-actions on this part of the front.

28. B—Q1   B—N3

Again a most obvious increase of the pressure against White's QNP. Black is threatening 29. ... B—N8; 30. R—R1, R × P.

29. B—R4   R—R4   31. R × B   K—N3
30. B—B2   B × B   32. R—K2   R(4)—N4

No direct threat, but Black maintains his pressure, which ties both Rooks to the defence of the QNP.

33. N—Q1

To release the Rooks from the 'eternal' task, but as suggested, the move represents a kind of a compromise.

33. ... B—B1

Keeps the B ready to go to N2 in order to prepare the advance of the centre Pawns (P—K4 and P—Q5) and thus strengthen the pressure against White's weak point.

34. R—R1   P—R4   35. P—B3

Or 35. P × Pch, K × P and 36. ... K—N3, which would not have made a great difference, but allows Black to continue his initiative by P—B4 or P—K4, after sufficient preparation.

35. ...   P × P   37. P × Pch   P × P
36. P × P   P—B4!

Now Black has attained a Pawn majority on the Kingside, and the possibility of bringing his Rooks directly from the eastern front (Queenside) to the western front (Kingside).

38. R—B1   R—KB3   40. R—K8
39. R(1)—B2   B—Q3

The White R ventures out, without success.

40. ... K—B2   41. R—K1

A wise decision; after 41. R—KR8, Black occupies the K-file (41. ... R—K3). Black has no vulnerable spots in his position; thus the White Rooks have no special targets.

41. ... P—B5   42. P—N4

White does not like to open the position.

D

42. ...   P—B6ch

In combination with the next move, Black's advance is very strong: the beginning of a 'petite combinaison'.

43. K—B2   R—R3

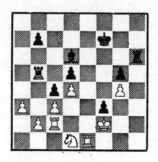

A Pawn sacrifice which White should not have accepted although other moves would not have saved the game either. One example: 44. N—K3, B—B5 (better than 44. ... R—R7ch; 45. K × P, R × R; 46. N × R, R × P; 47. N—N4 with counterchances for White); 45. K—N1, R—R5; 46. R—B2, K—N3; 47. R × P, B × Nch; 48. R(1) × B, R × KNPch; 49. K—B1, R × NP and Black must win.

44. K × P   R—R6ch
45. K—K2

After other moves White loses a Rook.

45. ...   R—R7ch
46. N—B2

Now White has fallen into the eternal pin.

46. ... B—N6	48. K—B3 B—R5
47. R—KB1 R—N3	

The pin is maintained.

49. R—K2 R—KB3ch	50. K—K3 P—N4

White can now only move his R to and fro along the second rank.

51. R—Q2   K—K2

The strategic plan is as follows: Black's K goes to N6, then Black exchanges all pieces on KB7 and finally the King captures White's Queenside Pawns. This is the end of the 'petite combinaison', admittedly a little combination with a long tail!

52. P—N4

Despair.

52. ... P×P *e.p.* **53. N—Q3** R(7)×R
White resigns (54. R × R, R × Nch; 55. K × R, K × R).

Our next game bears a great resemblance to the previous one: Capablanca allows the exchange of queens on his QN3, thus accepting an isolated double-Pawn which he brings back to life by the same manœuvre N—R4—B5 as in his game with Kostic. After having fixed the situation on the Queenside, his attack with rooks and bishop at the other wing bursts out with decisive force.

Game 9   *White:* D. Janowski   New York 1916
          Black: J. R. Capablanca   Slav Queen's Gambit

1. P—Q4, N—KB3 (a harmless transposition of moves); **2. N—KB3, P—Q4; 3. P—B4, P—B3; 4. N—B3, B—B4; 5. Q—N3, Q—N3; 6. Q×Q** (present-day theory gives 6. P×P as better), **6. ...** P×Q; **7. P×P, N×P; 8. N×N, P×N; 9. P—K3, N—B3; 10. B—Q2, B—Q2!** (It is really unbelievable that Capablanca can play for a win in this almost symmetrical simplified position, but the continuation shows there is some justification for this ambition. The text is forerunner of the plan to be carried out on the Queenside. For that purpose Black's QB had to go back to control his QN4 square.) **11. B—K2** (White should have developed this B to QN5 in order to cross Black's plans), **11. ...** P—K3; **12. 0—0, B—Q3; 13. KR—B1, K—K2; 14. B—B3, KR—QB1; 15. P—QR3, N—R4** (carrying out the plan already announced); **16. N—Q2** (White parries the threat 16. ... N—N6 and prepares the counterpush P—K4), **16. ...** P—B4 (directed against White's plans); **17. P—KN3, P—QN4!; 18. P—B3, N—B5** (the standard manœuvre); **19. B × N** (Not immediately necessary, but it is a little awkward for White to have a hostile N continually controlling important squares in his position.), **19. ...** NP×B; **20. P—K4** (a counterpush which looks promising), **20. ...** K—B2; **21. P—K5?** (This means that White gives up all chances for a possible initiative. Correct would have been 21. P × BP, P × P; 22. P—B4, followed by 23. N— B3 and 24. N—K5), **21. ...** B—K2; **22. P—B4, P—QN4.**

Black has built up an ideal position on both wings. On the Queenside Black can play P—QN5 at the right moment and on the Kingside P—KN4. First, though, he must regroup his pieces.

23. K—B2 R—R5   **24. K—K3** R(1)—QR1
Threatening 25. ... P—N5.

25. QR—N1 P—R3
Preparing P—N4.

26. N—B3   P—N4   27. N—K1

White brings his N to another square in order to strengthen the defence of KB4. It does not appear to be a very efficient idea.

27. ...   R—KN1

Black shifts his attention to the other wing where the possibilities for a decisive breakthrough are more concrete. The doubling on the QR file has apparently been only a demonstration of power.

28. K—B3   P × P   30. N—N2
29. P × P   R(5)—R1

It soon appears that the N on this square is only a target for the Black Rooks. Better would have been 30. N—B2.

30. ...   R—N5   31. R—N1

A self-pin, but what else can he do? After 31. N—K3, R—R5; 32. R—KR1, R—N1 followed by 33. ... R—R6ch, White would have been in greater trouble.

31. ...   R(1)—KN1

Black is ready for the advance of his KRP with all its disagreeable consequences for White.

32. B—K1

White hopes to avert the danger by bringing a new piece to the threatened wing, but he should first have played 32. R—QR1 in order to avoid the advance, which follows.

32. ...   P—N5!

A fine Pawn-sacrifice to bring the QB to the centre of the struggle via R5, B7 and K5.

33. P × P

After 33. B × P, B × P; 34. P × P, Black would have resumed his original plan, the advance of the KRP, and since there is no possibility of protecting the KR for a second time (as it was before by B—B2) this advance would have led to a complete success. It should be

(Position after White's 32nd move)

added that White's K—B2 would never have solved the problem, for the N could not have moved, as it had to protect the KBP.

| 33. ... | B—R5 | 34. R—QR1 |

34. R—QB1 to prevent the penetration of the Black QB would have failed: 34. ... R×Pch!; 35. K×R, B—KN4ch or 35. N×R, R×R. One of those pretty 'petites combinaisons'.

34. ... B—B7

Directly to the battlefield.

35. B—N3

White considered this move a sufficient defence against Black's threat 35. ... B—K5ch, etc.

| 35. ... | B—K5ch | 36. K—B2 P—R4 |

With the deadly threat 37. ... B×N and 38. ... P—R5 winning a piece.

| 37. R—R7 | B×N | 39. B×P |
| 38. R×N | P—R5 | |

A last try. White restricts the damage to the exchange.

| 39. ... | R×Rch | 41. B×B |
| 40. K—B3 | R×RP | |

If 41. R×Bch, K—B1; 42. B—B6 then 42. ... R(1)—R1 and mate (43. ... R(1)—R6).

41. ...	R—R6ch	44. R—K7 R×P(7)ch
42. K—B2	R—QN6	45. K—B3 R—QR1!
43. B—N5ch	K—N3	

Mate is inevitable (46. K—N3, R—R6ch; 47. K—R4, R—KR7 mate).

46. R×Pch K—R4

White resigns

A remarkable game by Capablanca though his opponent was not

always equal to the situation. Janowski was not among the very top players of that time. That Capablanca could employ similar stunts against the strongest opponents is shown by the next game.

Game 10 White: Dr E. Lasker   10th Game World Championship
Black: J. R. Capablanca   Match, Havana 1921
Queen's Gambit, Orthodox
Defence

1. P—Q4, P—Q4, 2. P—QB4, P—K3; 3. N—QB3, N—KB3; 4. B—N5, B—K2; 5. P—K3, 0—0; 6. N—B3, QN—Q2 7. Q—B2, P—B4; 8. R—Q1, Q—R4; 9. B—Q3, P—KR3; 10. B—R4, P × QP; 11. KP × P, P × P; 12. B × P, N—N3; 13. B—N3, B—Q2; 14. 0—0, QR—B1. (So far in accordance with the prevailing theory of the opening: White has accepted the isolated QP, and for this he obtains greater freedom of movement. Capablanca has developed in his usual sound way.) **15. N—K5** (White takes immediate advantage of his preponderance in space. He could have avoided the now following complications by 15. Q—K2. Bogoljubov gives the following nice little combination: 15. ... B—B3; 16. N—K5, QN—Q4; 17. P—B4!, N × N; 18. P × N, Q × P??; 19. B—K1 and wins.), **15. ... B—N4; 16. KR—K1, QN—Q4?**

This position contains a curious combination, which was overlooked by both world champions. Probably both relied on their intuition: after a series of mutually solid moves, it seems almost impossible that a forced combination should exist in a position without clear weaknesses on either part. And yet it does! Young Breyer, one of the most talented chess-players who ever lived (he died when he was twenty-seven years old), discovered the following beautiful combination: **17. B × N (3)** and now

(1)   17. ... N × B looks very solid but is refuted by the surprising **18. N—N6!**

(a) 18. ... P × N; 19. R × P, and White regains the sacrificed piece, thus winning a Pawn, overall.

(b) 18. ... KR—K1; 19. R × P!, P × R; 20. B × Pch, K—R2; 21. N × B dis. ch, etc.

(2) 17. ... B × B (After this move one can really expect a combination, since now Black's QP will become weak, Black's QB is vulnerable and—as it will soon appear—Black's QR too); 18. B × N, P × B; 19. N—N4! (now the B does not have many squares at his disposal).

(a) 19. ... B—Q1; 20. Q—B5 (attack on Black's QR), and 21. Q × QP winning a Pawn.

(b) 19. ... B—N4; 20. P—B4! (Better than 20. Q—B5 after which Black saves himself: 20. ... B—QB3; 21. P—B4, P—KN3; 22. Q—K5, KR—K1), 20. ... B × P; 21. Q—B5.

(i) 21. ... B—N1; 22. Q × QP, P—R3; 23. P—R4 wins a piece.

(ii) 21. ... B—B2 (protects the Q in order to answer 22. Q × QP by 22. ... B—B3); 22. N × QP!, K—R1 (relatively best is 22. ... B—B3; 23. N—K7ch, K—R1; 24. Q × Q, B × Q; 25. N × R, B × R; 26. N × QRP and White has reached an ending in which he has a plus Pawn); 23. N × P!, P × N (if 23. ... B—B3, then 24. N × Pch, R × N; 25. Q × QRch, etc.); 24. N—B6, B—Q6! (the only move; 24. ... K—N2 leads to mate after 25. N—R5ch, etc.); 25. Q × B, K—N2; 26. Q—R7ch, K × N; 27. Q × Pch, K—B4; 28. P—N4ch!, K × P; 29. R—K4ch, K—B4; 30. Q—R7ch, K—B3; 31. R—KB1ch, K—N4; 32. P—R4 mate.

The conclusion is that the best Black could hope for was an ending with one Pawn less.

17. B × N(5)?   **N × B**   **19. Q—N3**
18. B × B   **N × B**
This shows what Lasker is striving for: he hopes to get a positional advantage because Black must accept the isolation of his Queenside Pawns.

19. ...   B—B3
After 19. ... B—R3 the answer 20. N—Q7 is strong (20. ... KR—Q1; 21. N—B5).

20. N × B   P × N
It is noteworthy that in this position White's QP is weaker than Black's QBP; the main reason for this is that Black's Q4-square is very strong.

21. R—K5   Q—N3   23. N—K2
22. Q—B2   KR—Q1

Preferable was 23. N—R4, after which White could still hope for
complete equality.

23. ...   R—Q4!   24. R × R(?)

After this move Black's position is certainly superior, but Lasker's
recommendation after the game 24. R—K3, N—B4; 25. R—N3,
Q—Q1, also gives Black some advantage.

24. ...   BP × P   26. P—QN3
25. Q—Q2   N—B4

Commentators rightly recommend 26. P—KN3.

26. ...   P—KR4   27. P—KR3(?)

Again a dubious move which worsens White's position. Better would
have been 27. P—N3. Bogoljubov recommended 27. N—N3;
after 27. ... N × N; 28. RP × N, Black's advantage is minimal.

27. ...   P—R5!

Fixes the White K-wing, and from now on Black applies continued
pressure until the giant Lasker collapses.

28. Q—Q3   R—B3   30. Q—N1   Q—N5
29. K—B1   P—N3   31. K—N1

White is not quite aware of the dangers that threaten from the
advance of Black's QRP. Better would have been 31. Q—N2.

31. ...   P—R4

The advance to R5 can be prevented no longer. If the White Q had
been on its N2, White could have played 32. P—R3 in order to
answer a possible ... P—R5 by P—QN4.

32. Q—N2   P—R5   34. R × Q   P × P
33. Q—Q2   Q × Q   35. P × P   R—N3

Black now has attacking possibilities against two weak Pawns, which is the positive result of his minority attack.

36. R—Q3

Of course 36. R—N2, R—N5 would cost a Pawn at once.

36. ...   R—R3

We have seen this strategy by Capablanca in previous games. The R makes an encircling movement.

37. P—KN4

To give the K more freedom and also to abolish the blockade of White's Kingside.

37. ... P × P *e.p.*	39. N—B3
38. P × P R—R7	

White hopes to bring his N to a better square; after 39. K—B2, N—Q3 White can do nothing but wait for the deciding blow.

39. ... R—B7	40. N—Q1 N—K2

The N retires from the K-wing to become active on the other wing.

41. N—K3 R—B8ch	43. N—Q1 R—N8
42. K—B2 N—B3	

Black threatens to capture the hostile QNP by 44. ... N—R4. With the text, Black avoids a surprising trap: 43. ... N—N5 (looks very strong); 44. R—Q2, R—N8; 45. N—N2, R × N?!; 46. R × R, N—Q6ch; 47. K—K2, N × R; 48. K—Q2 and White recaptures the piece with equal chances.

44. K—K2?

White could not avoid the loss of a Pawn, but 44. K—K1 would have given much better chances: 44. ... N—R4; 45. K—Q2, R × P (45. ... N × Pch? then 46. K—B2); 46. R × R, N × Rch and the resulting Knight ending cannot be won very easily.

44. ... R × P!	45. K—K3

45. R × R, N × Pch would have cost another Pawn.

45. ... R—N5	46. N—B3 N—K2

The N returns to its earlier outpost, from which it can attack White's Pawns still more efficiently.

47. N—K2

It does not make much difference whether White plays P—N4 now or later.

47. ... N—B4ch	50. N—N1 N—K5ch
48. K—B2 P—N4	51. K—B1 R—N8ch
49. P—N4 N—Q3	

Black makes slow but sure progress.

52. K—N2	R—N7ch	55. K—B1	K—N2
53. K—B1	R—KB7ch	56. R—K3	K—N3
54. K—K1	R—QR7	57. R—Q3	

White cannot do anything but wait.

57. ...	P—B3	61. R—Q3	R—KB2ch
58. R—K3	K—B2	62. K—K1	R—KN7
59. R—Q3	K—K2	63. K—B1	R—QR7
60. R—K3	K—Q3	64. R—K3	P—K4!

Black has waited with this advance until the White R was at his K3.

65. R—Q3   P × P   66. R × P

If 66. N—K2 then 66. ... R—Q7; 67. R × P, N—N6ch; 68. K—B2, R × Nch; 69. K × N, K—K4. The rook ending is easily won.

66. ...	K—B4	68. R—B1ch	K—Q4
67. R—Q1	P—Q5		

White resigns. He has no defence against a further advance of Black's QP since 69. R—Q1 is refuted by 69. ... N—N6ch; 70. K—K1, R—KN7, and the White N cannot move on account of 71. ... N—K7 mate.

So far in his career, Fischer has not played many games of this kind, so there is not much evidence with which to compare Capablanca and Fischer in this area. Perhaps the game Petrosian–Fischer, discussed later, shows some analogy to the strategy and tactics Capablanca used in the three games just discussed.

7. CAPABLANCA'S MISTAKES

Chess is too complicated to be played to perfection. All chess players without exception make mistakes. Of course, the greatest players make fewer errors, but from time to time even they fall victim to the ever-present tendency to go wrong.

There are all kinds of mistakes and it is interesting to know which type of error a given player is likely to make and to compare Capablanca and Fischer in this respect. One could perhaps expect that Capablanca and Fischer, belonging to the same group of players, experts on strategy and the endgame, would be apt to make the same kind of error—probably outside their area of specialization.

This does not appear to be true, first in that the errors made by Capablanca and Fischer are on the whole different in character, and second in that their errors for the greater part are in the area(s) in which they excel. This is certainly the case with Fischer. He is great in endings—we have seen that in the examples—yet most of his misjudgments are in this field. Capablanca is a great man in 'petites combinaisons' but sometimes (though seldom) he overlooks a little combination by his opponent. We may add that Capablanca's mistakes are usually the direct consequence of his having too much confidence in a solid position. We have seen an example of this in game 10. We could call these errors psychological mistakes. They occur very seldom—Capablanca lost only twelve games in his career until his loss of the world title—and they can be more or less attributed to a state of absentmindedness.

Capablanca was not always equally serious. To a certain extent he considered chess as a kind of hobby. It is said that even in his fatal match with Alekhine in 1927, on free evenings instead of preparing openings, he played cards until late in the night. He was confident that he could find everything over the board. This over-confidence may have cost him the championship, and is also responsible for many of the mistakes he made.

Game Extract 1

Black: Sir G. A. Thomas
White: J. R. Capablanca

This was the position reached after Black's 25th move (Tournament, Hastings 1919). There followed: **26. N—N6ch** (26. R—N8 would be answered by 26. ... R—B8ch; 27. K—B2, R × R and Black can still play), **26. ... N × N; 27. P × N, R—K2; 28. R—N8, R—K1.** (Now 28. ... R—B8ch; 29. ... K—B2 would not have saved Black because his Q is not protected.)

The position now reached is an easy win for White. The simplest line would be 29. R × R, Q × R; 30. Q—R4! winning the R (30. ... R—B8ch; 31. K—B2). Capablanca, however, convinced of the absolute superiority of his position played without thinking: 29. Q—R8??. His opponent could now have given the game an unexpected turn by playing 29. ... R × RP!, after which White must simplify and can hope for a draw at best. Instead Black resigned!

Game 11   *White:* J. R. Capablanca   St Petersburg 1914
              Black: Dr S Tarrasch   Four Knights' Game

1. P—K4, P—K4; 2. N—KB3, N—QB3; 3. N—B3, N—B3; 4. B—N5, B—N5; 5. 0—0, 0—0; 6. P—Q3, B × N; 7. P × B, P—Q4 (the so-called Svenonius variation); **8. B × N, P × B; 9. N × P, Q—Q3; 10. B—B4, R—K1; 11. Q—B3, P × P; 12. P × P, R × N.**

13. KR—Q1?
The wrong Rook, as will appear a few moves later. Capablanca falls a victim to his opponent's 'petite combinaison'.

13. ...   B—N5
The only way to save the exchange.

14. Q—N3?
With 14. R × Q, B × Q; 15. R × N, P × R; 16. B × R, B × KP, White still could have reached a draw.

14. ... B × R   15. B × R   Q—Q7!

If White had played his QR on the 13th move, Black's only response would have been 15. ... Q—Q1, after which 16. B × N, Q × N; 17. R × B, would have given White a favourable ending.

16. P—B3   N—R4

Black kept the piece which White had intended to sacrifice only temporarily. He won the game in 82 moves, despite the stubborn resistance of Capablanca.

This was not the only time that Capablanca moved the wrong Rook. Seventeen years later the same happened to him, though in a different position.

Game 12   White: J. R. Capablanca   9th Match Game, Amsterdam
        Black: Dr M. Euwe   1931

1. P—Q4, N—KB3; 2. N—KB3, P—Q4; 3. P—B4, P—B3; 4. N—B3, P × P; 5. P—QR4, B—B4; 6. N—K5, QN—Q2; 7. N × QBP, Q—B2; 8. P—KN3, P—K4; 9. P × P, N × P; 10. B—B4, KN—Q2; 11. B—N2, B—K3; 12. N × N, N × N; 13. O—O, Q—R4; 14. N—K4, R—Q1; 15. Q—B2, B—K2; 16. P—QN4!, B × P; 17. Q—N2, P—B3.

White's position is far superior. He will win back the Pawn sacrificed anyhow and will then be able to demolish the hostile position completely.

18. KR—N1?

The wrong rook. Namely, White does not threaten 19. Q × B at all because this would cost a R on account of 19. ... R—Q8ch!. After 18. QR—N1 Black's B would have been forced to retreat and then 19. Q × N would have been practically decisive.

18. ... 0—0(?)

This compensates for White's blunder. Correct would have been 18. ... N—B5 and White is in great trouble.

19. B×N   P×B   **20. N—N5!   B—B6**

What should come next? After 20. ... B—B4; 21. Q—N3ch, White wins the exchange (and more!).

21. Q—B2   B—B4   **23. Q—R2ch   K—N2**
22. B—K4!   P—N3   **24. R×Pch** and White won easily.

It is remarkable that in all these three 'error-games' Capablanca had the White pieces, a further indication of the psychological nature of his mistakes: over-confidence and carelessness.

The following game gives another accident with a happy ending—at the same time a phenomenal performance by Capablanca.

Game 13   *White:* A. Nimzowitsch   St Petersburg 1914
            Black: J. R. Capablanca   Ruy Lopez

1. P—K4, P—K4; 2. N—KB3, N—QB3; 3. N—B3, N—B3; 4. B—N5, P—Q3 (transposition from Four Knights to Ruy Lopez); **5. P—Q4, B—Q2; 6. B×N, B×B; 7. Q—Q3, P×P; 8. N×P,**

8. ...   P—KN3?

Carelessly played. It was not so difficult to foresee the loss of a Pawn by force in two or three moves, but Capablanca apparently did not imagine that such a thing could happen in the solid Steinitz defence of the Ruy Lopez. Capablanca's mistakes are just as clear as his good moves.

9. N×B   P×N   **10. Q—R6   Q—Q2**

Practically forced; after 10. ... P—B4; 11. Q—B6ch, N—Q2; 12. B—N5 White would get a powerful attack which would certainly have been decisive.

11. Q—N7   R—B1   13. 0—0   0—0
12. Q × RP   B—N2

White has a sound plus Pawn. However, Black has a fianchettoed Bishop directed against a vulnerable Queenside.

14. Q—R6   KR—K1   15. Q—Q3   Q—K3

The black Q also looks eagerly at White's Queenside.

16. P—B3   N—Q2!

Brings the N to the battlefield, either via B4 or K4—B5.

17. B—Q2

To support the threatened wing, but 17. B—B4 would have been better in order to exchange the N as soon as this piece appeared on its K4.

17. ...   N—K4   18. Q—K2   N—B5

White is already in difficulties. He cannot play 19. P—QN3 on account of 19. ... B—Q5ch; 20. K—R1, N × B; 21. Q × N, Q—K4, etc.

19. QR—N1   R—R1   20. P—QR4

20. P—QN3 would not have been better: 20. ... N × B; 21. Q × N, R—R6, and Black recaptures at least the sacrificed Pawn.

20. ...   N × B   21. Q × N   Q—B5!

Prevents 22. P—QN3 and guarantees not only the recapture of the pawn but also an important positional advantage.

22. KR—Q1   KR—N1

The exchange 22. ... B × N would probably lead only to a draw: 23. Q × B, Q × Q; 24. P × Q, R × P; 25. R—N7. Now all the black pieces are directed against the Q-wing. Black already threatens the sham sacrifice 23. ... R × NP.

23. Q—K3   R—N5

Threatens 24. ... B—Q5. The heavy artillery comes into action.

24. Q—N5

Better perhaps would be 24. Q—Q3.

24. ...   B—Q5ch   25. K—R1   QR—N1

Decisive.

26. R × B

If White does not make this sacrifice, he will lose all his Queenside Pawns.

26. ... Q × R

and Black won: **27. R—Q1, Q—B5; 28. P—R4, R × NP; 29. Q—Q2, Q—B4; 30. R—K1, Q—KR4; 31. R—R1, Q × Pch; 32. K—N1, Q—R4; 33. P—R5, R—R1; 34. P—R6, Q—B4ch; 35. K—R1, Q—B5; 36. P—R7, Q—B4; 37. P—K5, Q × KP; 38. R—R4, Q—R4ch; 39. K—N1, Q—B4ch; 40. K—R2, P—Q4** (Just like Fischer, Capablanca takes his time when cashing material.); **41. R—R4, R × RP,** White resigns (42. Q—R6, Q × N).

8. FISCHER'S ERRORS

As already stated, we find Fischer's mistakes for the greater part in his special field, the ending. On a full board his strategically clear vision usually shows him the right way, and Fischer is too intent on the position to make the obvious mistakes we have seen in Capablanca's games. But in endings, Fischer certainly is not free from error. First, an example that might have influenced chess history of the last ten years.

Game Extract 2

White: M. Botvinnik   *Black:* R. Fischer

Olympiad, Varna 1962

Fischer, after having won a pawn in the opening, has managed to keep his plus pawn until the endgame. The above position arose after White's 41st move. Botvinnik states that White is in a kind of zugzwang: after a King move by White, Black continues . . . K—R5 and . . . N—K3—B5; after B—N1 Black wins by . . . R—Q8; and if the White R moves, the reply . . . R—QB5 is decisive. It must be added that after 41. . . . R—QN5; 42. R—K3, R—QB5; 43. B—N3, Black exchanges the B under more favourable circumstances than in the game. After 43. . . . N × B; 44. P × N, R—QN5, the White R does not have the possibility of a sally to the seventh rank, as in the game. There followed:

41. ... N—K5ch(?)
I do not consider this as a typical Fischer error. The consequences were very difficult to foresee and the move was played in the fifth hour, i.e. after a tiring day. Moreover, after the text the game could also have been won, but only with considerable effort.

42. B × N   R × B   43. R—R3
More forcing was 43. R—B7, although this would amount to about the same thing in a few moves.

43. ...   R—K2   45. P—QR4   R—B4
44. R—KB3   R—QB2
The sealed move.

46. R—B7   R—R4   47. R × KRP
After 47. R—B4?, R—KB4; 48. R—B4, R—B2, Black could bring his K to the other wing and then the win is no longer a problem.

47. ...   R × P   49. R—B7ch   K—K4
48. P—R4ch   K—B4   50. R—KN7   R—R8
Indirect protection of the KNP.

51. K—B3   P—QN4?

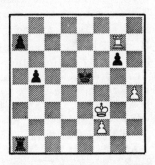

This is a real error. An extensive analysis by Fischer shows that 51. ... K—Q5 probably would have won. In the race between passed Pawns, Black queens first.

52. P—R5!   R—R6ch   54. R—N5ch   K—Q3
53. K—N2   P × P   55. R × NP
The draw is assured. There follows:

55. ... P—R5; 56. P—B4, K—B3; 57. R—N8, P—R6ch; 58. K—R2, P—R4; 59. P—B5, K—B2; 60. R—N5, K—Q3; 61. P—B6, K—K3; 62. R—N6ch, K—B2; 63. R—R6, K—N3; 64. R—B6, P—R5; 65. R—R6, K—B2; 66. R—B6, R—Q6; 67. R—R6, P—R6; 68. K—N1. Draw agreed.

E

In those days much was said about the possibility of a World Championship match outside the FIDE cycle. Many grandmasters expressed their sympathy towards this move, the intention of which was to organize a match between Botvinnik, at that time the World Champion, and Fischer. However, since the above game ended in only a draw, the interest in such a match faded, and Botvinnik declared that Fischer would have to wait some years more. And so it came about.

Game Extract 3

White: R. Fischer   *Black:* S. Reshevsky

(Position after Black's 39th move; played in the U.S.A. Championship 1962/63)

White has attained a decisive advantage, both positional and material. He can now crush his opponent.

40. P—B3ch   K—N6   41. K—Q3?

Unbelievable; after 41. K—B1! Black could resign. White threatens 42. B—B2ch and 43. R—KR7 mate. After 41. ... K—R6 or 41. ... K—R5 the answer 42. K—B2, threatening 43. R—KR7 mate, is decisive. With the text move White still wins, but it takes more time. There followed: **41. ... P—K5ch; 42. P × P, R—Q1ch; 43. B—Q4, K—N5; 44. R—B1, B—K4; 45. K—K3, B—B2; 46. R—KN1ch, K—R5; 47. K—B3, R—Q2; 48. P—K5, R—B2ch; 49. K—K4, R—B4; 50. P—K6, B—Q1; 51. B—B6, B × B; 52. P × B, R × P; 53. K—Q5, R—B7; 54. R—K1,** Resigns.

Game Extract 4

White: S. Reshevsky   *Black:* R. Fischer

(Position after White's 49th move; played in a match in New York 1961)

Black, to move, missed a simple win: 49. .... K—K5; 50. P—N8 = Q, R—R7ch and mate or 50. K—Q2, P—N8 = Q; 51. P—N8 = Q, Q—K6ch and mate follows.

Instead Black played:

49. .... P—N8 = Q?

After **50. P—N8 = Qch, K—B4; 51. Q—KB8ch, K—K5; 52. Q—QR8ch, K—Q5; 53. Q—Q8ch, K—B5; 54. Q—Q3ch, K—B4; 55. Q—B3ch, K—Q3; 56. Q—Q2ch, K—K4; 57. Q—QN2ch, K—B4;** White resigned.

Fischer also made slips from time to time in the match for the World Championship (1972). I don't agree with those who consider the level of this match below normal in view of the many mistakes made by both players. This was to be expected. Matches for the *highest* title are played under extreme pressure and in almost every match for the World Championship there are blunders. In the matches Botvinnik–Smyslov, Botvinnik–Petrosian, Petrosian–Spassky and even in the match Capablanca–Alekhine some incomprehensible errors occurred.

Game Extract 5

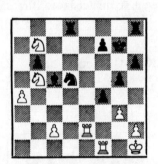

White: B. Spassky   *Black:* R. Fischer

(Position after White's 31st move; 7th Match Game, Reykjavik 1972)

Here Black could obtain a decisive advantage by 31. .... N—K6. Some variations:

(1)   32. N × R, N × R; 33. R—K1 (Black threatened 33. .... P—B6), 33. .... N—K6; 34. N—N7, P—B6; 35. N × B, P—B7 and wins.

(2)   32. KR—K1, P—B6; 33. N × R, R × N.
        (a)   34. R × N, B × R; 35. R × B, R—Q8ch; or 35. P—R3, R—Q7.
        (b)   34. R—B2, N—N5; 35. R × P, R—Q7 threatening mate.

(3)   32. R—R1, P—B6; 33. R(2)—K1, N × P or 33. R—B2, N—N5, etc.

(4)   32. R × N (the strongest move but still insufficient here),

32. ... B × R; 33. N × R, R × N and the black Rook will penetrate.

Instead Fischer played 31. ... R—QB1 and the game ended in a draw.

Game Extract 6

White: B. Spassky   *Black:* R. Fischer

(Position after White's 34th move; 13th Match Game, Reykjavik 1972)

34. ...   K—B2?

With this move Black gives his opponent an important tempo which enabled him to obtain counterchances after 35. N—K5ch, N × N; 36. B × N, P—N4; 37. R—KB1 threatening 38. R—B4 and 39. R—R4.

Smyslov recommends in the diagram 34. ... P—R6; 35. N—K5, N × N; 36. B × N, KR—Q1 (not 36. ... R—R5 at once on account of 37. B—B6, threatening 38. P—Q7); 37. R—KB1, R—R5! and Black wins easily since the counterattack R—KB4—KR4 is eliminated.

Game Extract 7

White: R. Fischer   *Black:* B. Spassky

(Position after Black's 20th move; 14th Match Game, Reykjavik 1972)

White's position is alarming: his QNP is *en prise* and his QB is in trouble from the threat of ... P—N4 and ... P—KR4. The only way to fight back consisted in 21. P—QN4, P—N4; 22. B—N3, P—KR4; 23. P—N5, P—R5; 24. B × P or 24. P × N. Fischer, however, blundered away a Pawn:

21. B—QN5? Q × P   22. B × N   N—B6!
This in-between move wins a Pawn.

23. Q—N4   Q × Q   24. P × Q   P × B
This game ended in a draw because three moves later Black also
made a blunder which cost a Pawn: 25. B—K5, N—N4; 26. R—B1,
R—B1; 27. N—Q4, P—B3?; 28. B × P!, etc. The Dutch grandmaster Donner states that in the Spassky–Fischer match the latter
missed his chances several times in the transition from middlegame
to endgame.

Comparing Capablanca's errors with Fischer's it appears that
apart from the extremely rare case (such as the example above)
Fischer's errors are of a more subtle nature. In general, Capablanca's
mistakes can be ascribed to oversight and lack of attention.

9   PERFORMANCE BY CAPABLANCA IN FIELDS OTHER THAN STRATEGY AND ENDGAMES

We conclude this chapter by giving a few performances by Capablanca in completely closed position, and then in attack.

Game 14 White: J. R. Capablanca   Karlsbad 1929
    Black: Dr K. Treybal Slav Defence (Stonewall Variation)

**1. P—Q4, P—Q4; 2. P—QB4, P—QB3; 3. N—KB3, P—K3;
4. B—N5, B—K2; 5. B × B, Q × B; 6. QN—Q2, P—KB4; 7. P—
K3, N—Q2; 8. B—Q3, N—R3** (a well-known manœuvre in the
Stonewall: both Ns are ready to control the important square K4);
9. 0—0, 0—0; 10. Q—B2, P—KN3 (extra protection of the KBP;
in case of White's P × P, Black wishes to retake with his KP);
11. QR—N1, N—B3 (more in agreement with the idea of this opening
would have been 11. ... N—B2 controlling Black's K4); **12. N—K5,
N—B2; 13. P—B4** (with his last moves White has improved his
position considerably), **13. ... B—Q2** (preferable is 13. ... N × N
and 14. ... N—N5. Now Black will be completely tied up.);
**14. QN—B3, KR—Q1; 15. P—QN4, B—K1; 16. KR—B1, P—
QR3; 17. Q—B2, N × N; 18. N × N, N—Q2; 19. N—B3** (White
avoids the doubled pawn; he wishes to attack with a 'clean' front),
**19. ... KR—B1; 20. P—B5, N—B3; 21. P—QR4, N—N5; 22. Q—
K1, N—R3; 23. P—R3** (after having temporarily shored up the
Queen's wing, White now takes action against the King's wing),
**23. ... N—B2; 24. P—N4, B—Q2; 25. R—B2, K—R1; 26. R—
KN2, R—KN1; 27. P—KN5, Q—Q1; 28. P—R4, K—N2; 29. P—
R5, R—R1; 30. R—KR2, Q—B2; 31. Q—B3, Q—Q1; 32. K—B2**
(Equal treatment on both wings: White has one possibility of opening

a line of attack on each side. On the Q-wing there is P—QN5, and on the K-wing P × P. White first regroups his troops and leaves the opponent in doubt as to where the battle will start.) **32. ... Q—B2; 33. R(1)—KR1, QR—KN1; 34. Q—R1, R—N1; 35. Q—R3, QR—N1.**

36. P—N5
D-day has come.

36. ... RP × P
Certainly not 36. ... BP × P; 37. P—R6ch, K—B1; 38. P—B6ch.

37. P—R6ch
Before the attack on the Queenside breaks out in full violence, first the Kingside must be closed.

37. ...	**K—B1**	**39. P—N6!**	
38. P × P	**K—K2**		

Only one open file is left, but this is sufficient to decide the battle in Capablanca's favour.

39. ...	**Q—N1**	**41. Q—N4**	**KR—Q1**
40. R—R1	**R—QB1**		

The Black forces, compressed in such a limited space, have difficulties in finding the right squares. It reminds one of a Chinese puzzle box.

42. R—R7	**K—B1**	**46. Q—R3**	**K—N1**
43. R(2)—R1	**B—K1**	**47. K—N3**	**B—Q2**
44. R(1)—R1	**K—N1**	**48. K—R4**	**K—R1**
45. R(1)—R4	**K—B1**		

A series of moves without much significance.

49. Q—R1	**K—N1**	**51. K—N2**	**B—K1**
50. K—N3	**K—B1**	**52. N—Q2!**	

At last the winning manœuvre: the N could not leave its place before ... N × NP was made harmless.

52. ... B—Q2   53. N—N3 R—K1

If 53. ... B—K1; 54. N—R5, R—Q2 then 55. N × NP!, R × N; 56. R—R8, etc.

54. N—R5 N—Q1   55. B—R6! P × B

There was nothing better.

56. R × B R—K2   58. N × P Black resigns
57. R × Nch! R × R

Game 15   *White:* J. R. Capablanca   San Sebastian 1911
               Black: Dr O. Bernstein   Ruy Lopez

1. P—K4, P—K4; 2. N—KB3, N—QB3; 3. B—N5, N—B3; 4. 0—0, B—K2; 5. N—B3, P—Q3; 6. B × Nch, P × B; 7. P—Q4, P × P; 8. N × P (A well-known position of the Steinitz defence often played in those days.) **8. ... B—Q2; 9. B—N5, 0—0; 10. R—K1, P—KR3; 11. B—R4, N—R2; 12. B × B, Q × B; 13. Q—Q3, QR—N1; 14. P—QN3, N—N4; 15. QR—Q1, Q—K4; 16. Q—K3, N—K3; 17. QN—K2, Q—QR4.**

(Bernstein apparently plays for a win against the newcomer—the game was played in the first round of Capablanca's first European tournament.)

18. N—B5!

White sacrifices his RP.

18. ... N—B4

Black could not take: 18. ... Q × P; 19. Q—QB3 (threatens 20. R—R1), 19. ... Q—R3; 20. N—B4!, P—B3 (White threatened 21. N × N); 21. Q—N3 and Black loses at least his KRP. This variation proves the strength of the White N on the outpost KB5. This explains the text: Black wants to eliminate the N.

19. N(2)—Q4

Threatens both 19. N × BP (19. ... B × N; 20. N—K7ch) and
19. Q—N3.

19. ...   K—R2   20. P—KN4!

An attacking move without an exact goal. The advanced KNP will
prove its importance later.

20. ...   QR—K1   22. N—K2!
21. P—KB3   N—K3

White again offers his RP, and this time his opponent accepts.

22. ...   Q × P

With 22. ... Q—N3 Black could have forced the exchange of
Queens, but after 23. K—N2, Q × Q; 24. N × Q, White would have
had a better endgame, which, in view of Capablanca's great strategical
capacities, certainly would have led to a win.

23. N(2)—N3

White continues his attack and does not worry about losing a second
Pawn.

23. ...   Q × P

With 23. ... Q—R4; 24. R—R1, Q—N3, Black again could have
entered into a somewhat disadvantageous endgame (after 25. R × P,
Q × Qch; 26. N × Q), but this is the least Capablanca would have
feared.

After the text there is no longer any compromise: White must
attack, and he does this with the skill of a perfect technician.

24. R—QB1   Q—QN7   25. N—R5

The White position contains a few possible threats such as P—K5
or either N × NP, but the main threat is N(B5) × P after the Black
Q will have been driven away from the diagonal.

25. ...   R—KR1

After 25. ... P—N3; 26. Q × Pch, K—N1, White wins: 27. P—
K5!, P × N (R4) (forced in view of the threat 28. N—B6ch); 28.
P × P, followed by 29. K—R1 and 30. R—KN1ch. Since White is
two Pawns down, the anti-positional 25. ... P—N4 has to be
examined too. In that case 26. P—K5 is again a killer and after
26. ... P—B3; 27. Q—Q3! (Prins) Black must lose his KRP and
more.

26. R—K2   Q—K4   27. P—B4   Q—N4

The driving away of the Queen is completed.

28. N(B5) × NP!   N—B4

The main variation is 28. ... N × N; 29. N—B6ch, K—N3;
30. N × B, P—B3 (White threatened 31. P—B5ch, K—R2; 32. N—
B6 mate); 31. P—K5!, QP × P; 32. P × P. Black has no longer any
proper defence and in addition must lose material in the next few
moves.

With the text Black loses the exchange without compensation.

29. N × R	**B × N**	**32. N—R5**	**R—N1**
30. Q—B3	**P—B3**	**33. P—B5ch**	**K—N4**
31. N × Pch	**K—N3**	**34. Q—K3ch**	**Resigns**

Fischer has shown similar ability in the attack, starting with unclear
Pawn sacrifices (compare the games Fischer–Najdorf (Varna 1962)
and Fischer–Addison (Palma 1970) which will be discussed in a later
chapter.

In our comparison between Capablanca and Fischer we have
seen how both excel in the field of strategy. It is impossible to
decide who of the two is the greater champion. They both have
their strong and weak points. In general, Capablanca's way of
playing is clearer and he possessed the power of winning almost
even, and apparently dull, positions. Fischer for his part has a fine
positional judgment, unlimited energy and great fighting spirit.

CHAPTER II

ALEKHINE AND FISCHER

1. GENERAL

A comparison between Alekhine and Fischer cannot be determined just by stating that Alekhine excels in tactics and Fischer in strategy. We have already noted that world champions are outstanding in practically all areas. In his match with Capablanca, Alekhine had to defeat his opponent mainly by strategic play or, more precisely, by his superior judgment in the field of strategical combinations. When Fischer beat Spassky he showed himself at least equal to the latter tactically and superior in strategy. As a matter of fact, Alekhine and Fischer have much in common. Many of Fischer's brilliant games could have been played by Alekhine, and vice versa. Considering the time in which each played their knowledge of openings is equally good. Their preference for Pawn sacrifices in the opening, without other compensation than better development or a preponderance in space, can be found in a number of games.

The difference in style between Alekhine and Fischer appears particularly in tournament games, in which the stronger players always have to play for a win, in contrast to their general attitude in match games. Under tournament conditions Alekhine prefers combinations and attack, Fischer strategy (which may also result in attack). Alekhine has enriched chess literature with a number of magnificent combinations. A characteristic of his combinations is that the point of the combination is often found only in the last move. The preparation of the attack is also a characteristic of Alekhine. He starts an attack with threats here and there; the opponent defends himself as well as possible and after having done this feels very satisfied with himself, thinking the storm is over. But then the real attack breaks out with irresistible force. It is not just a single attack—it consists of successive waves of attacks. And, equally important, during these attacking combinations, Alekhine never loses sight of the possibility of simplifications which could bring him into a favourable or a won ending.

We shall consider the play of Alekhine and Fischer under the following headings:

Pawn sacrifices in the opening,
Strategic combinations in general,
Attacking combinations and
Mating combinations

2. PAWN SACRIFICES IN THE OPENING—ALEKHINE

The concept is simple and has much in common with Morphy's
strategy. The opponent loses time by taking the pawn(s) when an
advance in development may be worth more. Morphy made sacrifices
only in open positions where better development might be a decisive
factor. By sacrificing a Pawn Alekhine generally tended to get a
better starting-point for a later attack, no matter whether the game
was open or closed.

Game 16 White: Dr A. Alekhine   Bled 1931
    Black: E. Colle   Queen's Gambit, Orthodox Defence

**1. P—Q4, N—KB3; 2. P—QB4, P—K3; 3. N—QB3, P—Q4;
4. B—N5, QN—Q2; 5. N—B3, P—B3; 6. P—K4, P × P; 7. N × P,
Q—N3.**

8. B—Q3!
The sacrifice of a Pawn to win a few tempi for development and
attacking chances.

| **8. ...** | **Q × NP** | **10. B × N** | **N—B3** |
| **9. 0—0** | **N × N** | **11. B—Q3** | **Q—N3** |

Black must lose a second tempo in order to bring his Queen out of
enemy territory.

| **12. R—K1** | **B—K2** | **14. B—Q2** | **P—B4** |
| **13. Q—B2** | **P—KR3** | | |

After 14. ... 0—0 nothing spectacular would have happened for
the moment. White would have strengthened his position with

moves such as B—B3, N—K5, R—K3, etc., and the attack would
have come of itself. The text intensifies the struggle and therefore
emphasizes White's advance in development.

15. B—B3   P × P   17. N—B5!   Q—Q1
16. N × P   0—0

An attempt to take advantage of the vulnerable position of the
White Rook after 17. ... P × N; 18. R × B, B—K3 would be fatal:
19. B × N, P × B; 20. B × P, Q—B4?; 21. B × B, Q × R; 22. Q—
N6ch, K—R1; 23. Q × RPch, K—N1; 24. B—B5 and mate.

18. N × Bch   Q × N   19. QR—N1!

Threatening 20. B—N4. White keeps his opponent busy all the time.

19. ...   R—Q1   21. Q—K2   B—N2
20. R—K3   P—QN3

White threatened 22. Q—B3, B—N2; 23. B × N!

22. R—N3   N—K1

Not at all good is 22. ... R × B in order to continue by 23. ...
B—K5 after 23. Q × R or 23. R × R. White simply inserts the move
23. B × N, and then the text would lose the exchange.

23. R—K1

Threatens 24. Q—N4, after which neither 24. ... P—B4 (25. Q ×
BP), nor 24. ... P—B3 or 24. ... P—K4 would work (25. R × KP).

23. ...   K—B1

Perhaps hoping for 24. Q—N4, P—B4; 25. B × P, P × B!; 26. Q ×
BPch, Q—B2.

24. Q—N2!

The beginning of the decisive attack. The Black defensive Pawn
front gradually crumbles.

24. ...	P—B3	26. R(3)—K3	K—B2
25. B—N4	N—Q3		

Black makes forced moves all the time; 26. ... P—K4; 27. P—B4 would immediately cost a Pawn.

27. P—B4
Of course, not 27. R × P, Q × R; 28. R × Q, K × R, after which White must play the difficult ending between Queen and two Rooks.

27. ...	Q—Q2	28. Q—K2

With this move White threatens both 29. R × P and 29. Q—R5ch. It is remarkable how simply Black is overwhelmed.

28. ...	R—K1	30. Q—N6
29. Q—R5ch	K—N1	

With new threats: 31. Q—R7ch, K—B1; 32. B—N6, etc.

30. ...	P—B4	33. Q—R7ch	K—B1
31. B × N	Q × B	34. B—N6	
32. B × P	Q × P		

Threatens 35. Q—R8ch, K—K2; 36. R × Pch, etc.

34. ...	Q—Q5	36. K—R1
35. B × R	R × B	

Unpins the Rook and threatens 37. Q—R8ch, K—B2; 38. R—B1ch, K—K2; 39. R × Pch, etc.

36. ... Q—B3
Black resigned without waiting for his opponent's answer. There could have followed 37. Q—R8ch, K—B2; 38. Q × Rch, K × Q; 39. R × Pch, etc.

Game 17	*White:* Dr A. Alekhine	Bled 1931
	Black: A. Nimzowitsch	French Defence

1. P—K4, P—K3; 2. P—Q4, P—Q4; 3. N—QB3, B—N5. This is called the Winawer variation of the French Defence. **4. N—K2, P × P; 5. P—QR3, B × Nch; 6. N × B.**

White has sacrificed a Pawn, which advantage Black can keep only by allowing a serious weakness in his position.

6. ... P—KB4(?)
Too risky. Satisfactory for Black is 6. ... N—QB3; 7. B—QN5, KN—K2.

7. P—B3
Preparing the sacrifice of a second Pawn which, as Alekhine himself remarks, is not necessary since White can get a very good game after 7. B—KB4, N—KB3; 8. P—B3! The difference between this and the text is that after 8. ... P×P; 9. Q×P, Black cannot take the second Pawn: 9. ... Q×P?; 10. N—N5, etc.

7. ... P×P   8. Q×P   Q×P
Here Black could have checked on KR5: 8. ... Q—R5ch; 9. P—N3, Q×QP. The difference is that the square KN3 is then no longer available for the White Q (compare White's next move). In that case White would have continued with 10. N—N5, Q—N3; 11. B—KB4, N—QR3; 12. 0—0—0, and Black's position is not enviable.

9. Q—N3!
After 9. N—N5 Black would have consolidated his position by 9. ... Q—R5ch and 10. ... Q—K2.

9. ... N—KB3!
The best strategy: Black returns one of his plus Pawns. The text is better than 9. ... N—K2, which is answered by 10. B—K3, Q—B3; 11. 0—0—0, and White has an ideal attacking position. The value of Black's 9. ... N—KB3 lies in eventually playing the N to K5 or N5 with chances of a counterattack.

10. Q×NP   Q—K4ch?
This in-between move is the cause of the quick deterioration of the Black position. Consistent would have been 10. ... R—N1; 11. Q—R6 (11. Q×BP is too risky on account of 11. ... N—B3; 12. N—N5?, Q—R5ch; 13. P—N3, Q—K5ch; 14. K—B2, Q×Pch and 15. ... N—K5), 11. ... R—N3, and the White Q does not have the square KR4 at its disposal (as in the game).

11. B—K2   R—N1   13. Q—R4
12. Q—R6   R—N3
In this position Black is completely lost, notwithstanding his plus pawn. His pieces are either inactive or vulnerable, and White can develop his pieces in the most effective way.

13. ... B—Q2
13. ... R × NP is refuted by 14. B—B4, Q—Q5; 15. R—Q1, and White wins a piece. Preferable, however, was 13. ... N—B3, in which case White continues as follows: 14. B—B4, Q—R4; 15. B—KN5!, Q—K4 (15. ... N—K5; 16. B—R5); 16. R—Q1, B—Q2; 17. 0—0, 0—0—0; 18. B—R5 winning the exchange.

14. B—KN5 B—B3
A worthless demonstration.

15. 0—0—0 B × P
Snatching a Pawn when his house is on fire. But 15. ... N—Q2; 16. KR—K1 is also hopeless for Black.

16. KR—K1 B—K5   17. B—R5! N × B
Forced.

18. R—Q8ch K—B2   19. Q × N
Black resigns. He has no reasonable continuation. E.g.:

  (1) 19. ... K—N2; 20. N × B, P × N; 21. B—R6ch, etc.
  (2) 19. ... Q—N2; 20. N × B, P × N; 21. R—B1ch, etc.
  (3) 19. ... P—KR3; 20. N × B, P × N; 21. R—B1ch, K—N2;
     22. B × Pch, etc.

This was a game 'à la Morphy', the sacrifice of two Pawns in an open position.

Game 18   *White:* Dr A. Alekhine   Kemeri 1937
                 Black: S. Reshevsky   Alekhine's Defence

1. P—K4, N—KB3; 2. P—K5, N—Q4; 3. N—KB3, P—Q3; 4. P—Q4, B—N5; 5. P—B4, N—N3; 6. B—K2. (This move already involves a Pawn sacrifice.) **6. ... P × P; 7. N × P** (Of course not 7. P × P, Q × Qch; 8. K × Q, which would give Black at least equality.) **7. ... B × B; 8. Q × B, Q × P.**

Here we have the same type of Pawn sacrifice as in the other game: the vulnerable position of the Black Queen must compensate for the loss of material.

9. 0—0   N(1)—Q2   10. N × N   N × N
After 10. ... Q × N White continues his attack by 11. P—QR4, N × RP?; 12. Q—B3, N—B4; 13. P—QN4.

11. N—B3   P—QB3
Necessary to prevent 12. N—N5.

12. B—K3   Q—K4   14. Q—B3!
13. QR—Q1   P—K3
With the threat 15. R × N, K × R; 16. Q × KBPch, which practically forces Black to give his Pawn back.

14. ...   0—0—0
Entails a nice trap: 15. Q × BP, B—Q3; 16. P—KN3, KR—B1, and the White Queen is caught.

15. B × RP!   Q—QR4   17. Q—N3
16. B—Q4   Q—KB4
With 17. Q × Q White could have obtained a practically won endgame, but Alekhine prefers to win in the attack. So he does, and how!

17. ...   P—K4   20. P—B4   B—B2
18. B—K3   B—N5   21. P—N3   P—B3
19. N—R4   B—R4   22. P × P   Q—K3
Black could not play: 22. ... Q × P; 23. B—B4, etc.

23. P—KR3!
This move serves two purposes. it prevents a later ... Q—N5 after ... N × P, and it gives the White Queen a retreat square without leaving the diagonal KR2—QN8.

| 23. ...   KR—N1 | 25. Q—QB3 |

24. B—Q4   N × P

Threatens both 26. N—N6ch and 26. N—B5.

| 25. ...   N—Q2 | 27. P—QN4!   N—N1 |

26. P—B5   KR—K1

It seems that Black has built up an absolutely safe defensive position.

| 28. N—N6ch   B × N | 30. Q—N3!   R—Q2 |
| 29. P × B   Q × P(?) | 31. B—B5 |

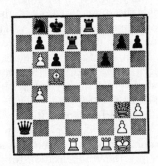

White's attack has reached its maximum: he threatens 32. R × R and 33. Q—B7ch.

| 31. ...   Q—B2 | 32. R—R1 |

The logical continuation: Black has opened the QR-file by accepting the Pawn sacrifice on his 29th move.

| 32. ...   Q—N3 | 33. Q—R2! |

Compare White's 23rd move.

33. ...   R—K4

Apparently this solidly closes the White Queen's diagonal.

34. R—R8   R—Q7?

Black is unaware of the danger. Preferable would have been 34. ... Q—K1, after which White continues by 35. Q—N3 and 36. Q—R3.

| 35. R × Nch!   K × R | 36. Q × Rch!! |

Black resigns (36. ... P × Q; 37. R—B8ch, etc.). A magnificent example of Alekhine's combinative powers. This game could also find a place in the fourth section (mating combinations) of this chapter.

F

3. PAWN SACRIFICES IN THE OPENING—FISCHER

We have said already that the games of Alekhine and Fischer, both characterized by Pawn sacrifices in the first phase, show a marked resemblance.

Intuition plays the greatest part in such sacrifices; it has to, for an exact calculation of the numerous continuations is impossible. We know that both Alekhine and Fischer are outstanding experts in the opening, and that both are accustomed to prepare their opening strategy for games against particular opponents. This implies that, apart from intuition, preliminary study is also important for them, though the main function of the study is to check their intuition. The outcome of a number of variations—though only a small proportion of the total—should give a definite answer as to the correctness of a Pawn sacrifice. Although in most cases there is no question of a spontaneous action or a momentary brainstorm, *these* performances show great chess powers. They require a refined judgement in complicated positions.

Comparing Alekhine's performances in this field with Fischer's, it may appear that Alekhine's concept is often simpler and at the same time of longer duration, which means that it may take a greater number of moves before the compensation for the sacrificed Pawn will become completely clear. On the other hand, in Fischer's games of this type we often see an intense struggle in the first phase and a quick dénouement. This is particularly true in the first of the games that follow.

Game 19	*White:* R. Fischer	Bled 1961
	Black: E. Geller	Ruy Lopez

1. P—K4, P—K4; 2. N—KB3, N—QB3; 3. B—N5, P—QR3; 4. B—R4, P—Q3; 5. 0—0, B—N5;

The position looks favourable for Black. As a general rule in the KP-openings after the opponent has castled, the pinning of the KN is very strong because White can liquidate the pin only by a serious weakening of his Kingside (P—KR3 and P—KN4). And that is just what Fischer does! By intuition (or by calculation) Fischer knows that in this case Black cannot take advantage of this weakening. Fischer is not prejudiced; he is courageous and examines even dangerous-looking variations. He does not need *rules*; he is above them.

6. P—KR3 B—R4

A separate problem is the sacrifice 6. ... P—KR4. Leading from this, here are a few possibilities:

(1) 7. P—Q4, P—QN4; 8. B—N3, N × P? (preferable is 8. ....
Q—B3, preventing White from accepting the sacrifice);
9. P × B, P × P; 10. N—N5, and White is better.

(2) 7. P—B4,
  (a) 7. ... Q—B3; 8. Q—N3, 0—0—0; 9. B × N, P × B;
10. P × B, P × P; 11. N—R2, Q—R3; 12. Q—N3. In this
position Fischer recommends 12. ... P—Q4.
  (b) 7. ... P—QN4; 8. P × P, N—Q5; 9. P × Pch, P—B3;
10. N × N!, B × Q; 11. B × Pch, K—K2; 12. N—B5ch,
K—B3; 13. B × R, Q × B; 14. R × B. This occurred in a
game Grabezerski–Brzuska, Warsaw 1961. It seems that
White has the better of it.

7. P—B3 Q—B3

Obvious, but not the best. It soon appears that the Black Queen is the object of various threats, correct would have been 7. ... N—B3; 8. P—Q4, N—Q2.

However, 7. ... B × N; 8. Q × B, Q—B3, should also be considered if Black wishes to play for a draw.

8. P—KN4!

We give this game as an example of a Pawn sacrifice in the opening, but properly speaking, the text move already involves a sacrifice in the sense that the safety of the Kingside is at stake. However, Fischer has very carefully calculated the advantages and the risks of his strategy.

8. ... B—N3 9. P—Q4!

This Pawn sacrifice is combined with the threat to win a piece by 10. B—KN5, Q—K3; 11. P—Q5.

9. ... B × P

In view of the threats mentioned, Black has no choice.

10. QN—Q2.

10. ...   B—N3

Black returns the Pawn, which perhaps is best. Other possibilities:

(1) 10. ... B × N; 11. N × B, P—K5 (Black can no longer play a 'quiet' game; he has to go into complications. After 11. ... P—QN4; 12. B—N3, it is not clear how he should continue his development.); 12. R—K1, P—Q4; 13. B—N5, Q—Q3 (If 13. ... Q—N3; 14. Q—N3, or 13. ... Q—K3; 14. P—B4!); 14. P—B4, P × P (White threatened 15. P × P, Q × P; 16. B—N3, with the capture of Black's KP); 15. P—Q5, P—N4; 16. P × N, P × B; 17. R × Pch, N—K2; 18. B × N, B × B; 19. Q—K2, etc.

(2) 10. ... B—Q6; 11. B × Nch, P × B; 12. R—K1, 0—0—0; 13. R—K3, B—N3; 14. Q—R4, K—N2; 15. N—B4 and wins.

11. B × Nch   P × B   12. P × P

Wins back the Pawn with an overwhelming position. Perhaps still better for White, as Fischer himself remarks was: 12. Q—R4! and now

(1) 12. ...   N—K2; 13. P × P, P × P; 14. R—K1, P—K5; 15. N × P!, Q × N; 16. Q × BPch!!, N × Q; 17. N—B6 double ch and mate.

(2) 12. ... K—Q2. This move, which Fischer believed would enable Geller to put up some resistance, is rejected by Keres in the following way: 13. P × P, P × P; 14. N—B4, B—Q3; 15. R—Q1, R—K1; 16. N × B, P × N; 17. Q—N4!, K—B2; 18. Q—R5ch, K—Q2 (18. ... K—N2; 19. B—K3, P—B4; 20. B × P); 19. Q—B5, and Black cannot prevent the Queen from penetrating any more. Remember that the Black Rook must protect his KP.

12. ...   P × P   13. N × P

White has recaptured his Pawn in the simplest way and he has a considerable lead in development. The only thing still to be proved is that his weakened Kingside does not seriously impair his chances.

13. ... B—Q3
If 13. ... 0—0—0, then 14. Q—K2, K—N2; 15. N—N3 with a strong attack.

14. N × B!
Unbelievable. White gives his opponent the open R-file against his King. Fischer again shows that rules do not count.

It is clear that after 14. N × QBP, P—KR4!, Black would indeed have obtained a strong attack.

14. ... Q × N
Black does not accept the gift. After 14. ... RP × N; 15. N—K4, Q—K4; 16. N × Bch, Q × N; 17. Q—B3 White wins at least a Pawn, e.g. 17. ... N—K2; 18. B—B4, Q—Q4; 19. Q—N3, while the KR-file does not offer any trace of attacking possibilities.

15. R—K1ch K—B1
The alternative was 15. ... N—K2, but after 16. N—B4 Black cannot castle Kingside, and 16. ... 0—0—0; 17. Q—R4 is too risky for him.

16. N—B4 P—KR4
Now or never!

17. N × B P × N?
Correct was 17. ... Q × N. True, the ending after 18. Q × Qch, P × Q; 19. B—B4, R—Q1; 20. QR—Q1, P—Q4; 21. B—K3, P—N3 is favourable for White, but the win is not yet simple.

After 17. ... Q × N; best is 18. Q—R4, P × P (the only possible counterchance); 19. B—B4, Q—B3 (Or 19. ... Q—B4; 20. R—K5); 20. Q—N4ch, N—K2; 21. B × P, R—K1 (If 21. ... P × P, then 22. R × N too—Black has no direct threats; White comes first) 22. R × N!, R × R; 23. Q—N8ch, R—K1; 24. B—Q6ch, etc.

18. B—B4 P—Q4?

Leads to a quick catastrophe. The only defence would have been
18. ... R—Q1; 19. Q—K2, P × P; 20. P × P, Q—B3 (Not 20. ...
Q—R2?; 21. B × Pch; 20. ... P—KB4 is answered by 21. P—N5);
21. Q—K3, and the threat 22. B—N5 can be parried only by 21. ...
Q—N3. White continues 22. P—B3, and Black cannot move hand
or foot.

19. Q—N3!

Very strong. White threatens 20. Q—N4ch winning a piece.

19. ...   P × P

Despair; Black hopes to fish in troubled waters after 20. Q—N4ch,
N—K2; 21. Q × Nch, K—N1. Other moves don't help either, e.g.
19. ... N—K2; 20. R × N, K × R; 21. Q—N7ch, K—B3;
22. Q × QBPch, K—K2; 23. R—K1ch, etc. Finally, 19. ... N—B3
is refuted by 20. Q—N7, R—K1; 21. R × Rch, N × R; 22. R—K1,
Q—B3 (preventing 23. Q—K7ch); 23. Q—B8, etc.

20. Q—N7!!

Wonderful! Fischer is not satisfied with one piece (after 20. Q—
N4ch), and he has seen that Black's offensive does not mean a thing.

20. ... **P × Pch**	**22. Q—N4ch**
21. B—N3 R—Q1	

Black resigns (22. ... N—K2; 23. Q × Nch and 24. Q × Rch).

Here is another fine example more in line with the heading 'Pawn
sacrifices in the opening'.

Game 20   *White:* R. Fischer   Palma de Majorca 1970
          Black: W. G. Addison   Scandinavian (Centre Counter)

1. P—K4, P—Q4; 2. P × P, Q × P; 3. N—QB3, Q—Q1 (usual is
3. ... Q—QR4); **4. P—Q4, N—KB3; 5. B—QB4, B—B4** (not a
very good place for this Bishop. Preferable was 5. ... B—N5);
6. Q—B3, Q—B1; 7. B—N5!

Here we have the Pawn sacrifice. What does White get for the
Pawn? We can see in the game three (small) advantages: 1. better
development, 2. an open QB-file and 3. the possibility of doubling
Black's Kingside Pawns by B × N.

7. ... B × P

Declining the sacrifice would have been no better, e.g. 7. ...
P—K3; 8. B × N, P × B; 9. 0—0—0, or 7. ... P—B3; 8. KN—K2
and 9. 0—0—0, in both cases with powerful position for White.

8. R—B1   B—N3   10. 0—0
9. KN—K2   QN—Q2

White first castles and then attacks, but Keres recommended 10. P—
Q5, N—K4; 11. B—N5ch, P—B3; 12. Q—N3 as more energetic.

10. ... P—K3

Now things don't look so bad for Black.

11. B × N

Another method of attacking Black's position was 11. N—B4
(Keres). Some variations:

(1) 11. ... N—N3; 12. B × P (12. B—N5ch, P—B3; 13. P—Q5!
    is also strong, and so is 12. N × P, N × B; 13. N × BPch, Q × N;
    14. B × N—the house is on fire), 12. ... P × B; 13. N × P with
    all kinds of threats.
(2) 11. ...   B—Q3; 12. N—N5, Q—N1; 13. B × P P × B;
    14. N × KP with advantage to White.
(3) 11. ... B—K2; 12. B × P, P × B; 13. N × P, again with a strong
    attack. Fischer choses a much safer method: he aims at breaking
    open the hostile position by P—Q5.

11. ... P × B?

Facilitates White's task. After 11. ... N × B it would have been
more difficult to prove the superiority of the White position. There
follows: 12. P—Q5!, B—Q3. Keres now gives three promising
continuations:

(1) 13. P × P, 0—0; 14. N—Q4.
(2) 13. N—N5, B—QB4; 14. P—Q6.
(3) 13. B—N5ch, N—Q2; 14. P—KR4.

This shows how many opportunities the gambit player has. On the
other hand it also shows how difficult it can be to make the right
choice.

12. P—Q5 P—K4

Black made his previous move (a mistake) to make possible this answer. From now on the struggle takes on a positional character. Black's KB4-square is weakened, and the decision must come from this side.

13. B—N5
Threatens 14. Q × P.

13. ... B—K2   **14. N—N3**
The siege is starting.

14. ... P—QR3   **15. B—Q3!**
A new piece is directed against KB5.

15. ... Q—Q1   **16. P—KR4**
Threatening 17. P—R5, after which Black is forced to exchange Bishops and White's KN becomes the absolute master of the key square KB5.

16. ... P—KR4
If 16. ... P—KB4 (attacking White's KRP), then 17. N × P, B × N (17. ... B × P?; 18. N—N7ch wins); 18. B × B, B × P; 19. KR—K1, Q—K2; 20. B × Nch, and White's attack will succeed.

17. B—B5
Black is completely hemmed in.

17. ... N—N3   **18. QN—K4!**

A fresh success. The natural consequence of the domination of the KB5-square is that the point K4 has become another strong square for White.

18. ... N × P
After the more solid 18. ... N—B1, White continues by 19. R—B3, N—Q3; 20. N × Nch, B × N; 21. N—K4 (21. ... B—K2; 22. KR—B1) with an irresistible attack. The consequences of the text

are just as bad for Black, but for some time he can console himself with his two plus Pawns.

19. KR—Q1
Threatening 20. R × N, Q × R; 21. N × Pch.

19. ... P—B3 20. N—B3
Now Black has to give up one of his extra Pawns.

20. ... Q—N3 21. R × N!
Tactically crowning a consistent strategy, typical of Fischer's style.

21. ... P × R 22. N × P Q × NP
Or 22. ... Q—Q1; 23. B × B, P × B; 24. N—B7ch, etc. (24. ... K—B2; 25. Q—N3ch wins the Queen, or 24. ... K—Q2; 25. Q—Q5ch, etc.)

23. R—N1 Q × P 24. R × P Black resigns.
The struggle has suddenly come to an end. Black cannot keep his KBP(3), e.g. 24. ... B—Q1; 25. B × B, P × B; 26. N × Pch, etc. It is interesting to note the co-operation between the White pieces, in sharp contrast with the complete lack of collaboration in the spreadout formation of the Black troops.

In the following game, too, Fischer handles an attack against the hostile King with great skill.

Game 21 White: R. Fischer Varna 1962
Black: M. Najdorf Sicilian Defence, Najdorf Variation

1. P—K4, P—QB4; 2. N—KB3, P—Q3; 3. P—Q4, P × P; 4. N × P, N—KB3; 5. N—QB3, P—QR3; 6. P—KR3, P—QN4; 7. N—Q5!

A surprising move with a great number of possibilities. The simplest are:

(1) 7. ... QN—Q2?; 8. N—B6 wins the Queen.
(2) 7. ... KN—Q2; 8. B—N5, P—R3?; 9. N—K6!, Q—R4ch; 10. B—Q2, etc.
(3) After 7. ... P—K3; 8. N × Nch, Q × N; 9. P—QB4 or 9. B—K3 and White's position is preferable.
(4) Unclear is 7. ... N × P; 8. Q—B3, N—B4.

Fischer points out that winning the exchange by 9. N—B6ch, NP × N; 10. Q × R is not entirely satisfactory for White (10. ... B—QN2; 11. Q—R7, Q—B2). He prefers 9. P—QN4, though this does not achieve more than equality.

7. ...   B—N2(?)   9. P—QB4   P × P(?)
8. N × Nch   NP × N

Again not the best continuation. Black should play 9. ... P—N5, for 10. Q—R4ch, Q—Q2; 11. Q × NP does not have much significance on account of 11. ... B × P.

10. B × P   B × P?

Black wrongly accepts the gambit, as becomes clear from what follows. After 10. ... Q—R4ch; 11. B—Q2, Q—K4; 12. Q—N3, Q × Pch; 13. K—Q1 great complications would arise, with better chances for White.

11. 0—0

Typical of these kinds of gambits: castle first.

11. ...   P—Q4   12. R—K1

Indirect protection of White's QB.

12. ...   P—K4

Fischer gives a number of variations, all in White's favour. We list from his analysis the most important continuations:

(1) 12. ... R—N1; 13. R × B, P × R; 14. Q—R5, R—N3; 15. Q × P, R—N2; 16. Q × P, R—QR2; 17. N—B5, and White is better.
(2) 12. ... B × P; 13. K × B, P × B; 14. Q—B3, N—Q2; 15. N—B5, R—N1ch (15. ... P—K3?; 16. R × Pch) 16. K—R1, P—K4; 17. B—K3, and again White's chances are better, notwithstanding Black's two plus Pawns.
(3) 12. ... P × B; 13. R × B, Q—Q4; 14. Q—B3, P—K3 with still an advantage for White, but less than in the other variations.

13. Q—R4ch   N—Q2

Not 13. ... Q—Q2; 14. B—N5, and certainly not 13. ... K—K2; 14. R × B, P × R; 15. N—B5 mate!

14. R × B!

Fischer in his element: an attack on a hostile position with the King in the middle of the board.

14. ... P × R 15. N—B5
Just as in the previous game the occupation of the strong KB5 square is the guarantee of a successful action.

15. ... B—B4 16. N—N7ch K—K2
16. ... K—B1; 17. B—R6, K—N1; 18. Q—N3, etc.

17. N—B5ch K—K1
This little intermezzo has only served to rob Black of the possibility of castling.

18. B—K3
The right strategy: elimination of the defender's active pieces.

18. ... B × B 20. R—Q1
19. P × B Q—N3
Also good would have been 20. B × Pch, K—Q1; 21. R—Q1, Q—N4; 22. Q—R3.

20. ... R—R2 21. R—Q6 Q—Q1
Necessary to prevent 22. R × BP followed by R × BP or B × BP.

22. Q—N3 Q—B2
Or 22. ... R—B1; 23. N—N7ch, K—K2; 24. Q—R3.

23. B × Pch K—Q1 24. B—K6
Black resigns, although the win is not so easy. Fischer gives the following variation: 24. ... R—N2; 25. Q—R4, Q—B1; 26. Q—R5ch, K—K1; 27. Q × RP, K—Q1 (White threatened 28. B × Nch); 28. B × N, R × B; 29. R × Rch, Q × R (29. ... K × R; 30. Q—Q6ch and mate); 30. Q × Pch, etc.

4. STRATEGIC COMBINATIONS BY ALEKHINE

In §1 of this chapter we classified various types of combinations. Let us define more in detail what we mean by a strategic combination—namely, a series of moves with several branches, finally leading to a positional or material advantage. In such a combination the hostile King plays a role of only minor importance. Naturally you cannot completely leave out of consideration the most important piece on the board, but the combination as such should not be directed against the King, which at most can figure in certain subsidiary variations.

Alekhine was a 'maestro' in this kind of combination, which although in general not very deep, always contained one or more unexpected turns.

Game 22   *White:* Dr A. Alekhine   22nd Game Match 1937
              Black: Dr M. Euwe   Reti Opening

1. N—KB3, P—Q4; 2. P—QB4, P—Q5; 3. P—K3, N—QB3; 4. P × P, N × P; 5. N × N, Q × N; 6. N—B3, N—B3 (better 6. ... B—N5 or 6. ... P—K4); **7. P—Q3, P—B3; 8. B—K3, Q—Q2; 9. P—Q4, P—KN3; 10. B—K2, B—N2; 11. P—KR3, 0—0; 12. 0—0, P—N3; 13. B—B3, B—N2; 14. P—QR4!, QR—Q1; 15. P—R5, Q—B2; 16. Q—N3, N—Q2; 17. P × P, P × P; 18. R—R7, R—R1; 19. KR—R1, P—K3; 20. R × R, B × R** (After 20. ... R × R; 21. R × Rch, B × R; 22. Q—R3, B—N2; 23. P—QN4 White has a considerable positional advantage.)

21. P—Q5!
The beginning of a venomous combination. The text appears to offer Black the opportunity to escape from his inactive position.

21. ...   BP × P   22. BP × P   N—B4
Alekhine was playing for the following pitfall: 22. ... B × N?;

23. P—Q6!, Q × P; 24. Q × B, B × B; 25. B—R6, and White wins the exchange for a Pawn.

Instead of the text 22. ... P × P would also have been possible, but after 23. B × QP, B × B; 24. N × B, Q—K4; 25. R—R7, Black certainly does not have fewer problems than after the move played. In any case the weakness of his QNP is a source of trouble.

23. Q—B4

Black too tried to trap his opponent. After 23. B × N, Q × B; 24. P × P, B × B; 25. P × Pch, R × P; 26. P × B, B × N; 27. R—R7, Q—N4ch. Black forces perpetual check.

| 23. ... | P × P | 25. N × B | Q—K4 |
| 24. B × P | B × B | | |

A counterattack gives Black the best prospects for a draw.

| 26. R—N1 | N—R5 | 27. P—N3 | |

After 27. Q × N, Q × N; 28. B × P, R—N1, Black regains his Pawn (29. Q—R7, Q—N2).

| 27. ... | N—N7 | 28. Q—B6 | P—QN4 |

Again Black defends his QNP, the source of all his troubles, in an indirect way: 29. Q × QNP?, R—Q1.

29. B—B4 Q—K3(?)

29. ... Q—K7 would perhaps have offered better chances to draw, but Black does not like to leave his KB3-square unprotected. Moreover, he hopes to regain the Pawn if he can develop greater activity for his pieces.

30. Q × P Q—K5

Not 30. ... R—Q1 on account of 31. R—QB1!, R × N; 32. Q—N8ch, B—B1; 33. B—R6, Q—Q3; 34. Q × Q, R × Q; 35. R—B8, etc.

| 31. R—QB1 | N—Q6 | 32. Q—B4 | Q—K7 |

Not 32. ... B—Q5; 33. N—B6ch.

| 33. R—B1 | N × B | 34. Q × N | |

Not 34. N × N, Q × Q; 35. P × Q, R—B1; 36. R—B1, B—R3, and a draw will result.

| 34. ... | Q—N4 | 35. Q—B3 | |

After 35. Q—B4 Black would force a draw by 35. ... R—N1.

| 35. ... | R—N1 | 37. R—QB1 | |
| 36. R—N1 | Q—R3 | | |

Repetition of moves to gain time.

37. ...   **Q—R6**   **39. Q—Q3   B—Q5**
38. R—N1   Q—R7

Black tries to make things as difficult as possible for White and practically forces him to carry out a subtle and deep winning combination.

40. R—KB1   Q—N7

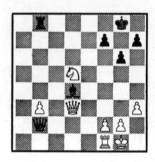

How should White proceed here? All Black's pieces are present to prevent the advance of White's only 'pride', the passed QNP.

41. N—K7ch!   K—B1

The first point is that 41. .... K—N2 is refuted by 42. N—B5ch, P × N; 43. Q—N3ch and 44. Q × R.

42. N—B6   B × Pch

This is Black's countercombination, which was taken into consideration by White. After 43. R × B, Q—B8ch; 44. Q—B1, Q × N; 45. R × Pch, K—N1, White has only a slight chance of winning.

43. K—R2!

The idea of this Pawn sacrifice will become evident five moves later.

43. ...   R—K1

Or 43. .... R—N2; 44. Q—KB3, B—N3; 54. N—Q8! winning the exchange.

44. Q—B3   R—K7

The only move. If on his 43rd move the White King had gone to R1, Black could have saved the game by 44. .... R—K8.

45. N—Q4   R—Q7   **46. N—K6ch   K—K2**
46. .... K—N1?; 47. Q—R8ch, etc.

47. N—B4

With the deadly threat, 48. N—Q3.

47. ... Q—Q5   48. K—R1!!
This wonderful move decides the game. White threatens 49. N—K2.

48. ... R—R7
The main variation continues as follows: 48. ... B—R5; 49.
Q—N7ch, Q—Q2 (49. ... K—Q3; 50. Q—N8ch, K—Q2; 51.
R—B1, or 49.... K—K1; 50. N × P, BP × N; 51. Q—B7ch,
K—Q1; 52. Q—B8ch, K—B2; 53. R—B7ch, etc.); 50. Q—N4ch,
K—K1; 51. N—K6!!, B—K2; 52. Q—N8ch, B—Q1; 53. N × B,
Q × N; 54. Q—K5ch, Q—K2; 55. Q—R8ch, K—Q2; 56. Q × P,
R—KB7; 57. R—Q1ch, K—B2; 58. Q—R8 and, with the Black
King in the field exposed to the checks of the heavy pieces, the win
should no longer be a great problem.

49. N—K2 R—R8
Hoping for 50. N × Q, R × Rch; 51. K—R2, B—N8ch, etc.

50. Q—N7ch K—B3(?)
50. ... K—B1 would have prolonged the death struggle.

51. N × Q R × Rch   52. K—R2 B—N8ch
Not 52. ... B × N on account of 53. Q—R6ch and 54. Q × R. This
explains the difference between 50. ... K—B3(?) and 50. ...
K—B1.

53. K—N3 B—B7ch   55. K—K4 R—Q8
54. K—B3 B × Nch
Forced.

56. Q—Q5?
Having attained his goal, White commits a slight error. 56. Q—B6ch
and 57. Q—B2 would have won immediately.

56. ... K—K2
The Pawn ending after 56. ... R—K8ch; 57. K × B, R—Q8ch;
58. K—B5, R × Qch; 59. K × Q leads to an easy win for White.

57. P—KN4 P—R4   58. P × P P—B4ch

Despair. After 59. K—B3, R—Q6ch; 60. K—K2, R—K6ch;
61. K—Q2, R—K5; 62. P × P Black resigned. A great game!

Certainly the Black King played his part in this game, but on the
whole his was a minor role. The same is true in the following two
games.

Game 23 *White:* Dr A. Alekhine   Margate 1923
     Black: A. Muffang Queen's Gambit, Orthodox Defence

**1. P—Q4, P—Q4; 2. P—QB4, P—K3; 3. N—KB3, N—KB3;
4. N—B3, B—K2; 5. B—N5, QN—Q2; 6. P—K3, 0—0; 7. R—B1,
P—B3; 8. Q—B2, P × P; 9. B × P, N—Q4; 10. N—K4** (Alekhine
preferred this and similar continuations to avoid the exchange of
too many light pieces), **10. ... Q—R4ch; 11. K—K2** (for the moment
the White King is just as safe in the centre as on the flank), **11. ...
R—K1** (Preferable is 11. ... P—B3; 12. B—R4, QN—N3;
13. B—N3, N—N5, and it will be difficult for White to seize the
initiative.); **12. KR—Q1, QN—N3; 13. B—N3, Q—N4ch; 14. Q—Q3**
(White could also play 14. K—K1, but Alekhine has sufficient
confidence in his position to play for a win without Queens), **14. ...
Q × Qch; 15. R × Q, B × B; 16. KN × B, N—B3; 17. N—Q6** (Apart
from an advantage in space, the occupation of this square (Q6) is
White's only trump, but Alekhine knows how to make the most
of it.) **17. ... R—K2; 18. P—K4** (occupying the centre and increasing
the mobility of the White pieces), **18. ... P—KR3; 19. N—B3,
R—N1** (prepares the development of the QB).

Black's plan is now ... B—Q2 and ... N—B1, to drive the White
Knight away from its powerful position. It seems very difficult for
White to improve his attacking chances in the remaining time (only
two moves).

20. P—N4!!
A Pawn sacrifice without direct threats. This is the beginning of a strategic combination which leads not only to the recapture of the Pawn, but also to the complete opening of the position and the exposure of the Black Kingside to the combined attack of the White forces.

20. ... N × NP
The alternative consisted of inserting 20. ... R—Q2; 21. P—K5, N × P (21. ... KN—Q4; 22. K—Q2 gives White an attack without the loss of a Pawn); 22. R—KN1, P—KR4; 23. P—R3, N—R3; 24. N—K8! and wins. White threatens both 25. R × Pch and 25. N—B6ch.

21. R—KN1 N—B3   22. N—K5
If Black should now carry out his original plan 22. ... B—Q2, he loses after 23. R—KB3!, K—B1 (to parry the threat 24 R × N); 24. N(5) × KBP. Black cannot take the White Knight: 24. ... R × N because of 25. N × R, K × N; 26. P—K5, and White wins the exchange.

22. ... QN—Q2
Black no longer has any defence against the threat 23. R—KB3.

23. N(5) × KBP
White regains his Pawn with an overwhelming position.

23. ... N—R4
23. ... R × N; 24. B × P would cost the exchange. All White's pieces are active. Black now threatens 24. ... N—B5ch.

24. R—KB3 K—R2
To defend the KRP.

25. P—K5! N—B1
White threatened 26. B—B2ch.

26. N × RP! P—QN3
A little trap: 27. R × N?, B—R3ch.

27. N(R)—B7 K—N1
The Black position is completely ruined.

28. K—K3
Avoids the check on R3 and threatens to win the Black Knight on its R4 by 29. R—R3.

G

28. ...	P—N3	30. R—N5
29. B—B2	K—N2	

Black resigns. There is no defence against 31. R × N, P × R; 32. R—N3 mate. The teamwork on the part of White's Rooks and light pieces was wonderful.

Game 24   *White:* Dr A. Alekhine   Berlin 1921
                   Black: F. Samisch   King's Indian Defence

1. P—QB4, P—K4; 2. N—QB3, N—KB3; 3. P—KN3, P—KN3; 4. B—N2, B—N2; 5. N—B3, P—Q3; 6. P—Q4 (with transposition of moves we have reached a well-known variation of the King's Indian) 6. ... P × P (Nowadays this early abandonment of the centre is considered positionally inferior); 7. N × P, 0—0; 8. 0—0, QN—Q2; 9. P—N3, N—B4; 10. B—N2, R—K1; 11. Q—B2, N—K3; 12. QR—Q1, Q—K2; 13. KR—K1, R—N1 (Preferable was 13. ... N × N; in positions with restricted movement it is advantageous for the defending side to exchange pieces.) 14. N—B3, Q—B1; 15. P—K4, N—Q2.

White has a powerful position: he controls important squares in the centre, has more space at his disposal and excellent activity for all his pieces. But how is he to make use of these advantages?

16. B—QR3!
The preparation for a clever combination. The text threatens not only 17. P—K5, but also gives the QN the opportunity to jump to QN5 or Q5 without having to fear the simplification of the position by the exchange of Bishops.

16. ... N—K4
With 16. ... N(2)—B4; 17. N—Q5, Black does not solve his problem, e.g. 17. ... B—Q2; 18. P—K5, P × P; 19. N × BP, N × N; 20. R × B.

17. N×N   B×N   19. K—R1
18. P—B4!   B—Q5ch
White now threatens 20. P—KB5, B×N; 21. Q×B and 22. B—N2.

19. ...   Q—N2
With this move Black expects to retain control over the important diagonal, but his hopes are not realized.

20. N—Q5!
Again with the threat 21. P—B5, which cannot be parried by 21. ... P—QB4 (notice that 21. ... P—QB3 is refuted simply by 22. B×P); 22. P—B5, N—B1; 23. P×P, RP×P; 24. R×B!, P×R (24. ... Q×R; 25. B—N2 would cost the Queen); 25. B×P, and White reaches an ending with at least one plus Pawn.

20. ...   B—B3
The easier part of the combination.

21. N×Bch   Q×N   22. B—N2
The Bishop returns to the diagonal as the undisputed victor.

22. ...   Q—K2   23. Q—B3   P—B3
Forced.

24. Q×P   Q×Q   25. B×Q
The end of the combination. White turned his material advantage into a quick win after 25. ... P—QN4; 26. P×P, R×P; 27. P—K5, P×P; 28. B×P (not 28. B—B6 on account of 28. ... B—N2), 28. ... B—N2; 29. B×B, R×B; 30. R—Q7, P—KR4; 31. R(1)—Q1, K—B1; 32. R—KB1, R—K2; 33. P—B5!, P×P; 34. R×Pch, K—K1; 35. R×Rch, K×R; 36. R×P, Black resigns.

Finally, the deepest strategical combination with Rooks and light pieces ever played.

Game 25   *White:* R. Reti   Baden-Baden 1925
              Black: Dr A. Alekhine   King's Fianchetto

1. P—KN3, P—K4; 2. N—KB3 (Alekhine's Defence with colours reversed and one tempo more for White), **2. ... P—K5; 3. N—Q4, P—Q4** (Under the altered circumstances Black should have chosen another variation: 3. ... P—QB4; 4. N—N3, P—B5; 5. N—Q4, B—B4; 6. P—QB3, N—QB3. In this variation the King's fianchetto does not mean a plus but a minus.) **4. P—Q3, P×P; 5. Q×P, N—KB3; 6. B—N2, B—N5ch; 7. B—Q2, B×Bch; 8. N×B, O—O; 9. P—QB4** (White's chances are on the Queenside because of his fianchettoed Bishop) **9. ...N—R3; 10. P×P, N—QN5; 11. Q—B4,**

N(5) × P; **12. N(2)—N3, P—B3; 13. 0—0, R—K1; 14. KR—Q1, B—N5; 15. R—Q2, Q—B1; 16. N—QB5, B—R6; 17. B—B3,** (Not 17. B × B, Q × B; 18. N × NP?, N—KN5; 19. N—B3, N(4)—K6; 20. P × N, N × KP; 21. Q × BPch, K—R1!; 22. N—R4, R—KB1, and Black wins. A clever combination!), **17. ... B—N5; 18. B—N2, B—R6; 19. B—B3, B—N5; 20. B—R1** (White avoids the draw by repetition.), **20. ... P—KR4** (Black continues his attack on the Kingside to get some counterweight against White's activities on the other wing.); **21. P—N4, P—R3; 22. R—QB1, P—R5; 23. P—R4, P × P; 24. RP × P, Q—B2** (the Black Queen also looks towards the hostile Kingside); **25. P—N5** (White underrates the coming attack. He should have played 25. P—K4.); **25. ... RP × P; 26. P × P, R—K6!!** (White cannot take this Rook on account of 27. ... Q × Pch, etc. Furthermore, Black is already threatening 27. ... R × Pch); **27. N—B3** (Alekhine gives as the only possible defence 27. B—B3), **27. ... P × P; 28. Q × P, N—B6!; 29. Q × P** (If 29. Q—B4, then 29. ... P—N4); **29. ... Q × Q** (This is stronger than 29. ... N × Pch; 30. R × N, Q × Q; 31. R × R, and White has drawing chances.); **30. N × Q, N × Pch; 31. K—R2** (better than 31. K—B1, N × Pch).

Now two White pieces and two Black pieces are in the air. It is very difficult for Black to maintain his advantage, for since the Pawns on the Queenside have disappeared, the winning of a single Pawn is not sufficient to win the game.

31. ... N—K5!
To make things still more complicated. We calculate: 32. P × R, N(5) × R, and Black wins the exchange or a piece.

32. R—B4
White also brings new threats onto the scene. If now 32. ... R × N, then 33. R × N (2), and if 32. ... N × R, then 33. N × N, R—Q6; 34. N—B5, in both cases with equal material.

32. ... N × BP

In one move all direct threats have disappeared. Now Black threatens (indirectly) 33. ... N × B; 34. K × N, B × Nch. Notice that 33. ... B × N is no threat (34. B × B, R × B; 35. R × N), neither is 33. ... R × N (34 R × N).

33. B—N2   B—K3

Threatens both 34. ... B × R and 34. ... N—N5ch, followed by a discovered check. White cannot parry both threats at the same time, and he has to wait to see what his opponent can do with his discovered check.

34. R(4)—B2

The threat R × N now forces Black to a dénouement. After other moves Black has time to strengthen his position, or he can win a second Pawn by N—K5 and N(5) × P.

The introductory moves have been made, and now the real combination follows—the third successive one.

34 ...   N—N5ch   35. K—R3

Or 35. K—R1, R—R8ch and mate.

35. ...   N—K4 dis. ch   36. K—R2

Or 36. K—R4, R—K5ch, etc. (37. K—N5, P—B3ch and mates).

36. ...   R × N!   37. R × N

What else? After 37. B × R, N × Bch; 38. K—N2, N × R White is a piece down.

37. ...   N—N5ch

Again the well-known combination with discovered check.

38. K—R3

Not 38. K—R1, R—R8ch, etc.

38. ... N—K6 dis. ch   39 K—R2

It does not make any difference whether White plays 39. P—N4 here, or even 39. K—R4. The same series of moves will follow.

39. ... N × R   40. B × R

After 40. R × N, R—B4 Black is the exchange and a Pawn ahead, still has an attack and will certainly win.

40. ... N—Q5!

White resigned; he did not wish to wait for the final blow after 41. R—KB2, N × Bch; 42. R × N, B—Q4!!, capturing the Knight.

As we have already mentioned, the point of several combinations by Alekhine is the final move.

5. STRATEGIC COMBINATIONS BY FISCHER

It can easily be proved that a deep combination with a number of branches can never be calculated completely and exactly by a human being unless he can reduce the extensive spread of variations in a drastic manner. This is possible only by a combination with a well-defined goal, when all continuations with no bearing on the goal can be disregarded. Intuition is sometimes a reliable substitute for calculation, but there are positions in which intuition does not count. Then, nothing else remains other than to calculate more and more deeply. Fischer has the great talent of being able to figure out long series of moves, sometimes between 10 and 20, without relying on hidden possibilities in future positions. The remark 'If I come to that, I'll look further' is never used by Fischer. He demands absolute clarity.

A good example of such a deep combination without a guiding beacon, and with the material state of affairs the only characteristic, is given by the following game.

Game 26   *White:* A. Bisguier   Bled 1961
              Black: R. Fischer   Queen's Gambit, Semi-Classical

1. P—Q4, N—KB3; 2. N—KB3, P—Q4; 3. P—B4, P—K3; 4. P—K3, P—B4; 5. N—B3, N—B3; 6. BP × P, N × P(4); 7. B—Q3, B—K2; 8. 0—0, 0—0; 9. P—QR3, P × P; 10. P × P, N—B3 (a well-known theme: advantages and disadvantages of the isolated Pawn); **11. B—K3, P—QN3; 12. R—B1, B—N2; 13. Q—K2, N—KN5** (The actual beginning of the combination. Black forces the exchange of White's QB, unless White is prepared to offer the sacrifice of a Pawn the acceptance of which looks more than risky); **14. B—B4**.

White offers his isolated Pawn. Can Black take it? The answer cannot be given until 13 moves later.

14. ...   N × P
This is unbelievable, considering the many obvious resources which White has at his disposal, which will soon become clear.

15. N × N   Q × N   16. Q × N
White could have recaptured the Pawn by 16. B × Pch, K × B; 17. Q × N. After 17. ... Q—B3 Black would then have obtained what he wanted with his 14th move: the exchange of a White Bishop. It is understandable that White does not follow course in view of the prospects opened by the continuation.

16. ...   Q × B   17. KR—Q1
Apparently with terrible consequences: the Rook will go to the seventh rank, attacking two Bishops at the same time.

17. ...   Q—N3!
Not 17. ... Q—R3 (to protect one of the Bishops), on account of 18. B—K5, P—N3 (18. ... P—B3; 19. Q × KPch); 19. R—Q7, B—B4; 20. Q × KP, or 19. ... KR—K1; 20. R × KB, R × R; 21. Q—N5.

18. Q × Q   BP × Q!
The point is that White's Bishop is now attacked. However, the affair has still not ended by far.

19. R—Q7   B—B4
After 19. ... R × B; 20. R × KB White recaptures his Pawn since 20. ... B—Q4 is refuted by 21. N × B, P × N; 22. QR—B7.

20. B—K3

If now 20. ... B × B; 21. P × B Black is still in trouble: after 21. ... B—B3; 22. R—Q6 White recaptures the Pawn, and after 21. ... R—B2; 22. R × R, K × R; 23. N—N5 White stands best.

20. ... B—B3!   **21. R—B7 KR—B1!**

If Black first plays 21. ... B × B he runs into trouble after 22. P × B, KR—B1; 23. R × Rch, R × R; 24. N—N5.

The position now reached is almost the same as the position which will soon arise in the game, but White has just one tempo more, which makes a decisive difference: 24. ... B—Q2; 25. R × Rch, B × R; 26. N × P, B—Q2; 27. K—B2, K—B2; 28. K—K2, K—K2; 29. K—Q3, K—Q3; 30. K—B4 and 31. N—N5.

22. R × Rch   R × R   **23. N—N5 B—Q2!**

Now 24. N × P is not possible on account of 24. ... R—R1.

24. P—N4   B × B

After 24. ... B × N; 25. P × B, P × P; 26. R × P, R × R; 27. B × R Black cannot play for a win because of the Bishops of opposite colours.

25. R × Rch   B × R   **27. N—Q6**
26. P × B   B—Q2

White retires. It is necessary to examine the consequences of 27. N × P to get a complete idea of the extent of the combination: 27. ... K—B2; 28. K—B2, K—K2; 29. K—K2, K—Q3; 30. K—Q3, P—QN4! (Black must prevent 31. K—B4); 31. K—Q4, P—K4ch; 32. K—K4, P—N4, and now White runs out of tempi (owing to Black's double Pawn!). As soon as the White King retreats, the Black King captures the White Knight via B2 and N2.

27. ... K—B1

The combination has come to an end. Black has maintained his plus Pawn, and although this is only a doubled Pawn, it seems sufficient for the win, taking into consideration the slight superiority of the Bishop over the Knight. There followed: 28. P—K4, P—K4; 29. K—B2, B—B3; 30. N—B4, B × P; 31. N × KP, K—K2; 32 N—B4, K—K3; 33. N—K3, K—K4; 34. K—K2, K—Q5; 35. K—Q2, B—B3; 36. P—N3, B—Q2; 37. N—Q1, K—K5; 38. N—K3, K—B6; 39. K—Q3, P—KN4; 40. K—Q4, B—K3; 41. K—K5, K × N; 42. K × B, K—B6; 43. K—B5, K—N7; 44. K × P, K × P; 45. P—N4, P—N4; 46. K—B5, K—N6; 47. P—N5, P—N3ch, White resigns.

In the next game the goal of Fischer's combination is his opponent's QN Pawn which, being on the open file, is exposed to the attack of the heavy pieces. Fischer works consistently on this theme.

Game 27 White: M. Bertok   Stockholm 1962
         Black: R. Fischer   Queen's Gambit, Orthodox Defence

1. P—Q4, P—Q4; 2. P—QB4, P—K3; 3. N—QB3, B—K2; 4. N—B3, N—KB3; 5. B—N5, 0—0; 6. P—K3, P—KR3; 7. B—R4, P—QN3 (the Tartakover variation, another way of solving the problem of Black's QB in the Orthodox Queen's Gambit); **8. P × P, N × P** (After 8. . . .P × P; 9. B—Q3, B—N2; 10. N—K5 White can build up an excellent attacking position, which 70 years ago was especially favoured by Pillsbury.); **9. B × B, Q × B; 10. N × N, P × N; 11. B—K2, B—K3; 12. 0—0** (sharper is 12. Q—R4 to answer an eventual 12. ... P—QB4 by 13. Q—R3), **12. ... P—QB4; 13. P × P** (White should postpone this move and exchange the Pawns only if Black threatens to advance his QBP. This is not the case here: 13. ... P—B5 can be answered favourably by 14. P—QN3, P—QN4; 15. P—QR4), **13. ... P × P** (Now Black has the so-called 'hanging Pawns', which in some positions can be considered weaknesses. Here, however, the White pieces are not placed particularly well for an attack against the hanging Pawns, while the Black pieces can counterattack early); **14. Q—R4, Q—N2; 15. Q—R3** (The right place at the wrong moment; better is 15. P—QN3); **15. ... N—Q2; 16. N—K1, P—QR4!** (Black already has an overwhelming position. E.g. if White now plays 17. P—QN3 there can follow 17. ... Q—N5; 18. Q—B1, P—R5, and White must at least accept the weakening of his Queenside Pawns, whereas nothing can be gained from an attack on Black's hanging Pawns.); **17. N—Q3, P—B5; 18. N—B4, KR—N1!**

Completing the mobilization of the Black forces. The text is the beginning of a combination with a number of branches. White's QNP seems to be doomed, and afterwards Black's QBP will be a dangerous element. So White must look for compensation, and the obvious 'victim' is Black's QP. So let us try: 19. B—B3, N—B3; 20. KR—Q1, Q×P; 21. Q×Q, R×Q; 22. N×P, N×N; 23. B× N, B×B; 24. R×B, P—B6! and wins (25. R—B5, P—B7; 26. R— B1, R—Q1, or 25. R(5)—Q1, P—B7; 26. KR—QB1, QR—N1; 27. K—B1, R—N8). This is one of the main branches of the combination.

19. QR—N1?
White has found another way to protect his NP, but this does not prove sufficient. There was only one move to equalize, discovered by Keres: 19. P—K4!, Q×P (If 19. ... P×P, then 20. N×B and 21. B×P); 20. Q×Q, R×Q; 21. P×P, B×P!; 22. KR—B1, etc.

19. ... B—B4
The obvious answer, naturally expected by White.

20. QR—Q1 N—B3   21. R—Q2
This is what White wanted: protection of his NP from the side, at the same time pressure against Black's weak QP. It is important to note that 21. B—B3 does not equalize either. Fischer gives the following variations: 21. ... Q×P; 22. Q×Q, R×Q; 23. N×P, N×N and now:

(1)   24. R×N, B—K3; 25. R—B5, R—QB1; 26. R×RP, P—B6;
        27. R—B1, P—B7; 28. B—K4, R—N8, etc.
(2)   24. B×N, R—QB1; 25. P—K4, B—K3; 26. B×B, P×B;
        27. P—QR4, P—B6; 28. R—B1, P—B7, and Black must win
        at least one Pawn.

21. ... P—N4!
The deciding blow. Black wishes to play his Knight to K5 in order to drive the Rook to a bad square. Therefore, he must first drive away

the Knight, because an immediate 21. . . . N—K5 could be answered simply by 22. R × P.

22. N × P

Despair. The main variation runs: 22. N—R5, N—K5; 23. R—B2, and now not 23. . . . N—N6??; 24. BP × N, B × R; 25. Q—B3!, but 23. . . . Q—N5!, and White must lose material in a bad position. This would have been the logical end of Black's combination.

22. ... N × N   23. B × P

If 23. B—B3, then 23. . . . B—Q6

23. ... B—K3   24. KR—Q1?

Hastens the loss of the game. More chances would have been offered by 24. B × N, B × B; 25. Q—Q6, since 25. . . . B × NP would be very risky on account of 26. Q × P. So Black has to play 26. . . . B—K3, and a careful follow-up would bring him victory.

24. ... N × P

Wins a Pawn and increases Black's material advantage. The rest is simple. 25. Q × N, B × B; 26. P—KR4, R—K1; 27. Q—N3, Q—K2; 28. P—N3, B—K3; 29. P—B4, P—N5; 30. P—R5, Q—B4ch; 31. R—B2, B—B4. White resigns.

Much more complicated and at the same time very surprising is the chain of combinations in the next game. This game was also important because it practically decided the match for the world championship in Reykjavik 1972. The endgame is one of the finest examples of Fischer's skill in this field.

Game 28   White: R. Fischer   10th Match Game, Reykjavik 1972
       Black: B. Spassky   Ruy Lopez, Closed Variation

1. P—K4, P—K4; 2. N—KB3, N—QB3; 3. B—N5, P—QR3; 4. B—R4, N—B3; 5. O—O, B—K2; 6. R—K1, P—QN4; 7. B—N3, P—Q3; 8. P—B3, O—O; 9. P—KR3 (A well-known position in this variation.), **9. ... N—N1** (So far the moves of both sides were directed towards development and control of the centre. The text is a terrible loss of two tempi, but it serves to maintain the centre by QN—Q2. The Knight on this square is more flexible than on QB3; moreover, the diagonal of Black's QB remains free and may be used by the QB to exert pressure on White's KP); **10. P—Q4, QN—Q2; 11. QN—Q2** (Sharper, although no more effective, is 11. P—B4, P—B3; 12. P—B5, Q—B2), **11. ... B—N2; 12. B—B2, R—K1** (directed against White's KP; better perhaps was 12. ... P—B4, trying to force White to a declaration in the centre); **13. P—QN4**

(White takes the initiative on the Queenside), **13. . . . B—KB1;
14. P—QR4** (consistent), **14. . . . N—N3** (according to a Russian
analysis, White gets a promising position after 14. . . . P—B4;
15. NP × P, P × QP; 16. P × P(Q4), P × BP; 17. P—K5); **15. P—
R5, QN—Q2; 16. B—N2** (16. P—Q5 would soon be answered by
16. . . . P—B3, after which Black has the initiative), **16. . . . Q—N1**
(an original preparation of . . . P—B4); **17. R—N1.** (Better perhaps
was 17. P—B4, P × P; 18. B—R4, as played by Kavalek against
Reshevsky.)

17. . . . P—B4 (very enterprising. Another possibility would have
been 17. . . . P × P; 18. P × P, P—Q4; 19. P—K5, N—K5; 20. N ×
N, P × N; 21. B × P, B × P, and things look pretty fair for Black.
However, White can better play 21. R × P, B × R; 22. B × B, and has a
very strong attack.); **18. NP × P, QP × P; 19. P × KP, N × P;
20. N × N, Q × N; 21. P—QB4, Q—B5.**

White could now have obtained a magnificent attack by 22. P—
K5, QR—Q1 (seemingly the refutation); 23. P × N! R × N; 24. Q ×
R, Q × Q; 25. R × R, Q × B; 26. P × KNP, Q × Rch; 27. K—R2
and wins (Timman's analysis).

22. B × N
Here the combinations from both sides start.

22. . . . Q × B
Fine recommends 22. . . . P × B in order to maintain the pressure
against White's Knight. After 23. P × P?, QR—Q1; 24. R—K2,
P × P, Black stands better.

23. P × P   KR—Q1   24. Q—B1!
A very strong move, introducing a hidden combination which not
only prevents any disadvantage, but also gives possibilities of playing
for a win.

24. ... Q—B6
This is what Bobby was waiting for.

25. N—B3   Q × P
Safer was 25. ... P × P, but Black hoped to get an advantage.

26. B—N3!
White immediately exploits the most vulnerable point of the Black position: it is very difficult for Black to find a reliable defence for his KB2.

26. ...   P × P
Two connected passed Pawns. What more can happen to Black?

27. Q—KB4!   R—Q2
After 27. ... P—B5; 28. B × P, P × B; 29. R × B, P—B3; 30. P—K5 White also has the better chances.

28. N—K5   Q—B2
Pinning the Knight. It seems as if White's attack has come to a standstill, but Fischer has calculated deeper.

29. QR—Q1!

With the nice little point: 29. ... R × R?; 30. B × Pch, K—R1; 31. N—N6ch, P × N; 32. Q—R4 mate.

29. ...   R—K2
It is difficult to decide whether 29. ... QR—Q1; 30. B × Pch, R × B; 31. Q × Rch, Q × Q; 32. N × Q, R × R; 33. R × R, B × P, would have given better chances to save the game.

30. B × Pch   R × B   32. N × Q
31. Q × Rch   Q × Q
The end of the combination. White has won the exchange for one Pawn.

32. ... B × P!

Black's best chance. After 32. ... K × N; 33. R—Q7ch the win is easier.

33. R × B   K × N   35. R—N7
34. R—Q7ch   K—B3

White must immediately blockade the Black passed Pawns. If they could advance only one square, he would probably lose the ending.

35. ...   R—R8ch

Black uses the opportunity to drive the White King away from the centre, and at the same time he develops his Bishop. After the obvious 35. ... P—N5; 36. R—N6ch, K—B2 (36. ... K—B4?; 37. P—B3, and the Black King is in a mating net); 37. P—B4, R—B1; 38. R—B4, White's chances are also very good.

36. K—R2   B—Q3ch   38. K—N2   P—R4
37. P—N3   P—N5

Many other moves were suggested in this position, such as 38. ... K—B4, 38. ... B—K4; 38. ... R—QB8 and 38. ... R—R3. Analyses have shown that the outcome is always the same: Black cannot reach an absolutely safe position, and in any case White has the opportunity for a number of promising manœuvres, which may lead to a win. The text has the advantage that the creation of a mating net by an advance of the White Pawns right down the line (P—B4, P—N4 and P—R4) is prevented.

39. R—N6   R—Q8   40. K—B3

In order by 41. K—K2 to drive Black's Rook to Black's Q4 where it has restricted possibilities of movement, so that (a) the dangerous looking Black Pawns are definitely blockaded, and (b) White can work with zugswang.

40. ...   K—B2(?)

All commentators agree that 40. ... P—N4 would have given better drawing chances.

41. K—K2   R—Q4

42. P—B4!

The way in which White brings this difficult ending to a win is exemplary. The advance of White's Kingside Pawns forces Black to new concessions again and again.

42. ...   P—N3   44. P × P   P—N4
43. P—N4   P × P

The natural looking 44. ... K—B3 is answered by 45. R—N5!, K—B2; 46. P—N5 (Timman shows that the ending after 46. R(4) × P, P × R; 47. R × R, B × P is a draw), 46. ... R—B4; 47. K—K3, R—Q4 (What else? If 47. ... K—N2, then 48. R—N6, R—Q4; 49. R—K6, etc.); 48. R(4) × P, etc.

45. P—B5   B—K4

Black tries to bring the Bishop to a better square. This, however, is at the expense of the safety of Black's King. After 45. ... R—K4 White wins as follows: 46. K—B3, R—Q4; 47. R—N7ch, K—B1 (47. ... K—B3; 48. R—K6 mate); 48. K—K2, R—K4; 49. R × R, B × R; 50. K—Q3, and White wins.

If White had exchanged Rooks immediately (46. R × R) without driving the King to the eighth rank, the win would have been very difficult, perhaps impossible.

46. R—N5!

Threatening 47. R(4) × P.

46. ...   K—B3

Black has no defence: 46. ... B—Q5; 47. R—N7ch, K—B1 (47. ... K—B3; 48. R—K6 mate); 48. R(4)—K7 or 48. R—K6 with a mating attack.

47. R(4) × P   B—Q5

At last a safe square for the Bishop, but it is already too late.

48. R—N6ch   K—K4   49. K—B3

Threatens 50. R—K6 mate.

49. ...   R—Q1   50. R—N8

Typical of Fischer's style: he gets the most out of his position. Other players would perhaps have first brought the attacked Rook into safety by 50. R—R4, but the text is much stronger and more energetic.

50. ...   R—Q2

After 50. .. P × R; 51. R × R, P—N6; 52. R—N8, P—N7; 53. R—N5ch, K—B3; 54. K—K4, B—B6; 55. K—Q3, B—K4; 56. K—B2, White wins just as easily as in the game.

51. R(4)—N7	R—Q3	54. R × P	B—K4
52. R—N6	R—Q2	55. P—B6!	
53. R—N6	K—Q4		

Witty till the end. After 55. . . . R—KB2 Black loses the Bishop:
56. R—Q8ch, K—K3; 57. R—K8ch.

55. . . . K—Q5   **56. R—N1!** Black resigns.
Against the threat 57. R—Q1ch there is no defence. E.g. 56. . . .
B × P; 57. R—Q1ch, K—B5; 58. R × Pch and 59. R × R.

It does not often happen that Fischer is playing for some trap. In
general he follows the strategical lines, and, if the position involves
seeing a number of moves ahead he recognizes his task and performs it.

But in the following game things are perhaps a little different.
On his 18th move Fischer intends to make a combination, but he
sees that it would not work. However, he discovers that if his
opponent's King were on QN1 instead of QB1, it *would* work.
So Fischer makes a rather indifferent move, and his opponent falls
into the trap. The combination is magnificent in all variations.
The point is the completely unexpected capture (or recapture) of
the hostile Queen.

Game 29   *White:* R. Fischer   Buenos Aires 1970
                 Black: S. Schweber   French Defence

**1. P—K4, P—K3; 2. P—Q4, P—Q4; 3. N—QB3, B—N5; 4. P—
K5, P—QB4; 5. P—QR3, B × Nch; 6. P × B, Q—B2; 7. N—B3,
N—QB3; 8. B—K2, B—Q2; 9. 0—0, KN—K2; 10. P—QR4,
N—R4** (Perhaps 10. . . . P—B3 would have been a little better);
**11. R—K1, P × P; 12. P × P, N—B5; 13. B—Q3, P—KR3; 14. N—
Q2, N × N; 15. B × N, N—B3; 16. Q—N4, P—KN3; 17. R—K3,
0—0—0.** (Castling Kingside was of course impossible in view of
White's concentration of forces on this side and the weaknesses
caused by Black's moves P—KR3 and P—KN3.)

At this point White considers 18. R—B3, but he sees that Black has a strong answer in 18. ... P—B4!. After 19. P × P e.p. (19. Q × NP, N × QP), 19. ... P—K4 wins a piece: 20. Q—N3, P—K5. However, if the Black King were on QN1, then the fork would not work on account of 21. B—KB4. Fischer, hoping that his opponent will soon play his King to the forbidden square, makes an indifferent move.

18. R—N3
This move does not accomplish anything, but neither does it do any harm.

18. ... K—N1?
Black swallows the bait.

19. R—B3
Waiting for the following mistake.

19. ... P—B4?
Black has been trapped. Any other move to protect the KBP would have been better (B—K1, B—B1, QR—B1 or R—R2).

20. P × P e.p. P—K4   21. Q—N3!
Not 21. Q × P, QR—N1; 22. Q—B7, R × Pch! (23. K × R, B—R6ch) or 22. Q—R5, B—N5.

21. ... N × P
Of course, not 21. ... P—K5 on account of 22. B—KB4, but the text seems strong enough.

22. R—K3 P—K5
Consistent. After 22. ... QR—K1; 23. B × NP White has one Pawn more and a strong passed Pawn.

23. R × P!!
Looks like a bad error. It is clear that Black cannot now play 23. ... P × R on account of 24. B—B4, but he can first exchange Queens.

23. ... Q × Q   24. R × N!!
This is the point of the whole combination. One is so accustomed to retaking after Q × Q that only a few players would have considered other possibilities in such a case. A miracle has happened: the Black Queen has no safe retreat (see diagram overleaf).

24. ... Q—N5
By this move Black gets the most for his lost Queen.
H

(Position after White's 24th move)

25. R × Q   B × R   26. B × NP

The combination has led to a material advantage: a Bishop and two Pawns for a Rook. In view of the strength of White's passed Pawn, supported by two Bishops, the win is quite safe.

26. ...   KR—N1   28. B—Q3   QR—K1
27. B—R7   R—R1

28. ... KR—B1 is answered by 29. B × P, R × P; 30. B—KN5.

29. P—B7!

White is going to sacrifice his passed Pawn to win back the exchange.

29. ...   R—K2

After 29. ... QR—KB1; 30. B—B3 the Black KR has no move, and after another move of the QR, e.g. 29. ... R—K3, White plays 30. B—N4.

30. P—B8 = Qch!   R × Q   32. B × R   R × B
31. B—N4   R(1)—B2

With a sound plus Pawn, the win for White is no longer difficult.

33. P—KB3   B—Q2   35. K—B2
34. P—R5   K—B2

Now White is ready to advance his Kingside Pawns.

35. ...   R—B2   37. P—N3   K—B4
36. K—K3   K—Q3   38. P—KB4   B—N5

All efforts by Black to stop the advance are in vain.

39. R—QN1   R—K2ch   41. P × P   P × P
40. K—Q2   P—N3   42. P—R3!

After White has exchanged his vulnerable RP he can turn his full attention to the other side.

42. ...,   B—Q2

Also 42. ... B × P; 43. R—R1, B—B1; 44. R × P, R—N2; 45. R—N6, and the two passed Pawns must win.

43. P—N4   P—Q5   **45. P—B6!   R—B6**
44. P—B5   R—K6

Not 45. . . . R × P; 46. P—B7, R—B6; 47. B—B5, etc.

46. R—KB1   R × R   **47. B × R   B—K3**

and Black resigned without awaiting the answer. White will soon
have two connected Pawns, which will win easily.

6. ATTACKING COMBINATIONS BY ALEKHINE

It is not necessary to give a firm definition of these kinds of combinations. We accept that 'attack' in this sense means attack against the
hostile Kingside. Alekhine was a master at building attacking
positions. He did not usually employ direct threats. The light pieces
and Rooks were brought into the vicinity of the battlefield, and then
suddenly the storm broke out. We have already noted that Alekhine's
attacks were in fact sometimes of a series of smaller attacks, ever
increasing in fierceness and strength. The following game gives a
good example of this.

Game 30   *White:* Dr A. Alekhine   Match, 3rd Game 1927
              Black: Dr M. Euwe   King's Indian Defence

**1. P—Q4, N—KB3; 2. P—QB4, P—KN3; 3. N—QB3, B—N2;
4. P—K4, 0—0; 5. B—K3, P—Q3; 6. P—B3** (White strengthens
his centre), **6. . . . P—K4; 7. P—Q5** (White's strategy is now clear:
he will castle Queenside and then march against the Black King),
7. . . . P—B3; 8. Q—Q2, P × P; 9. BP × P, N—K1 (to get some
counterweight against the White attack); **10. 0—0—0, P—B4;
11. K—N1, N—Q2** (Alekhine criticizes this move and prefers
11. . . . P—QR3 followed by 12. . . . P—QN4); **12. N—R3, P—
QR3** (Black could have closed the position on the King's wing by
12. . . . P—B5, but in the long run White would have succeeded in
opening up the Kingside by such moves as P—KN3, P—KR4
and P—R5); **13. P × P, P × P** (White strives for more space
on the Kingside, as is particularly evident from his next move);
14. P—KN4!, P × P; 15. N—KN5 (threatens 16. N—K6), **15. . . .
N(2)—B3** (White has sacrificed a Pawn for more freedom for the
attack; see diagram overleaf).

16. B—Q3

A bit later the characteristics of an attack against the King will
appear. As yet there are no direct threats, but White is building up
a concentration of force.

16. ... Q—K2

After 16. ... P × P White would have mobilized his QR by 17. QR—
KB1 and 18. R × P.

(Position after Black's 15th move)

17. P—B4

Breaking open the position further and also playing with the idea of
continuing by 18. P—B5 and 19. N—K6.

17. ... P—K5!

Black gives the Pawn back in order to activate his KB.

18. N(5) × KP	**N × N**	**20. N—N3**	**B × Bch**
19. N × N	**B—B4**	**21. Q × B**	

Black has sustained the first wave of attacks, and his position looks
satisfactory.

21. ... Q—B3

Threatens mate and forces the Rook to leave the first rank, which
may be of importance later.

22. R—Q2 Q—B2

To prevent 23. N—R5.

23. P—KR3!

The attack proper starts.

23. ...	**P × P**	**25. P—B5**
24. R × P	**Q—N3**	

White must certainly avoid the exchange of Queens, but the other
method, 25. N—K4, would perhaps have been better. The drawback of the text move is that the Black Bishop can eventually go to
K4.

25. ... Q—N5 26. R(2)—R2 R—B1

Black places his pieces on the most active squares. What else can
happen? White cannot play 27. R × P on account of 27. ... Q × N.

27. P—B6!

The second wave. The combination runs as follows: 27. .... N × P; 28. N—B5!, Q—QB5 (White threatened 29. R—N3, etc.); 29. N—K7ch, K—B2 (29. .... K—R1?; 30. Q × Pch and mate); 30. Q—B5!, K × N; 31. Q—K6ch, K—Q1; 32. B—N6ch (This again shows how dependent a combination is on details. If Black's Queenside formation had been R2—N3 instead of R3—N2, the combination would have failed), 32. .... R—B2; 33. R—QB3, Q—B8ch; 34. K—B2, N—K1; 35. B × Rch, N × B; 36. Q × Pch and wins. A wonderful combination.

27. ...	**R × P!**	**29. R—R1**
28. Q × Pch	**K—B1**	

Compare Black's 21st move.

29. ...   Q—N3ch

Relief again. The attack is repulsed, because White's strongest piece will disappear.

30. Q × Q   R × Q   31. N—B5!

Alekhine once again shows his skill at attacking with light pieces. The text threatens 32. N × B, R × N; 33. B—R6, or 32. .... N × N; 33. R—R8ch.

31. ...   B—K4

31. .... R—B2 would have made things more difficult: 32. B—Q4, B × B; 33. N × B, N—N2, and although Black is threatened from all sides, it is not so easy to demonstrate a forced win.

32. R—B3   N—B3(?)

Not the best way of interposing. True, 32. .... R—B3 would have been equally bad: 33. B—N5, R—KB2; 34. B—K7ch, R × B; 35. N × P dis. ch, etc. However, after 32. .... B—B3 Black could still play: 33. B—Q4, R—B2; 34. N × P, N × N; 35. B × B, R—B2. Black was confident that everything was all right having survived such serious attacks.

33. R—R8ch

The simple refutation.

33. ...	R—N1	35. N—K7ch
34. R × Rch	**K × R**	

Black resigns.

An example of a very quiet preparation of the attack on the King is given by the following game.

Game 31 White: Dr A. Alekhine   Baden-Baden 1925
            Black: F. J. Marshall   Queen's Gambit, Irregular
                                                                      Defence

1. P—Q4, P—Q4; 2. P—QB4, N—KB3 (favourite of Marshall's);
3. P × P, N × P; 4. P—K4 (Preferable is first 4. N—KB3), **4. ...
N—KB3; 5. B—Q3** (5. N—QB3, P—K4 would give Black a good
game), **5. ... P—K4; 6. P × P, N—N5; 7. N—KB3, N—QB3;
8. B—KN5** (White rightly does not make any effort to keep the
gambit Pawn. After 8. B—KB4, N—N5; 9. B—QN5ch, B—Q2;
10. B × Bch, Q × B; 11. Q × Qch, K × Q, Black is quite happy.)
**8. ... B—K2; 9. B × B, Q × B; 10. N—B3, N(3) × P; 11. N × N,
Q × N; 12. P—KR3, N—B3; 13. Q—Q2!.**

Who would think of a Kingside attack in such a position?
Answer: Alekhine. From here on, Black gradually gets into difficulties but without having made an obvious error.

13. ...   B—Q2   14. Q—K3!

Preparing the advance of his KP and KBP without leaving the Black
squares (Q4 and QB5) in his opponent's hands.

14. ...   B—B3   15. 0—0—0

The consequence of White's strategy.

15. ...   0—0   16. P—B4   Q—K3

Perhaps 16. ... Q—QR4 would have been a little better, but after

17. P—K5 the Knight cannot go to Q4 on account of 18. N × N,
B × N; 19. B × Pch, K × B; 20. Q—Q3ch and 21. Q × B, winning a
Pawn.

17. P—K5   KR—K1

17. ... N—Q4?; 18. N × N, B × N; 19. B × Pch, etc.

18. KR—K1

White puts his pieces into battle array. His KP needed extra protection in view of P—B5 to follow.

18. ... QR—Q1

'If two people do the same thing, it is not the same.' Preferable was
18. ... N—Q2.

19. P—B5   Q—K2   20. Q—N5

The storm breaks. Black, himself a fine combinative player, has
confidence in the possibilities of his counteraction, which will soon
follow.

20. ...   N—Q4   22. B—B4!
21. P—B6   Q—B1

Opens a new line of attack against the Black King.

22. ...   N × N

Not 22. ... P—KR3; 23. P × P!, and White wins a piece on Q5.

23. R × R   R × R   24. P × P

This looks very simple, but it is not.

24. ...   N × Pch

This is better than 24. ... Q—K1, after which 25. B × Pch decides:
25. ... K × B; 26. R—B1ch, K—K3; 27. R—B6ch, K—Q4;
28. R—B8, etc.

25. K—N1!

After 25. B × N, Black has a remarkable counterattack at his disposal. 25. ... Q—B4ch; 26. K—N1, B—K5ch; 27. K—R1, R—Q4! and now 28. B × R fails against 28. ... Q—R4ch; 29. B—R2, Q × Rch and mate.

25. ... Q—K1
There is no other answer.

26. P—K6!
The final blow.

26. ... B—K5ch   27. K—R1
Not 27. K × N, Q—R5 mate, and not 27. R × B either: 27. ... R—Q8ch; 28. K—B2, Q—R5ch with counterchances.

27. ... P—KB4
Or 27. ... P × P; 28. B × Pch, Q × B; 29. Q × Rch, K × P; 30. Q—Q4ch and 31. Q × B.

28. P—K7 dis. ch   R—Q4   29. Q—B6!
The final blow.

29. ... Q—B2   30. P—K8 = Qch
Black resigns; mate follows.

If the opposing King's position was not properly defended, Alekhine knew how to strike immediately.

Game 32   *White:* Dr A. Alekhine   Triberg 1921
            Black: E. Bogoljubov   Queen's Indian Defence

1. P—Q4, N—KB3; 2. N—KB3, P—K3; 3. P—B4, P—QN3; 4. P—KN3, B—N2; 5. B—N2, P—B4; 6. P × P (The simplest continuation. More energetic is 6. P—Q5, P × P; 7. N—R4, and White recaptures the Pawn, exercising pressure on Black's position), **6. ... B × P** (better 6. ... P × P); **7. 0—0, 0—0; 8. N—B3, P—Q4; 9. N—Q4,** (preventing the complete equalization in the centre) **9. ... B × N** (better 9. ... Q—B1); **10. Q × B, N—B3; 11. Q—R4!**.

The beginning of the preparation for the Kingside attack.

11. ...   P × P   12. R—Q1

Not 12. Q × BP, N—R4, with equal chances.

12. ...   Q—B1   13. B—N5!

Accumulation of power. White drives away the last Black defender.

13. ...   N—Q4

Better 13. ... N—Q2, but the text looks perfectly safe.

14. N × N   P × N   15. R × P!

The White Rook must also participate in the attack.

15. ...   N—N5

The obvious answer—with a striking refutation.

16. B—K4!

Four pieces against an undefended King's wing!

A number of pretty variations, some quite uncommon, result from this fine attacking move.

(1) 16. ... P—N3; 17. B—B6,
   (a) 17. ... Q—K3; 18. Q × Pch, K × Q; 19. R—R5ch and mate.
   (b) 17. ... N × R; 18. B × N, P—KR4; 19. B—QB3, and mate follows (19. ... Q—Q1; 20. Q—Q4).

(2) 16. ... P—KR3; 17. B × P,
   (a) 17. ... P × B; 18. R—N5ch! and mate.
   (b) 17. ... P—B4; 18. Q—N5, R—B2 (18. ... Q—B2;
       19. B × NP, Q × B; 20. Q × Qch, K × Q; 21. R—Q7ch, etc.);
       19. R × P, B × B; 20. R × R, K × R; 21. Q × Pch, K—K3;

22. R—Q1, and, with three Pawns for a piece in an over-whelming positon, White has nothing to fear.

(c) 17. ... N × R; 18. Q—N5, P—N3; 19. B × N, K—R2; 20. B × R, etc.

(d) 17. ... P—B3; 18. B × P, B × R (or N × R); 19. Q—R7ch, K—B2; 20. Q—R5ch!, K—K2; 21. B × Rch, and 22. B × B. White has won two Pawns.

(3) 16. ... P—B4. See the game.

16. ...   P—B4   18. R—Q8ch
17. B × P!   R × B
Very original.

18. ...   Q × R   19. B × Q
With Queen and Pawn against Rook and Knight, the game is easily won by White.

There followed: 19. ... R—QB1; 20. R--Q1, R—KB2; 21. Q—N4, N—Q6; 22. P × N, R × B; 23. P × P, QR—KB1; 24. P—B4, R—K2; 25. K—B2, P—KR3; 26. R—K1, B—B1; 27. Q—B3, R(2)—KB2; 28. Q—Q5, P—KN4; 29. R—K7, P × P; 30. P × P, Black resigns.

7. ATTACKING COMBINATIONS BY FISCHER

Fischer's attacking games usually start with a positional struggle for small advantages. In the course of this the hostile King may appear in the picture, if so, there is a change in the evaluation of certain characteristics. Control of squares in the neighbourhood of the opponent's King becomes more important than control elsewhere. Sacrifices to open up the King's position must be considered at each move. In short, the calculations may become deeper but, on the other hand, sometimes less broad because moves outside the battlefield proper do not need to be considered. Anyhow, exact calculation comes to the fore, and it is superfluous to say that Fischer is most competent in this field. The difference between Fischer and Alekhine is that Fischer never seeks the attack—it comes to him of itself, while Alekhine—as we have seen—makes aggressive moves like Q—R4 and N—N5 to steer the game into the desired direction.

First, a game in which the better treatment of the opening and the exact calculation of a number of continuations give Fischer the possibility of attacking the opponent's Kingside. He carries out the attack with such intensity that even a defender like Petrosian is not equal to the difficult task.

Game 33   *White:* R. Fischer   1st Game   U.S.S.R.–Rest of
         Black: T. Petrosian   World, Belgrade 1970
                                                 Caro-Kann Defence

1. P—K4, P—Q3; 2. P—Q4, P—Q4; 3. P × P, P × P; 4. B—Q3
(Fischer plays a very quiet variation. He did not want to play
4. P—QB4, as was probably expected by his opponent) **4. ...
N—QB3; 5. P—QB3, N—B3; 6. B—KB4** (6. P—KR3 to prevent
the development of Black's QB, is energetically answered by 6. ...
P—K4) **6. ... B—N5; 7. Q—N3, N—QR4** (This was generally
considered the best counteraction. However, 7. ... Q—B1 seems
to entail fewer obligations.) **8. Q—R4ch, B—Q2; 9. Q—B2, P—K3;
10. N—B3, Q—N3; 11. P—QR4!** (A very powerful move which,
(a) prevents B—N4, the exchange of Black's bad Bishop for White's
good Bishop and, (b) in the long run prevents Black from playing
the minority attack, consisting in the advance P—N4 and P—N5,
the standard manœuvres against White's formation on the Queenside), **11. ... R—B1** (It is interesting that Black cannot take
advantage of the obvious weakness of White's QN3 square. We try:
11. ... Q—N6; 12. Q—K2, B × P?; 13. R × B, Q × R; 14. B—N5ch,
or 11. ... N—N6; 12. R—R2, R—B1; 13. 0—0, followed by
QN—Q2. White has the better development anyhow); **12. QN—Q2,
N—B3; 13. Q—N1** (to prevent 13. ... N—QN5), **13. ... N—KR4**
(unco-ordinated actions on both wings cannot be good in a position
where White has centralized his pieces and is more advanced in
development); **14. B—K3, P—KR3** (Perhaps Black is thinking in
terms of 15. ... P—N4, but it does not come to that. Instead
of the text, 14. ... P—B4 was not recommended on account
of 15. P—KN4, P × P; 16. N—N5, regaining the Pawn and
initiating a promising attack. Better, however, would have been
14. ... P—N3.); **15. N—K5!** (with the strong threat, 16. B—N6!),
15. ... N—B3 (Black retreats, leaving the initiative completely in
White's hands. Black could have tried 15. ... N × N; 16. P × N,
B—B4; 17. P—R5!, Q—B2; 18. P—KN4—winning a piece—
18. ... B × B; 19. P × B, Q × KP; 20. P × N, Q × Pch; 21. B—K2,
B—N4; 22. Q—Q1, 0—0; 23. N—B1, Q—K4; 24. N—N3, R—B5,
and White has a difficult defence, but in the long run his chances
will be better); **16. P—R3, B—Q3; 17. 0—0, K—B1** (The best
proof that Petrosian is not satisfied with his position. The normal
17. ... 0—0 would certainly have been better, although not
entirely satisfactory, for White can start an attack by P—KB4 and
P—KN4.)

18. P—KB4

White has built up an ideal attacking position, and we shall now see how Fischer handles this kind of position. First we have to examine 18. ... N × N?; 19. BP × N, B × P; 20. P—R5! (always a welcome in-between move), and White wins a piece.

18. ... B—K1   19. B—B2
To prevent once and for all the exchange on K5.

19. ... Q—B2
After 19. ... P—N3 White could have made a promising sacrifice: 20. P—B5, NP × P; 21. B × P, P × B; 22. Q × P.

20. B—R4 N—KN1
Steinitz redivivus!

21. P—B5!
The right method in attacking positions like this: open the files against the King.

21. ...   N × N   24. P × P B × KBP
22. P × N B × P   25. N—B3 B × B
23. P × P B—B3
Black's position is hopeless; he cannot build up a reliable defensive line around his King.

26. N × B N—B3   27. N—N6ch
The more defenders eliminated, the better. White could also play 27. B—N6, but in general Fischer has a certain preference for Bishops.

27. ...   B × N   28. B × B K—K2!
A last attempt to save the game. Black tries to bring his King to the Queenside.

29. Q—B5
Heavy artillery to prevent the flight.

29. ... K—Q1

29. ... KR—Q1 would not be in harmony with the flight plan:
30. QR—K1ch, K—B1; 31. R—K6, and there is no good defence
against 32. R × Nch.

30. QR—K1 Q—B4ch

After 30. ... Q—Q2; 31. R—K6 (threatens 32. R × N), 31. ...
R—B1; 32. Q—K5, R—B3; 33. Q—N8ch wins.

A pretty variation is 30. ... R—B1; 31. Q × Pch, N × Q; 32. R ×
Rch, K—Q2; 33. B—B5ch, K—Q3; 34. R × R and wins.

31. K—R1

White still has problems in securing the win. If, e.g., after 31. ...
R—B3 he plays 32. Q—K5, Black answers 32. ... Q—Q3, and
White can no longer make any progress. Keres gives the right
winning continuation after 31. ... R—B3; 32. P—QN4!, and now:

(1) 32. ... Q × BP; 33. Q—B4! and Black cannot prevent the
    White Queen from penetrating his position. (33. ... R—QB1;
    34. Q—Q6ch, or 33. ... R—B2; 34. R—B1.)
(2) 32. ... Q—Q3; 33. P—B4!, and the Black position falls apart
    (33. .... R × P; 34. R—K6, or 33. ... P—Q5; 34. P—B5,
    Q—Q2; 35. Q—K5).

31. ... R—B1   32. Q—K5 R—QB2

32. ... Q—B2 is answered by 33. Q × Pch! (Compare the comment
on Black's 30th move.)

33. P—QN4! Q—B3

If 33. ... Q × BP then 34. Q—Q6ch, and if 33. ... Q—K2, then
34. Q—Q4 and 35. Q × RP.

34. P—B4!

Breaks all resistance.

34. ... P×P   **35. B—B5 R(1)—B2**

Black cannot avoid the loss of at least the exchange.

36. R—Q1ch R(KB)—Q2

If 36. ... N—Q2, then 37. KR—K1.

37. B×R

The first material result of White's well-conducted attack.

37. ... R×B   **38. Q—N8ch K—K2**

38. ... Q—B1 is answered by 39. R×Rch, N×R; 40. Q—Q6, etc.

39. R(Q)—K1ch   Black resigns

(39. .... K—B2; 40. Q—K8 mate).

Here is another attacking game which, however, ends abruptly because of Fischer's precisely timed attack on his opponent's weakest point (KB2).

Game 34   *White:* R. Fischer   Vinkovci 1968
                  Black: D. Minic   King's Gambit

1. P—K4, P—K4; 2. P—KB4 (It is certainly a surprise to see Fischer play this wild opening, but as this gambit is handled here by both sides, it is not wild at all. It moves along regular positional lines.), **2. ... P×P; 3. B—B4** (White does not fear the check on R5 which, as is well known today, is more dangerous for Black than for White), **3. ... N—K2** (Unusual; Bogoljubov has recommended 3. ... N—KB3; 4. N—QB3, P—QB3.); **4. N—QB3, P—QB3; 5. N—B3** (With 5. Q—K2 White could prevent 5. ... P—Q4, but it is just this move that Fischer wants to provoke), **5. ... P—Q4; 6. B—N3, P×P** (Better perhaps is 6. ... B—K3); **7. N×P, N—Q4** (7. ... N—N3 is refuted by 8. QN—N5); **8. Q—K2, B—K2; 9. P—B4, N—N2; 10. P—Q4, O—O; 11. B×P, N—K3; 12. B—K3, B—N5ch; 13. K—B2** (castling in an artificial manner,) **13. ... N—Q2; 14. P—B5?!** (Typical Fischer: his KB is mobilized against Black's KB2, while the Black KB is cut off from the field of action. The only drawback of the text is the weakness of the Q5 square, but it will not be easy for Black to get at this weakness) **14. ... N—B3; 15. N×Nch, Q×N; 16. KR—KB1** (continuation of the castling process); **16. ... N—B5** (Things look very bright for Black, but this is just what Fischer wants: his opponent overrates his position); **17. B×N, Q×B; 18. P—N3!** (A weakening of the King's position. Not many players would have done this, because Black's QB can now come to R6), **18. ... Q—R3** (Favours White's plans. After 18. ... Q—B3; 19. K—N1, B—N5 Black would have had nothing to fear, and the same is also true after 19. Q—K5, Q×Q; 20. N×Q,

B—K3.); **19. K—N1, B—R6?** (Black falls into the trap; the bait was too tempting. With 19. ... B—K3 Black would have held his own.)

20. N—K5!
This powerful move decides the game; the attack against KB2 is worth more than the exchange. Some variations:

(1) 20. ... B—K3; 21. N × KBP! (the Black Queen is badly placed), 21. ... B × N; 22. R × B, R × R; 23. R—KB1, R—KB1 (with 23. ... K—R1, Black can hold out longer); 24. R × R, R × R; 25. Q—K8 mate.

(2) 20. ... B—Q7; 21. N × KBP, Q—K6ch; 22. R—B2!, Q × Q; 23. N—K5 dis. ch, K—R1; 24. R × Q, etc.

(3) 20. ... B × R, as in the game.

20. ... B × R   21. R × B B—Q7!
Two alternatives:

(1) 21. ... P—KN3; 22. N × BP, Q—N2; 23. N—Q8 dis. ch!, K—R1; 24. R × Rch, Q × R; 25. Q—K5ch and mate.

(2) 21. ... Q—Q7; 22. Q—K4, K—R1; 23. N × Pch, R × N; 24. R × R, R—Q1; 25. Q—K5, Q—K8ch (25. ... R—KN1; 26. Q × Pch! and mate); 26. Q × Q, B × Q; 27. R × QNP, B—Q7; 28. K—B2, P—N3; 29. P—Q5! and wins.

22. R—B3
To prevent Q—K6ch. Worth considering was 22. N × KBP, Q—K6ch; 23. R—B2, Q × Q; 24. R × Q, B—B8, but Black would have had drawing chances.

22. ... QR—Q1?
Only with 22. ... K—R1 could Black have prolonged the game: 23. N × Pch, R × N; 24. B × R, and in view of the Bishops of opposite

colours some drawing chances would still exist (24. ... B—N4!;
25. B—K8, B—B3).

23. N × KBP   R × N   24. Q—K7!
Black resigns (24. ... QR—KB1; 25. B × Rch and mate).

One of Fischer's best attacking games follows. It is also the most
difficult, and the complications, with numerous possibilities on both
wings, make mistakes unavoidable. I shall not go too deeply into
the analysis but indicate only briefly where each of the players went
wrong, mainly using Fischer's own comments and those of Keres.

Game 35   *White:* R. Fischer   Sousse 1967
                Black: L. Stein   Ruy Lopez, Closed Variation

**1. P—K4, P—K4; 2. N—KB3, N—QB3; 3. B—N5, P—QR3;
4. B—R4, N—B3; 5. 0—0, B—K2; 6. R—K1, P—QN4; 7. B—N3,
P—Q3; 8. P—B3, 0—0; 9. P—KR3, B—N2** (an unusual move
which, however, has the advantage of pressing against White's KP)
**10. P—Q4, N—QR4; 11. B—B2, N—B5; 12. P—QN3, N—N3;
13. QN—Q2** (13. P × P, P × P; 14. Q × Q, QR × Q; 15. N × P is
useless on account of 15. ... N × P!; 16. B × N, B × B; 17. R × B?,
R—Q8ch) **13. ... QN—Q2** (now we come to the well-known
variation with 9. ... N—N1); **14. P—QN4** (Compare game 28
Fischer–Spassky) **14. ... P × P** (This is a concession which enables
White eventually to start a Kingside attack. To be considered was
14. ... R—K1, similar to the game just cited, but Black has one
tempo less here); **15. P × P, P—QR4; 16. P × P, P—B4** (This is
stronger than 16. ... R × P, after which White can tie up Black's
Queenside by 17. P—Q5.)

17. P—K5!
The Kingside attack begins:

17. ...   P × KP

17. ... N—Q4 is inferior on account of 18. N—K4. After 17. ...
N—K1 Keres gives the variation 18. P × BP, N × BP; 19. N—N3,
N × N; 20. Q—Q3, P—N3; 21. B × N, with a strong attack for
White.

18. P × P   N—Q4   19. N—K4

The normal build-up of the Kingside attack, which we can also see
in many of Alekhine's games. White's light pieces are all ready for
battle.

19. ...   N—N5!

Black strikes back. After 19. ... R × P; 20. N(4)—N5, P—R3;
21. Q—Q3, P—N3; 22. N—K6 White would win immediately.

20. B—N1   R × P   21. Q—K2   N—N3

Fischer considers that Black should have played 21. ... R—K1,
but Keres shows a most interesting continuation of the attack after
this move: 22. P—K6, P × P; 23. N(4)—N5, B × N (If 23. ...
N—B1?, then 24. B × Pch, N × B; 24. Q × Pch, etc.); 24. B × Pch!
(Fischer considers only 24. N × B, N—B1; 25. Q—R5, P—N3),
24. ... K × B; 25. N × Bch, K—N3; (25. ... K—N1; 26. Q—R5
wins); 26. N × P, R × N; 27. Q—N4ch, K—R2; 28. R × R, N—B3;
29. Q—B5ch, K—N1; 30. Q × P, and White stands best.

22. N(3)—N5   QB × N

The best defence. After 22. ... P—R3; 23. N—R7! White wins
(23. ... K × N; 24. N × P dis. ch, or 23. ... R—K1; 24. N(7)—
B6ch, B × N; 25. P × B, P × P; 26. Q—N4ch).

More difficult is 22. ... P—N3. Keres analyses: 23. N × RP!,
K × N; 24. N—Q6!, B × N; 25. Q—R5ch, K—N1; 26. B × P,
P × B; 27. Q × Pch, K—R1; 28. B—N2!, and it seems as if White
(notwithstanding his enormous disadvantage of being three pieces
down) must win.

23. Q × B   P—N3   25. Q—N3
24. Q—R4   P—R4

25. P—N4 would simply be answered by 25. ... Q—Q5. Now
White has a number of threats, such as 26. N—K6, or 26. P—K6
or 26. N × BP.

25. ...   N—B5

Black wishes to see the proof of the threats in the previous comment,
hoping that the 'embarras du choix' will confuse his opponent.

On examining this position we come to the following conclusions:

(1) Black's 25th move has parried the threat 26. N—K6, because of: 26. ... B—R5; 27. N × Q, B × Q; 28. N—N7, R—R2; 29. N × P, B × KP!

(2) 26. P—K6 is still strong (Fischer). After 26. ... P—B4; 27. N—B3 (27. N—B7, R × N; 28. P × Rch, K × P looks very drawish).

    (a) 27. ... K—N2; 28. Q—B4, R—R1; 29. B × P leads to the game.

    (b) 27. ... R—B3; 28. B—N5, K—R2; 29. B × R, B × B; 30. B × P!, P × B; 31. QR—Q1, N—Q4 (Else 32. R—Q7ch); 32. P—K7, B × P; 33. R × N wins.

(3) Best seems Keres' recommendation 26. N × P. After 26. ... R × N, both 27. B × P, R—N2; 28. B—R6, and 27. Q × Pch, R—N2; 28. Q × P are very promising.

26. N—B3? K—N2?
With 26. ... N—Q6! Black could have stopped White's attack:

27. B × N (27. R—Q1, N × B!; 28. R × Q?, N—K7ch), 27. ... Q × B; 28. B—N5, R—R2!; 29. B × B, R × B; 30. Q—N5, KR—K1, and now 31. Q—R6 fails against 31. ... N × P; 32. N—N5, P—B3.

If in this variation White drives away the Black Queen by QR—Q1, the Queen goes to its KB4 and thus helps to eliminate all dangers.

27. Q—B4 R—R1   28. P—K6; P—B4
Fischer believed that 28. ... B—B3 would have been Black's best chance, but Keres in an excellent analysis shows that then White would also have won. We give from this analysis only the main variation: 28. ... B—B3; 29. P × P, B × R; 30. P—B8 = Qch, Q × Q; 31. Q—B7ch, K—N1; 32. B × P, N—Q4; 33. Q—N3!, Q—Q3; 34. Q—N5!, B—B3; 35. B—R7 db ch, K × B; 36. Q—R6ch, K—N1; 37. Q—N6ch, B—N2; 38. R—K8ch, Q—B1; 39. Q—K6ch, K—R2; 40. N—N5 mate.

29. B × P!   Q—B1

After 29. . . . P × B; White wins: 30. Q—N3ch, K—R2 (30. . . . K—B1; 31. Q—N6!); 31. N—N5ch, B × N; 32. B × B, Q—N1 (32. . . . Q—Q6; 33. Q—B7ch); 33. Q—R4, K—N3; 34. B—B6.

30. B—K4?

White does not persevere. Here Alekhine would certainly have played 30. N—R4!, e.g. 30. . . . B × N; 31. Q × B, Q × B; 32. Q—K7ch, K—N1; 33. Q—Q8ch, K—N2; 34. Q—B7ch, K—N1; 35. P—K7, etc.

30. . . .   Q × Q   31. B × Q   R—K1?

Time trouble; Black fails again. According to Fischer Black could have obtained some drawing chances by taking White's RP: 31. . . . R × P; 32. R × R, N × R; 33. N—K5, P—N4; 34. B—N3. Keres suggests 33. B—B6, N—B6; 34. N—K5.

32. QR—Q1   R—R3   33. R—Q7

Perhaps still better was 33. B—N7, R—R2; 34. R—Q7.

33. . . .   R × P   34. N—N5   R—KB3

Or 34. . . . R—R3; 35. B—N1, K—B3 (Black is completely tied up); 36. N—K4ch, K—B2; 37. N × P, etc.

35. B—B3

Wins the exchange.

35. . . .   R × B

If 35. . . . K—B1, then 36. N—R7ch.

36. N—K6ch   K—B3   38. R—N7   B—Q3
37. N × R   N—K4

38. . . . N × Bch; 39. P × N does not facilitate Black's task.

39. K—B1   N—B7

After 39. . . . N × B; 40. R × R, N—Q7ch; 41. K—K2, B × N White wins by 42. R—B8ch and 43. R × B.

40. R—K4   N—Q5, and White won after 16 more moves: 41. R—N6, R—Q1; 42. N—Q5ch, K—B4; 43. N—K3ch, K—K3; 44. B—K2, K—Q2; 45. B × Pch, N × B; 46. R × N, K—B3; 47. P—R4, B—B2; 48. K—K2, P—N4; 49. P—N3, R—QR1; 50. R—N2, R—KB1; 51. P—B4, P × P; 52. P × P, N—B2; 53. R—K6ch, N—Q3; 54. P—B5 R—QR1; 55. R—Q2, R × P; 56. P—B6, Black resigns (56. . . . R—KB5; 57. N—Q5 and 58. N × B).

White had to kill his opponent a third time, after having brought him back to life twice.

8. MATING COMBINATIONS BY ALEKHINE

The mating combination is the natural extension of the attacking combination, and it is more or less problematic whether such a combination will end in a mate. Certainly Alekhine's vigorous attacks lend themselves best to such a beautiful crowning of the attack. We start with a simple example, an exhibition game played by Alekhine against a weaker opponent who, however, builds up a solid position. Alekhine has to launch all his forces and exert his whole creative capacity to overpower the hostile position. A pretty mate by Knight and Bishop is his reward.

Game 36   *White:* Torres   Exhibition Game, Seville 1922
            Black: Dr A. Alekhine   Ruy Lopez

**1. P—K4, P—K4; 2. N—KB3, N—QB3; 3. B—N5, P—QR3;
4. B—R4, N—B3; 5. 0—0, P—Q3** (With the Black pieces, Alekhine generally chose some unusual line, because following the well-known theoretical paths could very easily lead to drawish positions.); **6. B × Nch, P × B; 7. P—Q4, N × P** (again an unusual move); **8. R—K1, P—KB4** (played very energetically, but Alekhine's build-up is not very solid, and he would never have taken the risk against a stronger opponent); **9. P × P, P—Q4; 10. N—Q4, B—B4; 11. P—QB3** (After 11. B—K3! Black might have got into trouble); **11. ... 0—0; 12. P—B4** (preferable 12. P—B3, N—N4; 13. K—R1); **12. ... Q—K1; 13. B—K3, B—N3; 14. N—Q2, B—N2; 15. N(2)—B3, R—Q1; 16. Q—B2, P—B4** (mobilization on all fronts); **17. N—N3, P—B5; 18. N(N3)—Q4, P—B4** (Black does not let up on his opponent); **19. N—K2, Q—B3; 20. QR—Q1, P—R3; 21. R—KB1, K—R1; 22. K—R1, Q—N3; 23. N(2)—N1, Q—R4** (now everything is ready for the final attack P—N4, etc.) **24. N—R3** (Black threatened 24. ... N—N6 mate). This move prevents the advance of Black's KNP, but now the blow comes from another and quite unexpected quarter.

24. ... P—Q5!

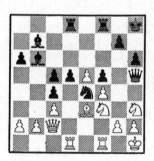

Though White controls this square 4 times and Black only 3 times, Black carries out this advance, since his only aim is to open the diagonal for his QB.

25. P×P   P×P   26. B×P?
This loses a piece, but 26. B—N1, P—N4! would have been hopeless for White as well.

26. ...   B×B   28. N×R
27. R×B   R×R
White has won the battle on Q4, but now he loses another battle.

28. ....   Q×N!   29. P×Q?
With 29. N—B3 or 29. R—B3 White could have extended the hopeless struggle, but he certainly appreciated Alekhine's last move and thus co-operated in completing a fine work of art.

29. ...   N—B7 double ch   30. K—N1   N×P mate.

Alekhine operated in this stormy manner not only against weaker opponents but also against colleagues of equal stature. Compare, e.g. his games with Nimzowitsch (No. 17) and Bogoljubov (No. 32).

Here follows his famous struggle with Dr Lasker, the only game he won against the ex-world champion. Even though Lasker was already 65 when this remarkable game was played, he was still able to gain high places in strong tournaments, e.g. in Moscow 1935 (third prize after Botvinnik and Flohr, but ahead of Capablanca, Spielmann and many others).

Game: 37   *White:* Dr A. Alekhine   Zurich 1934
             Black: Dr E. Lasker   Queen's Gambit, Orthodox
                                                   Defence

1. P—Q4, P—Q4; 2. P—QB4, P—K3; 3. N—QB3, N—KB3; 4. N—B3, B—K2; 5. B—N5, QN—Q2; 6. P—K3, 0—0; 7. R—B1, P—B3; 8. B—Q3, P×P; 9. B×P, N—Q4; 10. B×B, Q×B; 11. N—K4 (Alekhine preferred this move to 11. 0—0, to avoid the exchange of too many light pieces, which could easily result in a drawish position. Compare his game with Muffang, No. 23.), **11. ... N(4)—B3; 12. N—N3, P—K4** (In Alekhine's games with Capablanca, the latter, a few times, played 12. ... Q—N5ch, followed by the exchange of Queens, and succeeded in getting a draw, though not without great difficulty.); **13. 0—0, P×P; 14. N—B5, Q—Q1; 15. N(3)×P, N—K4; 16. B—N3, B×N; 17. N×B, Q—N3?** (With 17. ... P—KN3, as was played by Flohr against Euwe at Nottingham 1936, Black could have equalized. **18. Q—Q6**

is then answered by 18. ... R—K1, and 18. N—Q6 by 18. ... Q—K2.)

18. Q—Q6!   N(4)—Q2
18. ... N—N3; 19. N—R6ch, P × N (forced); 20. Q × N is also favourable for White.

19. KR—Q1   QR—Q1   20. Q—N3!
The attack has started.

20. ...   P—N3   21. Q—N5!
With the threat 22. R—Q6, N—K1; 23. R × Pch!, RP × R; 24. Q × Pch, K—R1; 25. Q—R6ch, K—N1; 26. N—K7 mate.

21. ...   K—R1   23. P—K4!
22. N—Q6   K—N2
The attack is going full speed ahead. The text gives White's KR the opportunity to participate and, with the intervention of a fourth attacking piece, the job is soon accomplished.

23. ...   N—N1
Protects the important square KR3, but now other dangers arise.

24. R—Q3!
In order to continue with 25. R—KB3.

24. ...   P—B3?
Loses in the grand manner, just as 24. ... P—KR3? would have done: 25. N—B5ch, K—R2; 26. N × P, P—B3 (26. ... N × N; 27. R—R3); 27. N—B5!, P × Q; 28. R—R3 and mate. The only way to continue would have been 24. ... Q—B2.

25. N—B5ch   K—R1   26. Q × NP!!
Black resigns (26. ... P × Q; 27. R—R3 mate).

Sometimes the mate is quite accidental; there is no attack, only a strategic fight for small advantages and suddenly—as happens in the following game—a mating pattern arises from 'scrap', so to speak.

Game 38   *White:* Dr A. Alekhine   Paris 1925
            Black: E. Colle   Queen's Gambit, Chigorin
                                                      Defence

1. P—Q4, P—Q4; 2. P—QB4, N—QB3 (seldom played, but not bad); **3. N—KB3, B—N5; 4. Q—R4, B × N; 5. KP × B, P—K3** (After 5. ... P × P White sacrifices a Pawn by 6. N—B3 to get a lead in development.); **6. N—B3, B—N5** (better 6. ... KN—K2); **7. P—QR3, B × Nch; 8. P × B, KN—K2; 9. R—QN1, R—QN1; 10. P × P, Q × P; 11. B—Q3, 0—0; 12. 0—0, Q—Q3; 13. Q—B2, N—N3; 14. P—B4, N(B3)—K2; 15. P—N3, KR—Q1; 16. KR—Q1, P—N3** (A difficult position. There is not much he can do, and it is instructive to see how Alekhine proceeds, managing to make something out of nothing.); **17. P—QR4, N—Q4; 18. B—Q2, P—QB4** (a disagreeable move for White); **19. P—B5, P × P; 20. B × P, P × P; 21. P × P, N(4)—K2; 22. B—QN4, Q—KB3; 23. B × N(2)** (White gives up the pair of Bishops in order to avoid any pressure against his isolated QP), **23. ... Q × B; 24. QR—QB1, R—Q4** (with 24. ... P—N4 Black could have increased his drawing chances); **25. B—K4, R—Q2; 26. P—Q5, Q—B3.**

27. R—K1!
The introduction to a deeply hidden mating combination.

27. ...   R(1)—Q1
Black concentrates his Rooks against White's passed Pawn.

28. Q—B6!   Q—N4?
The fatal square for the Black Queen. Correct would have been 28. ... Q—Q5, but what superman could have foreseen this?

29. B × N!   RP × B?

The obvious answer, since 29. ... Q × B?? would lose because of 30. Q × R!, while 29. ... BP × B seems a bit dangerous after 30. Q—K6ch, R—B2 (30. ... K—R1 ?; 31. Q × R again, or 30. ... K—B1; 31. R—B3); 31. R—B8, R × R; 32. Q × Rch, R—B1; 33. Q—K6ch, K—R1; 34. P—Q6, and the passed Pawn must decide.

30. Q × R!!

A very unusual mating combination. The 1st rank seems to be quite safe for Black, since his King has a flight square.

30. ...   R × Q   32. R(1)—B8
31. R—K8ch   K—R2

Threatening mate (33. R—KR8), which can be parried only by sacrificing the Queen. It now becomes clear why 28. ... Q—N4 was fatal.

32. ...   R—Q1

A last try, Black hopes for 33. R(B8) × R, after which he can still play (33. ... Q—B8ch and 34. ... P—KN4).

33. R(K8) × R   Black resigns.

9. FISCHER'S MATING COMBINATIONS

In Fischer's mating combinations we find the same characteristics as in Alekhine's. Sometimes they follow as the logical outcome of a carefully prepared and well executed Kingside attack. In other games the final blow appears quite unexpectedly as a bolt from the blue.

We start with an example of the first type.

Game 39   *White:* R. Fischer   Buenos Aires 1970
                   Black: O. Panno   Sicilian Defence

1. P—K4, P—QB4; 2. N—KB3, P—K3; 3. P—Q3 (Very unusual but not bad. The definite configuration of the centre will be decided later.) **3. ... N—QB3; 4. P—KN3, P—KN3; 5. B—N2, B—N2; 6. 0—0, KN—K2; 7. R—K1** (in order to answer 7. ... P—Q4 by 8. P—K5); **7. ... P—Q3; 8. P—B3, 0—0; 9. P—Q4, P × P; 10. P × P, P—Q4; 11. P—K5** (This decides the character of the game: White will attack on the Kingside, Black on the Queenside.) **11. ... B—Q2** (Black is perhaps too modest. He could attack White's QP. True, with 11. ... N—B4; 12. N—B3, Q—N3; he would not have attained anything on account of 13. N—QR4, but in combination with ... P—B3 now or later, perhaps this attack could have some success.); **12. N—B3, R—B1; 13. B—B4, N—R4; 14. R—QB1, P—QN4** (To be considered was 14. ... Q—N3; 15. P—N3, R—B2 and 16. ... KR—B1.); **15. P—N3, P—N5; 16. N—K2, B—N4** (Black has cleared the QB-file in order to exchange the heavy pieces in case the Kingside attack should become too dangerous.); **17. Q—Q2, N(4)—B3; 18. P—N4!** (the beginning of a methodical attack against the King), **18. ... P—QR4** (Better 18. ... B × N; this Knight will be an important help in the assault to come); **19. N—N3, Q—N3; 20. P—KR4, N—N1; 21. B—R6** one of the defenders must be eliminated); **21. ... N—Q2; 22. Q—N5!, R × R; 23. R × R, B × B** (Black does not wait for 24. B × B, K × B; 25. N—R5ch); **24. Q × B, R—B1** (the dangers are increasing on the other side); **25. R × Rch, N × R.**

It does not seem probable that White's attack with a Queen and two Knights will be conclusive.

26. P—R5! Q—Q1?
It is remarkable that an innocent transposition of moves does that much harm. If Black had first played 26. ... N—B1, then White could not have continued by 27. N—N5 on account of 27. ... Q × P. Now the attack will play itself.

27. N—N5   N—B1   28. B—K4!!
Unbelievable. It looked for a long time as if this Bishop was condemned to a passive role, and now suddenly he comes into play. Black cannot take it: 28. ... P × B; 29. N(3) × KP, Q—K2 (the KBP needed protection); 30. N—B6ch, K—R1; 31. N(5) × RP, etc.

28. ... Q—K2   29. N × RP!
Most remarkable. With a piece 'en prise' White can still sacrifice one of his two remaining pieces.

| 29. ...   N × N | 31. B × NP   N—N4 |
| 30. P × P   P × P | |

After 31. ... Q—N2; 32. B × Nch, K—R1 (32. ... Q × B; 33. Q ×
Pch and 34. Q × N) White has the choice between:

(1) A comfortable endgame with two plus Pawns after 33. Q × Qch,
K × Q; 34. B—N1, and
(2) An overwhelming middlegame after 33. Q × P, B—Q2; 34. Q—
QR6, Q × B; 35. P—K6, recapturing the piece and maintaining
the attack.

32. N—R5   N—B6ch
The last convulsions.

| 33. K—N2   N—R5ch | 35. N—B6ch   K—B2 |
| 34. K—N3   N × B | 36. Q—R7ch |

Black resigns (36. ... K—B1; 37. Q—N8 mate).

The following game is characterized by a wonderful inspiration.

Game 40   *White:* R. Fischer   U.S.A. Championship 1963/64
              Black: P. Benko   Pirc Defence

**1. P—K4, P—KN3; 2. P—Q4, B—N2; 3. N—QB3, P—Q3;
4. P—B4** (The most energetic continuation White has for building a
broad centre. However, his position may be somewhat vulnerable.);
4. ... N—KB3; 5. N—B3, 0—0; 6. B—Q3, B—N5 (?) (There is
not much sense in exchanging White's KN and furthering White's
development. Preferable is 6. ... N—B3 or 6. ... QN—Q2);
7. P—KR3, B × N; 8. Q × B, N—B3; 9. B—K3, P—K4 (to have
some counterweight in the centre); **10. QP × P, P × P; 11. P—B5!,
P × P** (Without this exchange, White could have continued with
P—KN4—KN5.); **12. Q × P** (After 12. P × P, Black gets counterchances by the Pawn sacrifice 12. ... P—K5), **12. ... N—Q5;**

13. Q—B2 (13. Q × KP is not advisable on account of 13. ...
N—N5); **13. ... N—K1; 14. 0—0** (one might expect 14. 0—0—0,
but White shows that after the text move a Kingside attack is also
possible); **14. ... N—Q3; 15. Q—N3, K—R1; 16. Q—N4, P—
QB3?** (Black should have played 16. ... P—QB4 to drive away the
White KB by P—QB5. Although for the time being blocked by his
own KP, it will soon appear that this Bishop plays an important
part in the Kingside attack.)

17. Q—R5
With the threat 18. B × N, P × B; 19. P—K5.

17. ... Q—K1?
Black expects to parry the threat 18. B × N, P × B; 19. P—K5 by
19. ... P—KB4! An original idea which, however, succumbs to
Fischer's outstanding counter-idea.

18. B × N   P × B   19. R—B6!!
Such moves continually bring a freshness into the game.

19. ...   K—N1
After 19. ... B × R; 20. P—K5, Black cannot parry the mate. The
same goes for 19. ... P × N; 20. P—K5.

20. P—K5   P—KR3   21. N—K2!

Black resigns. If the Black Knight moves, 22. Q—B5 decides, and after
21. ... B × R the mate is still there: 22. Q × P and 23. Q—R7 mate.

In the following game Black succeeds in an almost symmetrical
position, in taking the initiative which culminates in a deeply
calculated Knight sacrifice. The resulting complications then show
two main characteristics:

(1) Overworking of the defending pieces, and
(2) The K-wing open to attacks along the diagonal.

Game 41   *White:* R. Byrne   U.S.A. Championship 1963/64
              Black: R. Fischer   King's Indian Defence

1. P—Q4, N—KB3; 2. P—QB4, P—KN3; 3. P—KN3, P—B3; 4. B—N2, P—Q4; 5. P × P, P × P; 6. N—QB3, B—N2; 7. P—K3 (By developing his KN to K2 White deviates from complete symmetry); **7. ... 0—0; 8. KN—K2, N—B3; 9. 0—0, P—N3; 10. P—N3; B—QR3; 11. B—QR3, R—K1; 12. Q—Q2, P—K4!.** (With this courageous move Black definitely breaks the symmetry. His pieces will soon develop great activity, but he has to be careful with his isolated QP.); **13. P × P, N × P; 14. KR—Q1?** (This appears bad because White's KBP becomes weak. Preferable was 14. QR—Q1, after which Fischer recommends as best 14. ... Q—B1, in order to answer 15. N × P, N × N; 16. B × N by 16. ... R—Q1, threatening 17. ... R × B); **14. ... N—Q6.**

Black now threatens 15. ... N—K5, with complete restriction of the White position.

15. Q—B2

15. N—B4 is answered by 15. ... P—Q5! (analysis by Prins).

15. ... N × P!		**17. K—N1 N × KP**
16. K × N N—N5ch		**18. Q—Q2 N × B!**

Again a surprise; the elimination of White's KB is more important than winning the exchange.

19. K × N   P—Q5!

This powerful move opens Black's QB diagonal.

20. N × P   B—N2ch   21. K—B1

With 21. K—B2 White could have held his own a little longer. Fischer shows that after 21. ... Q—Q2; 22. QR—B1, Q—R6; 23. N—B3, B—KR3, Black also wins. Obviously incorrect is 21. K—N1, B × Nch; 22. Q × B, R—K8ch, etc.

21. ...   Q—Q2!

White resigns; he is helpless against 22. ... Q—R6ch; 23. K—N1,

B × Nch; 24. Q × B, Q—N7 mate. The most beautiful variation is
22. Q—B2, Q—R6ch; 23. K—N1, R—K8ch!! (White's Rook and
Queen are both overworked, the Rook controlling Q4 and K1, the
Queen controlling Q4, K1 and N2.); 24. R × R, B × N!; 25. Q × B,
Q—N7 mate.

10. ALEKHINE'S ERRORS

Alekhine did not lose many of his games, certainly not in the period
of his top performances (1927–1934). In the San Remo (1930) and
Bled (1931) Tournaments he did not lose a single game. In his match
with Capablanca (1927), he lost only three games out of thirty-four!

Playing with the Black pieces against strong opponents sometimes
gave him trouble. Unlike Capablanca, he could not equalize by
first simplifying the position and then 'softening up' his opponent
by endless manœuvring. He disliked this kind of slow strategy and
generally tried to overcome the disadvantage of having Black by
active counterplay. Against weaker players he almost always
succeeded, but against opponents of his own strength he failed from
time to time.

A characteristic example is shown in the seventh game of the
Capablanca–Alekhine match for the world championship.

Game 42   *White:* J. R. Capablanca   Buenos Aires 1927
                 Black: A. Alekhine

**1. P—Q4, P—Q4; 2. P—QB4, P—K3; 3. N—KB3, N—Q2;
4. N—B3, KN—B3; 5. B—N5, P—B3; 6. P—K3, Q—R4; 7. N—
Q2, B—N5; 8. Q—B2, 0—0; 9. B—R4, P—B4;** (better was 9. . . .
P—K4); **10. N—N3, Q—R5; 11. B × N, N × B; 12. P × BP,
N—K5?**

A bad mistake. Apparently Alekhine had not prepared this
opening thoroughly. Correct was first 12. . . . B × Nch. Black
almost equalizes after 13. Q × B, N—K5. Now Black must lose a
Pawn and the game.

13. P×P   B×Nch   15. R—Q1!   P×P
14. P×B   N×QBP (5)   16. R×P   N×N
With 16. ... P—QN3 Black could have offered more resistance.

17. P×N   Q—B3   19. B—Q3!
18. R—Q4   R—K1
Capablanca doesn't fear the following complications, which may
bring his King into an unsafe position.

19. ...   Q×NP   22. Q—Q2   B—K3
20. B×Pch K—B1   23. P—QB4   P—R4
21. B—K4   Q—R6   24. R—N1!
White returns his plus Pawn in order to play for a Kingside attack.

24. ...   Q×RP   26. Q—N2!
25. R—R1   Q—B2
White, having built up a powerful attack, won after **26. ...
Q—B4** (to parry 27. Q—R3ch); **27. B—Q5, R—R3; 28. R—K4,
R—Q3; 29. R—R7, K—K2** (if 29. ... P—B3 then 30. R—R8ch
and 31. R×R); **30. Q×P, K—Q1; 31. B×B, P×B; 32. Q×P,
Q—N5ch; 33. Q×Q, P×Q; 34. P—B5, R—B3; 35. R×P, R×P;
36. R—R7.** Black resigns.

This game illustrates the 'Achilles' heel' of Alekhine's style: his play
in positions in which he had to strive for equality, with no prospects
for a win. Consequently the opening meant more to Alekhine than
to his predecessors. If he managed to get a promising position after
the opening, there was little doubt about the outcome of the game.
But with a small disadvantage without any counter-play, he often
risked playing for all or nothing. In many cases he came off better
owing to his phenomenal capacities in combinations. Only 'once in a
blue moon' did his instinct fail, as happened in the following example.

Game Extract 8

White: Dr M. Euwe   Black: Dr A. Alekhine
(Position after White's 30th move, Zurich 1934)

Alekhine got a bad start in the opening, with a cramped position and having to continually fight against positional threats by his opponent. Now suddenly, after a simplification on White's K4, there is a gleam of light. True, White threatens the very strong 31. P—Q5!, but why not

30. ... P—B3?
This move seems to win material.

31. N—B7!
Not only avoids the loss of material but even leads to winning a Pawn. It is clear that Black cannot *take*: 31. ... K × N; 32. Q—R5ch, K—K2 (32. ... P—N3; 33. Q × RPch, etc.); 33. R × Rch, K × R; 34. R—K1, K—Q3; 35. Q—B5ch, K—Q2; 36. Q—B5ch, K—K3; 37. Q—K6 mate.

31. ...   Q—K1   33. N—Q8!
32. R × R   Q × R
This peculiar move wins an important Pawn.

The rest is easy: **33. ... Q—K5; 34. N × P, P—P3; 35. P—Q5, Q—Q6; 36. P—R3, Q—Q7; 37. P—N3, K—R1; 38. K—N2, Q—Q6; 39. R—K1, K—R2; 40. R—K3, Q—Q7; 41. R—K8, Q—Q6; 42. Q—Q4, Q—B5; 43. Q—K4ch, Q × Q; 44. R × Q, K—N1; 45. N—N8, K—B2; 46. N × P, R—Q2; 47. R—Q4, N—K2; 48. P—Q6, N—B4; 49. R—Q5, N × QP; 50. N—B5, R—Q1; 51. N—K4, N—N2; 52. P—R6!** (the last trick: if now 52. ... R × R, then 53. P × N, R—Q1; 54. N—Q6ch and 55. N—B8), **52. ... K—K3; 53. R × R,** Black resigns.

Alekhine rightly remarked that the probability that he would overlook the above combination is on a par with 'en plein win' at Monte Carlo.

Much more serious is Alekhine's false judgment in a relatively simple position.

Game Extract 9

White: Dr M. Euwe   *Black:* Dr A. Alekhine
(Position after White's 32nd move, 24th Match Game, Delft 1935)

This endgame can be won by Black. He has a clear majority of two Pawns on the Queenside, and White's majority on the other wing is handicapped by the doubled KBP. There followed

32. ... P—B4??
Carelessly played. The text gives White the opportunity to get rid of his doubled Pawn. After 32. ... P—R4! White would have been too late with the manœuvre 33. K—K3 and 34. P—B4. The White King would have been tied to the Queenside, while the Black King could also have marched to the Queenside to support the advance of his Pawns and returned to the Kingside as soon as White's Pawns advanced (P—N4 and P—R5).

33. K—K3!
Draw agreed. After 33. ... P—B5; 34. P—B4, P × Pch; 35. K × P, the White King remains inside the quadrant.
If he had won this ending, Alekhine could probably have saved his world title.

11

A summarizing sketch of Alekhine's ingenuity, strength and versatility would not be complete without the last game of his match with Capablanca (Buenos Aires 1927), which gave him the highest title in the chess world. Here we see the combinational genius Alekhine as the perfect positional player, slowly gathering small advantages and combining them into the material result of one Pawn, which proved to be sufficient for the win. It has already been remarked that great players excel in *every type* of play.

The reader may be somewhat surprised by the patience Alekhine showed in this 82-move game, but he *was* patient in positions in which he had an advantage or the initiative. He lacked patience only in (dull) positions in which he could hope for a draw at the most.

Game 43   White: Dr A. Alekhine   Match, 34th Game, Buenos
            Black: J. R. Capablanca   Aires 1927
                                                    Queen's Gambit, Orthodox
                                                                    Variation

1. P—Q4, P—Q4; 2. P—QB4, P—K3; 3. N—QB3, N—KB3; 4. B—N5, QN—Q2; 5. P—K3, P—B3; 6. P—QR3 (to avoid the Cambridge Springs variation after 6. N—B3, Q—R4), **6. ... B—K2; 7. N—B3, O—O; 8. B—Q3, P × P; 9. B × P, N—Q4; 10. B × B, Q × B; 11. N—K4** (compare game 23 against Muffang: White avoids the exchange of pieces), **11. ... N(4)—B3; 12. N—N3,**

P—B4; 13. 0—0, N—N3; 14. B—R2, P × P; 15. N × P, P—N3
(Black prepares the advance 16. ... P—K4 in case White should
play 16. P—K4 and in this way prevents the QN from jumping to
KB5); **16. R—B1, B—Q2; 17. Q—K2, QR—B1; 18. P—K4,
P—K4;** (compare Black's 15th move); **19. N—B3, K—N2; 20. P—
R3, P—KR3(?)** (Alekhine considers this a mistake which gives him
considerable chances to take a promising initiative.)

21. Q—Q2!
With threats in two directions. First, there is the threat 22. Q—R5
winning a Pawn. If Black parries the threat by the counterattack
21. ... B—B3 (against White's KP), then White's second threat
becomes visible: 22. N—R4! and now

(1) 22. ... N × P; 23. N(4)—B5ch, P × N; 24. N × Pch, K—B3
(the only move); 25. Q × Pch, K × N; 26. P—KN4 mate!
(2) 22. ... B × P; 23. Q—K3, and Black's QB can no longer
maintain control of KB5.
(3) 22. ... B—Q2; 23. Q—R5, R—QR1; 24. R—B7 with clear
superiority to White.

21. ... B—K3?
The decisive mistake. Lasker recommended 21. ... N—R5 as best.
After the text White wins a Pawn.

22. B × B   Q × B   23. Q—R5   N—B5
Or 23. ... Q—N6; 24. Q × KP, which also wins a Pawn.

24. Q × RP   N × NP   26. Q × P   N—B5
25. R × R   R × R   27. Q—N4
The complications are over. White has a 'pure' plus Pawn.

27. ...   R—Q1   29. P—QR4   N × P
28. R—R1   Q—B3   30. N × P
Not 30. N × N, Q × N; 31. R—QB1, R—QB1; 32. N × P?, N—K6!;
K

33. Q × Q, R × Rch; 34. K—R2, N—B8ch, and Black wins (35. ...
N—N6ch, etc.).

30. ...	Q—Q3		35. R × N	R—QN1
31. Q × N	Q × N		36. R—K2	R—QR1
32. R—K1	N—Q3		37. R—R2	R—R4
33. Q—B1	Q—B3		38. Q—B7	Q—R3
34. N—K4	N × N		39. Q—B3ch	

White has conquered the important diagonal QB3—KR8.

39. ...	K—R2	40. R—Q2	

Threatening 41. R—Q8, etc.

40. ...	Q—N3		46. P—R4	Q—KR1
41. R—Q7	Q—N8ch		47. Q—N6	Q—R8
42. K—R2	Q—N1ch		48. K—N2	R—B3
43. P—N3	R—KB4		49. Q—Q4	Q × Q
44. Q—Q4	Q—K1		50. R × Q	
45. R—Q5	R—B6			

This Rook ending is a sure win for White, whose plus Pawn is a
distant passed Pawn. However, it is not easy and requires time.
Alekhine shows that he has time. There followed:

50. ...	K—N2		53. R—Q4	R—R3
51. P—QR5	R—R3		54. R—R4	K—B3
52. R—Q5	R—B3			

Now the Black King can come to the Queenside, which would not
have been possible if White had been able to maintain his Rook on
Q5.

55. K—B3	K—K4		58. K—B3	K—B4
56. K—K3	P—R4		59. R—R2	K—N4
57. K—Q3	K—Q4		60. K—N3	K—B4

60. ... R × P would lead to a lost Pawn ending.

61. K—B3	K—N4	62. K—Q4	R—Q3ch

If 62. ... K—N5, then 63. R—R1.

63. K—K5	R—K3ch	66. K—R6	R—B4
64. K—B4	K—R3	67. P—B4	
65. K—N5	R—K4ch		

Alekhine gives 67. K—N7 as the simplest way to win.

67. ...	R—B4	72. P × P	R—Q4
68. R—R3	R—B2	73. K—N7	R—B4
69. K—N7	R—Q2	74. R—R4	K—N4
70. P—B5	P × P	75. R—K4!	K—R3
71. K—B6	P—B5		

Not 75. ... K × P on account of 76. R—K5ch.

76. K—R6	R × RP	80. R—KB5	K—N3
77. R—K5	R—R8	81. R × P	K—B3
78. K × P	R—KN8	82. R—K7	
79. R—N5	R—KB8		

Black resigns. After adjournment Capablanca convinced himself that the situation after 82. ... R × P; 83. K—N5 was hopeless. It is a well-known fact that the RP wins if the defending King is cut off three files from the passed Pawn.

CHAPTER III

LASKER AND FISCHER

1. GENERAL

A comparison between Dr Lasker and Fischer is much more difficult than the comparisons we have made in previous chapters. Lasker lived much longer ago, and, since his career spanned so many years, he was continuously modifying his methods of play, so that one can hardly speak of a single Lasker style.

Lasker won the world championship in 1894 by beating Steinitz. However, the defeated champion was so much older than Lasker that this victory alone did not completely convince the chess world. Lasker had to add successes in tournaments, and he did. He regularly won strong tournaments, and only seldom was he reduced to second or third place. Lasker kept his pre-eminent position, beating his rivals in matches or outpointing them in tournaments, until around 1910, when a new generation of masters appeared. This did not mean a turning-point in his career, but it did mean some change in his strategy and style.

Let us first attempt to characterize Lasker's style as a whole. Lasker was a supporter and a connoisseur of Steinitz's theory, which in short amounted to the main principle. 'Make a plan in agreement with the characteristics of the position.' However, Lasker did not always apply this basic principle. He was primarily a practical player because he had to win tournaments. But how can one beat a weaker man if one has the Black pieces and one's opponent is only playing for a draw? Chess is not mathematics; chess is a struggle. Sometimes one can win by making bad moves in a good position or by making good moves in a bad position. Chess is too complicated to be mastered completely. If one sees more moves ahead than one's opponent, one is likely to win, at least if the position is such that seeing far ahead is possible and fruitful. This means that the position should never be dull, although it need not necessarily be wildly complex. It should simply be interesting, with both sides having possibilities deserving calculation and evaluation.

One of Lasker's greatest capacities lay in ability to see ahead deeply and exactly, and he thus always sought double-edged positions. This often introduced an element of risk or gambling. If the best move at a certain point might lead to a dull position, or to a position too simple to induce the opponent to make a mistake, why not consider the second best move? This kind of tactic can be seen frequently in the first half of Lasker's career.

His game was never colourless; it had to have a character. I remember that once, when I was walking during a tournament game, I met Lasker and said to him, 'I have made a serious error. I have captured my opponent's Queen thinking I gave Rook and Knight for it, but I now see that I have miscalculated: the hostile Queen has cost me Rook and two Knights.' 'Don't worry,' Lasker replied, 'you have at any rate succeeded in giving the game a character.' In Lasker's practice this was the main principle: 'Give the game a character.'

To attain this, Lasker often took great risks: the King in the open field, pieces threatened everywhere, positions in which nobody could predict the outcome. I once heard that Fischer is supposed to have said, 'Lasker was a coffee-house player.' I do not know if he really said this, but there is some truth in it if we restrict this judgment to the games of the first phase of Lasker's career, when he had to play against relatively weak opponents. However, Lasker deliberately sought critical positions: he knew perfectly well what risks were involved, but he accepted them. In chess, sometimes the word 'swindle' is used for these tactics, not in the sense of cheating your opponent, but in taking risks. Spielmann, a great combinative player, felt at home in complicated attacking positions, and so did Alekhine. One could call them swindlers in a favourable sense. But they, in contrast to Lasker, were primarily looking for the opponent's King. Lasker's field of swindle was broader: his aim was the combat. He would only play for an attack if the characteristics of the position required it. In this way he followed Steinitz strictly, and went even further: if the characteristics justify the attack, attack one must. The positional characteristics dictate the plan of play, and one has no alternative.

It was often considered a piece of good luck when Lasker's opponents went wrong, but this was often not so, since it was part of Lasker's style to make things so difficult that the opponent could easily fail.

Speaking about Lasker's two lives, Lasker before 1910 and Lasker thereafter, with a period of transition in between, we can state that Lasker grew considerably in strength during his World Championship. Lasker's games in the second period of his career belong to the best that can be found in chess literature. Enterprising and flexible strategy, interwoven with tactical finesses based on seemingly small particularities in the position, was typical of his play. Lasker had no knowledge of openings, but this was of no great consequence at the time he achieved his greatest successes, since none of his contemporaries had made a special study of openings. This shortcoming was more than compensated for by his broad outlook on all types of chess positions. Only in the thirties, when Lasker was already sixty years old, did this handicap become apparent from time to time.

We now give a number of games which illustrate Lasker's play in different positions in each period of his career. A comparison with Fischer is hardly possible. Each is great in his own field. Except for the endgame, in which both champions excelled, they do not have much in common. Like all other world champions, Lasker knew how to exploit the slightest advantage in the endgame.

2. OLD TIMES

| *Game 44* | *White:* Dr E. Lasker | Tournament Berlin 1890 |
| | *Black:* Th. v. Scheve | Scotch Opening |

1. P—K4, P—K4; 2. N—KB3, N—QB3; 3. P—Q4, P × P; 4. N × P, B—B4; 5. B—K3, Q—B3; 6. P—QB3 (passive; 6. N—N5 would be more enterprising), **6. ... N—K2; 7. N—B2, B—N3** (in the tournament at St Petersburg 1914, Lasker played this variation with the Black pieces against Blackburne and continued with 7. ... P—QN3); **8. N—Q2, 0—0; 9. B—K2, P—Q4; 10. 0—0, P × P; 11. B × B, RP × B; 12. N × P, Q—N3; 13. N—N3, R—Q1; 14. Q—B1, B—K3** (This is not a position for White to be proud of. The advantage of the first move has vanished into thin air.); **15. P—KB4** (Indirect protection of White's QRP; after 15. ... B × P; 16. P—B5 Black would walk into difficulties.), **15. ... N—B4; 16. N × N, B × N; 17. N—R3** (One would have expected 17. N—K3, after which Black, with 17. ... P—R4, maintains some initiative. With the text White probably intends to play N—N5 eventually to force the Black pieces into a less aggressive position.), **17. ... B—K5; 18. B—B3, B—Q6; 19. R—K1, P—R4; 20. Q—K3, P—R5; 21. QR—Q1, P—R6?** (Apparently an oversight. After 21. ... R—Q3 Black's position would have remained superior.); **22. B × N, P × B; 23. Q × RP, P—N4** (Black still has a very good position, since the White Knight is paralysed by the Black Bishop.); **24. Q—B3, P—QB4??** (see diagram).

25. R × B!   Q × R
Not 25. ... R × R?; 26. Q × Rch, etc.

(Position after Black's 24th move)

26. R—K8ch!

Black resigns (26. ... K—R2; 27. Q—R5 mate, or 26. ... R × R; 27. Q × Q). A real 'coffee-house' game!

Game 45   *White:* Dr E. Lasker   Tournament Nürnberg 1896
             Black: E. Schallop   Queen's Gambit, Orthodox

1. P—Q4, P—Q4; 2. N—KB3, N—KB3; 3. P—B4, P—K3; 4. N—B3, B—K2; 5. B—B4, 0—0; 6. P—B5 (an unmotivated advance), **6. ... P—QN3; 7. P—QN4, P—QR4; 8. P—QR3, N—K5; 9. N × N, P × N; 10. N—K5, P—KB3; 11. N—B4, P × NP; 12. RP × P, R × R; 13. Q × R, N—B3** (wins a Pawn. Again one cannot admire Lasker's build-up.) **14. Q—B3, N × QP** (14. ... Q × P might have been still stronger.); **15. P—K3, N—B4** (After 15. ... N—N4; 16. Q—N3, P—K4; 17. B—N3, P × P; 18. P × P, P—B3, White would not have survived.); **16. N—Q2, B—N2?** (Better is 16. ... P—K4; 17. B—N3, N × B; 18. RP × N, B—B4.); **17. P—B6.**

17. ... B × BP

This is what Black had played for: he counts on the recapture of the piece.

18. Q × B   B × P   19. Q—B2   Q—Q4?

Black goes into the trap. However, 19. ... Q—Q2 would not have been much better: 20. B—B4!, R—Q1; 21. 0—0, B × N; 22. Q—N3, R—K1; 23. R—Q1. It is remarkable how, after such a silly opening, Lasker's pieces suddenly come into action.

20. B—B4!   B × Nch   21. K—K2!

This is what Black had overlooked. Now White must win a piece.

21. ...   Q—B3   23. K—K2   R—Q4
22. K × B   R—Q1ch

Black must lose at least one of his Pawns, and after that two Pawns are insufficient compensation for the Bishop.

24. Q—N3   R—B4   28. B—Q5 ` R—B7ch
25. B × Pch   K—B1   29. R—Q2   R × Rch
26. R—Q1   N—Q3   30. K × R
27. B × Nch   P × B

and White won after 14 more moves.

Game 46 The King Steps Out
White: Dr E. Lasker   Tournament Cambridge Springs 1904
Black: F. J. Marshall   French Defence

1. P—K4,   P—QB4; 2. N—KB3,   P—K3; 3. N—B3,   P—Q4; 4. P × P,   P × P; 5. B—N5ch,   N—B3; 6. 0—0,   N—B3; 7. P—Q4 (We are now in a well-known variation of the French Defence, the usual order of moves being 1. P—K4, P—K3; 2. P—Q4, P—Q4; 3. N—QB3, P—QB4; 4. P × QP, KP × P; 5. B—N5ch, N—B3.), **7. ... B—K2; 8. P × P, 0—0;** (Marshall was a born gambit player); **9. B—N5, B—K3; 10. B × QN, P × B; 11. P—QN4** (Lasker has accepted the challenge), **11. ... P—KR3; 12. B × N?** (Certainly not the best. After 12. B—K3 and 13. B—Q4 White would have a solid position.), **12. ... B × B; 13. Q—Q2** (Probably White believed that he could play 13. N—Q4 here, but then 13. ... P—QR4 is awkward: 14. N × BP, Q—B2.), **13. ... P—QR4; 14. P—QR3, Q—N1** (Black's counterattack is in full swing) **15. QR—N1, P × P; 16. P × P, R—R6; 17. N—Q4, Q—K4; 18. N(3)—K2, B—N5. 19. P—KB3, B—Q2; 20. P—B3, R—K1; 21. R—R1, R(1)—R1; 22. R × R, R × R; 23. R—K1, Q—B2; 24. N—B2** (White has succeeded in holding his own. Now he tries for more.), **24. ... R—R7; 25. R—R1, Q—R2; 26. Q—B1, B—B4** (Black keeps on pressing) **27. R × R, Q × R; 28, N(B2)—Q4, B—Q6;**

29. Q—K3, B × N(5); 30. N × B, Q—R8ch; 31. K—B2, Q—N7ch; 32. K—N3?! (Great; the consequences of this risky move will appear soon. After 32. K—N1, Black would have drawn by 32. ... Q—R8ch, etc.), **32. ... B—B8!** (Threatens mate in a few moves.)**: 33. K—B4, Q × KNP; 34. K—K5!**

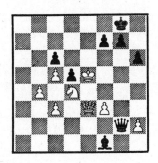

Have you ever seen such a King?

34. ...   Q—N3
Black is threatening mate all the time.

35. Q—B4   B—Q6
Threatens 36. ... P—B4 and 37. ... Q—B3 mate. White must simplify.

36. P—N5!   B × P
If 36. ... P—B4, then 37. P × P, and White has obtained a new flight square for his King.

37. N × B   P × N   38. K—Q4
Not 38. K × P, Q—K3ch; 39. K—Q4, Q—B5ch, and White loses his passed Pawn.

38. ...   Q—B7
Black must remain active. After a move like 38. ... Q—B3 he would get into difficulties: 39. Q—N8ch, K—R2; 40. Q—N6, etc.

39. P—B6
Looks very good for White, but Black shows his special skill in this complicated position, dangerous for both sides.

39. ...   Q—R5ch   40. K—K3
On K5 the White King would hamper the activity of its own Queen.

40. ...   Q—R2ch   41. K—Q3

Or 41. Q—Q4, Q—B2; 42. Q×P, K—B1, and Black can bring his King nearer and probably draw. White prefers to have his Queen controlling the QB7 square.

41. ...   P—N5!

Thus Black gives his Queen more freedom of manœuvre. White cannot take the NP because of 41. ... Q—R3ch, and Black wins the advanced passed Pawn.

42. P—B7	**Q—R3ch**	**44. K×P**	**Q—B3ch**
43. K—Q2	**P×Pch**	**45. K—Q2**	**P—B3**

Prevents 46. Q—K5.

Here the game was given up as a draw. After **46. K—Q1!** (threatening 47. Q—B1), **P—Q5; 47. Q—B1, Q×Pch** the White King cannot escape perpetual check.

We would wrong the chess masters of the previous century by evaluating their strength only on the basis of these three games. Lasker has played a number of other games which have taken a worthy place in chess literature, and great performances were also achieved at this time by Steinitz, Tchigorin, Tarrasch, Pillsbury and others. None the less, the impression remains that the decision too often was reached by relatively simple tactical turns and oversights.

3. THE PERIOD OF TRANSITION

Game 47 Endless Manœuvring Wears Out the Opponent
White: Dr E. Lasker   Tournament St Petersburg 1909
Black: G. Salwe   Ruy Lopez, Steinitz Defence

1. P—K4, P—K4; 2. N—KB3, N—QB3; 3. B—N5, P—Q3; 4. P—Q4, B—Q2; 5. N—B3, N—B3; 6. 0—0, B—K2; 7. B—N5, P×P; 8. N×P, 0—0; 9. B×QN, P×B; 10. Q—Q3, R—K1 (So far, nothing special.); **11. QR—K1, P—B4; 12. N—N3, N—N5; 13. B×B, R×B; 14. P—B4, R—N1; 15. P—KR3, N—R3; 16. P—B5** (This gives the game the necessary character. White gets space to attack Black's Kingside, but leaves his K5 square to Black), **16. ... P—KB3; 17. N—Q5, R—K1; 18. P—B4, N—B2; 19. Q—QB3, R—K4; 20. N—Q2, P—B3** (Drives away the powerful Knight but weakens the QP, which can eventually be of importance.); **21. N—B4, Q—N3; 22. P—QN3, QR—K1; 23. Q—N3, K—R1; 24. N—R5, R—KN1; 25. R—B4.**

White's attack looks promising, but Black has sufficient possibilities of defence. A long series of manœuvres—only some of them meaningful—will now follow.

25. ... Q—Q1; 26. N—B3, R—K2; 27. R—R4, Q—K1; 28. Q—B2, R—B1; 29. Q—Q2, Q—N1; 30. K—R1, R(1)—K1; 31. R—N4, R—N1; 32. R—Q1, Q—N5; 33. Q—B2, Q—B6; 34. Q—R4 (Threatens 35. N—B4, after which 35. ... N—R3 would lose a Pawn to 36. R × QP. Here we see the importance of Black's weakness on Q3. As a general rule the presence of two targets gives the attacker more chances to succeed), **34. .... N—R3; 35. R—B4, N—B2; 36. K—R2, R(1)—K1; 37. Q—N3** (Now White strives for the right formation: the Rook on the KR file and the Queen putting pressure on KN7, while the second Rook attacks Black's QP.), **37. ... R—KN1; 38. R—R4** (threatening 39. N—B4, N—R3; 40. R × P), **38. ... P—KN4** (practically forced); **39. P × P e.p., R × NP; 40. Q—B2, P—B4; 41. N—B4, R—B3; 42. N—K2, Q—N7** (Black wishes to have his R (3) protected); **43. R—Q2, Q—R8; 44. N—N3, K—N1** (Loses a Pawn; the necessary reaction was 44. ... P × P; 45. N × P, R—N3. However, Black, with his Kingside weakened and his QP helpless, would have lost anyway.); **45. P × P, B × P.**

46. N—Q4!
Wins a Pawn and the game. The Knight on Q4 intersects the diagonal QR1—KR8.

46. ... P×N   47. N×B K—B1
47. ... R(2)—K3; 48. Q×P leads to roughly the same position.

48. Q×P   Q×Q   50. R—R5
49. N×Q   N—K4
With the threat 51. N—B5.

50. ...   R(2)—KB2   52. R×N   P×N
51. P—B5   P×P   53. R×QP   R—B7
White, with a sound plus Pawn, won after: **54. R—Q8ch, K—N2;**
55. R—QR5, R—B7; 56. P—R3, P—B4; 57. R—QB8, R—N7
(57. ... R(2)—B7 is answered by 58. R×Pch, K—R3; 59. R—
KN8); **58. R—N5, R(2)—B7; 59. R—N7ch, K—N3; 60. R—B6ch,**
R—B3 (Other moves would lose one or two Pawns more with check.);
61. R×BP, R—R3; 62. P—QR4, R—KB3; 63. R—B3, P—QR3;
64. R—N3ch, K—R3; 65. R(3)—N7, Black resigns.

Game 48   Direct Kingside Attack
White: Dr E. Lasker   Tournament St Petersburg 1909
Black: R. Teichmann   Ruy Lopez, Closed variation

1. P—K4, P—K4; 2. N—KB3, N—QB3; 3. B—N5, P—QR3;
4. B—R4, N—B3; 5. 0—0, B—K2; 6. Q—K2, P—QN4; 7. B—N3,
P—Q3; 8. P—B3, 0—0; 9. P—Q4, P×P; 10. P×P, B—N5;
11. R—Q1, P—Q4; 12. P—K5, N—K5; 13. N—B3, N×N;
14. P×N (So far, according to the most modern theories), **14. ...**
P—B3? (Correct was 14. ... Q—Q2. The text gives White the
opportunity to launch a tremendous attack); **15. P—KR3, B—R4;**
16. P—N4!

16. ... B—B2

16. ... B—N3 would have been no better: 17. N—R4, P × P fails against 18. N × B, P × N; 19. P × P, etc.

17. P—K6 B—N3

Now the diagonal QR2—KN1 is blocked.

18. N—R4 N—R4

If 18. ... B—K1, then 19. Q—B3 wins a Pawn.

19. N × B P × N	**21. K—R1**
20. B—B2 P—B4	

Makes room for the rook. 21. P × P, P × P; 22. Q—R5 would be answered by 22. ... Q—K1.

21. ... B—Q3	**22. P × P Q—R5**

22. ... P × P; 23. R—KN1, Q—R5; 24. Q—B3 leads to the same position.

23. Q—B3 P × P	**24. R—KN1**

Not 24. B × P?, on account of 24. ... Q—B3.

24. ... P—B5

To prevent 25. B—N5, but the cure is worse than the disease.

25. R—N4 Q—R3	**26. P—K7! B × P**

Or 26. ... R—B2; 27. B—N6, R × P; 28. Q × Pch and 29. Q × Rch.

27. B × P Q—K3

27. ... Q—B3; 28. Q × Pch is also hopeless for Black.

28. R × Pch!

Black resigns (28. ... K × R; 29. R—N1ch, K—B2; 30. Q—R5ch, or 29. ... K—B3; 30. B—K5 mate).

Game 49 'Hours of Destiny in the Chess World' (Stefan Zweig, *Sternstunden der Menschheit*)

White: Dr E. Lasker   10th (last) match game, Berlin 1910
Black: C. Schlechter   Queen's Gambit, Slav Defence

1. P—Q4, P—Q4; 2. P—QB4, P—QB3; 3. N—KB3, N—B3; 4. P—K3, P—KN3 (leads to a kind of Grunfeld Defence); **5. N—B3, B—N2; 6. B—Q3, 0—0; 7. Q—B2, N—R3; 8. P—QR3, P × P; 9. B × P, P—QN4** (More solid is 9. ... N—B2 followed by 10. ... B—K3.); **10. B—Q3, P—N5; 11. N—QR4, P × P; 12. P × P** (not 12. Q × P on account of 12. ... N—QN5), **12. ... B—N2; 13. R—QN1, Q—B2; 14. N—K5** (simpler and much better was 14. 0—0 and 15. B—Q2), **14. ... N—R4; 15. P—N4?** (There was no need to complicate the game, since White still has an overwhelming position. He should consolidate by 15. P—B4.), **15. ... B × N; 16. P × N, B—N2; 17. P × P, RP × P; 18. Q—B4** (preferable is 18. P—B4, P—QB4; 19. R—N1), **18. ... B—B1** (which parries the threat 19. B × P, now answered by 19. ... B—K3; 20. Q × N, P × B, and Black has a strong attack for the sacrificed Pawn. Moreover, he then threatens 21. ... B—Q4.); **19. R—N1, Q—R4ch; 20. B—Q2, Q—Q4; 21. R—QB1, B—N2; 22. Q—B2** (White should have exchanged Queens), **22. ... Q—KR4; 23. B × P** (A sham sacrifice which, however, gives Black the opportunity to start a direct attack against the insecurely placed White King.), **23. ... Q × P; 24. R—B1, P × B; 25. Q—N3ch, R—B2!; 26. Q × B, QR—KB1.**

27. Q—N3

White could not take the Knight: 27. Q × N, R × P; 28. R × R, R × R, etc. Another possibility was 27. P—B4, P—K4!; 28. Q × N, P × QP; 29. P—K4, Q—N6ch; 30. K—K2, R—K1, giving Black a most promising attack: 31. Q × BP?, P—Q6ch leads to mate, or 31. P—K5, B × P, or 31. Q—Q3, Q—N7ch and 32. ... R × P.

27. ...	**K—R1**	**31. K—K2**	**Q—R7ch**
28. P—B4	**P—N4!**	**32. R—B2**	**Q—R4ch**
29. Q—Q3	**P × P**	**33. R—B3**	**N—B2**
30. P × P	**Q—R5ch**	**34. R × P**	

White's tragedy is that he has to play for a win in this bad position in order to retain his title.

34. ...	**N—N4**	**35. R—B4**	**R × P**

Black certainly believed that this sacrifice would lead to a draw at least. However, he had a stronger line: 35. ... R—Q1; 36. B—K3, P—K4, and the White position is blown up (37. R—B5, N × Pch; 38. B × N, Q—N5, etc.).

36. B × R   R × B   38. K—B2   Q—R7ch
37. R—B8ch   B—B1
Not 38. .... Q—R5ch; 39. K—N2, Q—N5ch; 40. R—N3, Q × R;
41. Q—N6!, and White wins.

39. K—K1

39. ...   Q—R8ch?
'Hours of destiny in the chess world': 39. .... Q—R5ch would have
led to a draw; Schlechter would have become world champion.
There would have been no Lasker–Capablanca match, and no
second glorious period for Lasker. Chess history would have
developed along other lines. Let us examine the consequences of
39. ... Q—R5ch:

(1) 40. K—B1?, Q—R6ch; 41. K—K2, R × R, and 42. ... Q × R.
(2) 40. K—K2, Q—R4 leads to a repetition of moves, or even
    stronger 40. ... N × Pch.
(3) 40. K—Q1, Q—N5; 41. K—K2, R × R and 42. ... Q × R.
(4) K—Q2, Q—R7ch; 41. K—K3 (the only move to escape the
    checks), 41. .... R × Rch; 42. K × R, Q—R6ch; 43. K—K2,
    Q × R; 44. Q × N, and Black stands better.

40. R—KB1!   Q—R5ch   41. K—Q2   R × R
41. ... R × P fails against 42. R(8) × Bch, K—N2; 43. R(1)—B7ch,
K—R3; 44. R—R7ch, etc.

42. Q × R   Q × Pch   44. K—Q1   N—Q3
43. Q—Q3   Q—B7ch
The storm is over. White's advantage is slight but sufficient for the
win. There followed: **45. R—B5, B—R3; 46. R—Q5, K—N1;
47. N—B5, Q—N8ch; 48. K—B2, Q—B8ch; 49. K—N3, B—N2;
50. N—K6, Q—N7ch; 51. K—R4, K—B2; 52. N × B, Q × N;
53. Q—QN3, K—K1; 54. Q—N8ch, K—B2; 55. Q × P, Q—N5ch;
56. Q—Q4, Q—Q2ch; 57. K—N3, Q—N2ch; 58. K—R2, Q—B3;
59. Q—Q3, K—K3; 60. R—KN5, K—Q2; 61. R—K5, Q—N7ch;**

62. R—K2, Q—N5; 63. R—Q2, Q—QR5; 64. Q—B5ch, K—B2; 65. Q—B2ch, Q × Qch; 66. R × Qch, K—N3; 67. R—K2, N—B1; 68. K—N3, K—B3; 69. R—B2ch, K—N2; 70. K—N4, N—R2; 71. K—B5, Black resigns. Lasker keeps his title!

4. TRIUMPH OVER THE YOUNGER GENERATION

In the 1914 St Petersburg tournament, Lasker won the first prize, half a point ahead of Capablanca, leaving Alekhine, Rubinstein, Nimzowitch, Marshall and others far behind.

Seven years later, Lasker lost the title in a match against Capablanca, simply because Capablanca's style did not suit him. His overall strategy, 'Make the second best move in order to complicate the postion', did not work against Capablanca. We have seen in the chapter on Capablanca (Game 10) how Lasker had no chances for his 'swindles', and this is still more evident in Game 55, in the section on Lasker's errors.

After Lasker's defeat, it seemed most unlikely that there would be another era in which he would excel, and yet it came. During the period 1923–1925 Lasker beat all the younger masters, and twice he was even placed ahead of Capablanca. He did not now take the risks he had taken twenty years before; it was no longer necessary to make concessions in order to create complications. His ambitious opponents did so, and this allowed Lasker to play under much more favourable circumstances than in the past. He was no longer the world champion, against whom a draw was considered a moral victory. Therefore Lasker did not have to fear simplifications and dull games, and could fight with equal weapons. The reigning world champion, Capablanca, was an exceptional opponent in that he could keep the position dull and still play for a win. Of the three games Lasker lost out of fifty-three during this golden age, one was against Capablanca.

It is so rare that a chess player in his fifties (Lasker was born in 1868) achieves such extraordinary results that one seeks an explanation. We can either state that a miracle which cannot be explained occurred, or accept Wildhagen's view (from his *Weltgeschichte des Schachs*) that

> Lasker's career is an exception in chess history. In order for him to produce top performances for so long a period, quite a few preconditions must have worked together: excellent health and endurance, spiritual freshness owing to a continuous capacity and desire for a natural and efficient way of life, an economic use of forces and a deeply rooted philosophic attitude.

There can be no doubt that Lasker belongs among the greatest
players in chess history.

Game 50 White: R. Reti   Tournament Mahrisch-Ostrau 1923
      Black: Dr E. Lasker   Queen's Gambit, Slav Defence

**1. P—Q4, P—Q4; 2. P—QB4, P—QB3; 3. N—KB3, N—B3;
4. N—B3, P × P** (As in most of his games in this glorious period,
Lasker did not improvise in the opening, as he had done formerly,
but followed instead the usual, often-played lines); **5. P—K3,
P—QN4; 6. P—QR4, P—N5; 7. N—R2, P—K3; 8. B × P, B—K2;
9. 0—0, 0—0; 10. Q—K2, QN—Q2; 11. P—QN3, P—QR4;
12. B—N2, P—B4; 13. KR—Q1, Q—N3; 14. N—B1, B—R3; 15.
P × P, N × P; 16. N—K5, B × B; 17. N × B, Q—R3; 18. B—Q4,
KR—B1; 19. B × N** (White had to eliminate Black's QN, which was
putting uncomfortable pressure on White's QNP), **19. ... B × B;
20. Q—B3, B—K2; 21. N—Q3, N—Q4** (Black has discovered a
strong square for his knight) **22. N(3)—K5, B—B3; 23. P—K4,
N—B6; 24. R—Q6** (24. R—Q7 is answered by 24. ... R—R2),
24. ... Q—N2; 25. R—K1, B × N; 26. N × B, Q—B2; 27. N—B4
(It is clear that 27. R—Q7 fails against 27. ... Q × N), **27. ...
P—K4** (Black doesn't want to permit 28. P—K5) **28. Q—B5,**
(threatening both 29. R—Q7 and 29. Q × KP).

28. ...   N—K7ch!

Very surprising. White cannot take on account of 29. ... Q × R!
(30. Q × BPch, K—R1!).

29. K—B1?
The obvious move, but not the best. It will soon become clear that the
White King would stand better at R1.

29. ...   N—Q5   31. N—N6   N—Q7ch!
30. Q × KP   N × P
If the White King was on his R1, then Black would have played

L

31. ... Q—B6, and after 32. Q × Q, P × Q; 33. N × R(8), P—B7;
34. P—R3, P—B8 = Qch; 35. R × Q, R × Rch, Black would have
to struggle for a draw, though most likely with success.

32. K—N1   N—B5!   **33. N × N   Q × N**
Now Black's superiority is clear.

34. Q—KB5   QR—N1   **35. P—K5   P—N6**
There is no cure for the advancing passed Pawn.

36. P—K6
White's only possible counterchance.

36. ...   **P × P**   **38. Q—K5   Q—B7**
37. R(6) × P   R—B1
Controls the promotion square and threatens Q × Pch at the same
time.

39. P—B4   P—N7   **41. P—B5   Q—KB3**
40. R—K7   Q—N3
Black could not take the Pawn (41. ... R × P; 42. Q × Rch).

42. Q—Q5ch   K—R1   **43. R—N7**
The last attempt.

43. ...   **Q—B6**
White resigns (44. R—KB1, Q—K6ch; 45. K—R1, Q—B8).

This victory over Reti may not be too convincing, since the latter
could have saved himself by 29. K—R1 (instead of 29. K—B1 ?).
Lasker's games against Reti at New York 1924, were more impressive. The following game in particular, in which Reti relied in vain
upon all his modern ideas and manœuvres, aroused great admiration.

Game 51   *White:* R. Reti   Tournament New York 1924
           Black: Dr E. Lasker   Reti's Opening

**1. N—KB3, P—Q4; 2. P—B4, P—QB3; 3. P—QN3, B—B4;
4. P—N3, N—B3; 5. B—KN2, QN—Q2; 6. B—N2, P—K3;
7. 0—0, B—Q3; 8. P—Q3, 0—0; 9. QN—Q2** (a well-known variation), **P—K4** (It is one of the principles of this opening that White
permits his opponent to occupy the centre in order to attack it
later.); **10. P × P** (later analyses have shown that 10. P—K4 is
stronger), **10. ... P × P; 11. R—B1, Q—K2; 12. R—B2, P—QR4;
13. P—QR4, P—R3; 14. Q—R1** (One of the ideas of the modern
set-up: piece pressure against the hostile centre. Exceptionally,

even the Queen helps.) **14. ... KR—K1; 15. KR—B1, B—R2; 16. N—B1, N—B4.**

17. R × N

Surprising. White sacrifices the exchange for a Pawn. He hopes, however, to win a second Pawn in the long run, since Black's QP is weak and White's minor pieces are becoming very active.

17. ...	**B × R**	**20. P—R3**	**B—Q3**
18. N × P	**QR—B1**	**21. R × R**	**R × R**
19. N—K3	**Q—K3**	**22. N—B3?**	

Much better would be 22. N(5)—N4, after which Black's QP would soon be irretrievably lost.

22. ...	**B—K2**	**24. K—R2**	**P—R4**
23. N—Q4	**Q—Q2**	**25. Q—R1**	

Again a most original manœuvre. Black's QP must now fall, and it looks as though White's strategy is going to triumph. However, Lasker has already taken his counter-measures, which culminate in a most tricky turn.

25. ...	**P—R5**	**27. P × P**	**N × N**
26. N × P	**P × Pch**	**28. B × N**	**B—B3!**

Black gives up a third Pawn for the exchange, but the pin of White's Knight will later yield a profit.

29. B × NP   R—B4!
29. ... R—B2 seems to be stronger, since two pieces are attacked. However, there follows 30. B—Q5, R—B4; 31. B—B4, and now 31. ... B × N; 32. B × B, Q × B, is not possible on account of 33. Q—R8ch.

30. B—R6
White's Knight is indirectly protected.

30. ...   B—N3
Now 31. ... B × N is threatened.

31. Q—N7
The only defence. 31. P—K3, B × N; 32. B × B, R—B7ch, etc., is no good.

31. ...   Q—Q1   32. P—QN4
The only move. After 32. P—K3, B × N; 33. B × B, R—B7ch; 34. K—R1, Q—Q3!, Black's attack is decisive.

32. ...   R—B2!   34. Q × Qch   R × Q
33. Q—N6   R—Q2!   35. P—K3
At last the pinned piece is safe, but now Black gets a dangerous passed Pawn.

35. ...   P × P   37. P × B
36. K—N2   B × N

After 37. B × B, Black cannot play 37. ... R × B; 38. P × R, P—N6 on account of 39. B—B4, P—N7; 40. B—R2, B × P; 41. P—R5, P—N8 = Q; 42. B × Q, B × B, and Black has a draw at best. After 37. B × B, the correct line is 37. ... B—B4; 38. K—B3 (38. B—B4, B—K3), 38. ... B—Q2; 39. P—R5, R—R1.

37. ...   B—B4   39. K—B3
38. B—N7   B—K3
If 39. P—R5, then 39. ... B—Q4ch, capturing White's last hope, the QRP.

39. ...   B—N6   42. K—K3   R—K3ch
40. B—B6   R—Q3   43. K—B4
41. B—N5   R—B3ch
43. K—Q2, R—KN3; 44. P—N4, R—KR3 is just as easy for Black.

43. ...   R—K7   45. B—K3 B—Q4
44. B—B1 R—B7

White resigns, since the advance of the QNP cannot be prevented.

Alekhine and Bogoljubov were the great rivals of the World Champion, Capablanca, at this time. Lasker beat them both (in fact he beat Bogoljubov three times). Let us see how Lasker managed this.

Game 52   White: Dr A. Alekhine   Tournament New York 1924
          Black: Dr E. Lasker   Queen's Gambit, Exchange
                                   Variation

1. P—Q4, P—Q4; 2. P—QB4, P—K3; 3. N—KB3, N—KB3; 4. N—B3, QN—Q2; 5. P × P, P × P; 6. B—B4, P—B3; 7. P—K3 (Perhaps 7. P—KR3, to prevent the exchange of the QB, would have been better), **7. ... N—R4; 8. B—Q3** (It is not such a good idea to have the Bishop exchanged at KB4, because White's QP will become a target later.), **8. ... N × B; 9. P × N, B—Q3; 10. P—KN3, 0—0; 11. 0—0, R—K1; 12. Q—B2, N—B1; 13. N—Q1, P—B3; 14. N—K3, B—K3; 15. N—R4, B—QB2; 16. P—QN4** (The minority attack, the logical consequence of White's exchange of pawns at the fifth move), **16. ... B—QN3** (White's QP is weak); **17. N—B3, B—KB2!** (threatening 18. ... B—KR4 with an indirect attack against the QP); **18. P—N5?** (Correct would have been 18. Q—N2, N—K3; 19. N—B2, and White doesn't need his knight on B3 for the defence of his pawn.), **18. ... B—KR4; 19. P—N4** (forced, but the weakening of the K-side will soon be avenged), **19. ... B—KB2; 20. P × P, R—B1; 21. Q—N2, P × P; 22. P—B5** (White must play this move sooner or later. Now the diagonal KR2—QN1 is open for a Black attack.), **22. ... Q—Q3; 23. N—N2, B—B2; 24. KR—K1, P—KR4** (Not only to undermine White's Pawn structure, but also to prepare the manœuvre N—R2 and N—N4.); **25. P—KR3, N—R2.**

Now Black is ready for the final attack: N—N4, soon followed by the deadly penetration of the Black Queen on KR7. Alekhine, a strong attacking player, does not wish to torture himself with a patient defence and thinks out a counter-combination which would certainly have succeeded against a weaker player than Lasker.

26. R × Rch   R × R   27. R—K1
First the king file must be cleared. As long as a Black Rook is on its K1, the penetration of the Black Queen would mean mate (on R8).

27. ...   R—N1!
After 27. ... N—N4; 28. R × Rch, B × R; 29. Q—K2, or 27. ... R × Rch; 28. N(2) × R, White can defend himself.

28. Q—B1   N—N4
The battle starts.

29. N—K5!
Alekhine's fine point. After 29. N × N, Q—R7ch; 30. K—B1, P × N, White's position is hopeless.

29. ...   P × N   30. Q × N   P—K5
Reopening the attacking line.

31. P—B6   P—N3
Black is not content with a single Pawn. Playing 31. ... Q—R7ch first would be bad: 32. K—B1, P—N3; 33. Q—R6 and mate.

32. P—B4
Again, a very original move. Bad would have been 32. P × P, Q—R7ch; 33. K—B1, P × B, and Black is ahead.

32. ...   P × P!
The right way. Not 32. ... P × B; 33. P × P, or 32. ... P × P e.p.; 33. R—K5, P × N; 34. B × P.

33. B—K2
After 33. P × P, Black could safely take the Bishop. Bear in mind that the move Q—R6 is harmless as long as the Black Queen is on its Q3 (33. Q—R6, Q × P(3)).

33. ...   P × P   34. B—R5   R—N7
It is remarkable that Lasker's pieces are always on the right squares at the right moment.

35. N—R4   Q × P(5)   36. Q × Q   B × Q
White resigns. His position has become completely hopeless in only
a few moves.

Game 53   *White:* E. Bogoljubov   Tournament New York 1924
             Black: Dr E. Lasker   Ruy Lopez, Berlin variation

**1. P—K4, P—K4; 2. N—KB3, N—QB3; 3. B—N5, N—B3;
4. P—Q4, P × P; 5. N × P, B—K2; 6. 0—0, P—QR3; 7. N × N,
NP × N; 8. B—Q3, P—Q3** (We have reached a kind of Steinitz
defence in which White has one tempo more.); **9. N—B3, 0—0;
10. P—B4, R—K1; 11. K—R1, N—Q2; 12. B—K3, B—B3;
13. Q—B3** (It was not necessary to give his opponent the opportunity
to mutilate White's Queenside, even though White does get some
counterchances. More solid was 13. Q—Q2.), **13. ... R—N1;
14. QR—N1, B × N; 15. P × B, R × R; 16. R × R, P—QB4; 17. P—
B4, Q—K2; 18. P—KR3, N—B3; 19. B—B2, B—Q2** (Black could
not take: 19. ... N × P; 20. B × N, Q × B; 21. R—K1, but now
White's KP is '*en prise*'); **20. P—K5** (leads to great simplifications
which look favourable for White), **20. ... P × P; 21. P × P, Q × P;
22. B—N3, Q—K3** (if 22. ... Q—K2, then 23. B—R4); **23. B × P,
B—B3; 24. Q—B5, Q × Q; 25. B × Q, B—K5** (elimination of
White's pair of bishops); **26. B × B, N × B; 27. R—N6, R—R1.**

Black finds himself in a rather cramped position. It is impressive to
see how Lasker frees himself and takes the initiative.

28. R—B6
Preferable is 28. P—N4 to prevent the following advance of Black's
KRP.

28. ...   P—KR4!   30. K—N1
29. B—N6   P—R5
White is aware of the danger. After 30. B × P, R—Q1; 31. B—K3,

R—Q8ch; 32. B—N1, P—N4; 33. R × P, R—Q7; 34. P—B5, P—N5; 35. P × P, P—R6, Black is just in time to stop White's QBP: 36. K—R2 (else 36. ... R × NP and 37. ... N—N6 mate), 36. ... R × Pch; 37. K × P, R × B; 38. P—B6, R—N6ch and 39. ... R—QB6.

30. ...   R—K1   31. B × P R—Q1

White has won a Pawn, but the situation on his Kingside is critical, e.g.: 32. B—K3, R—Q8ch; 33. K—R2, N—N6; 34. B—N1, P—B4; 35. R × P, P—B5, and 36. ... P—B6, winning a piece, cannot be prevented.

32. K—B1 R—Q7   33. P—R4

33. B—K3 loses after 33. ... N—N6ch, and 33. B—K7 is answered by 33. ... P—B3.

33. ...   R × BP   36. B—K1 R × P
34. B—N4 R—B7ch   37. B × P
35. K—N1 R—R7

The dangerous RP has disappeared, but now Black wins a Pawn, which proves to be sufficient.

37. ... N—Q7

There followed: **38. B—Q8, N × P; 39. P—N4, N—Q7; 40. R—B8, K—R2; 41. R—QR8, R—R7; 42. K—N2, N—N6ch; 43. K—N3, N—Q5; 44. P—R4, R—R6ch; 45. K—B2, N—B3; 46. B—B7, N—K2; 47. B—Q6, R—R7ch; 48. K—B3, N—B3; 49. B—B7, N—Q5ch; 50. K—N3, R—R6ch; 51. K—B2, R—R5; 52. K—N3, N—K3; 53. B—N6, R—R6ch; 54. K—N2, N—B5ch; 55. K—B2, N—Q6ch; 56. K—N2, N—K4; 57. P—N5, N—N3; 58. B—B2, N—B5ch; 59. K—R2, K—N3; 60. R—R7, P—R4; 61. B—N3, R—R7ch; 62. K—R1, N—R4; 63. B—K5, R—R5; 64. K—N2, R × P** (At last!); **65. R—R6ch, K × P; 66. R × P, K—N3; 67. K—B3, P—B4; 68. B—Q6, R—Q5; 69. B—B7, R—QB5; 70. B—Q6, R—B3; 71. B—N8, K—N4,** White resigns.

5. LASKER IN ENDGAMES

As has already been mentioned, and can be seen from the various games we have discussed, Lasker was especially strong in the ending. I cannot remember a single instance of Lasker's going wrong in the endgame. He could calculate quite a number of moves ahead most exactly, and he knew how to exploit the slightest advantage. Moreover, and this is very important in handling the endings, his patience was almost unlimited.

We have seen how Lasker, playing Schlechter (Game 49), grasped at a straw—the last remaining Pawn—and patiently converted his advantage to retain his title. Against Alekhine, at St Petersburg 1914, he won a similar endgame, with the exchange ahead and only one pawn left. Against Bogoljubov (Game 53), he capitalized on his plus pawn after endless manœuvring.

To these endgame performances we will add two more, both from the St Petersburg Tournament 1914: his wins against Rubinstein and Capablanca. Strictly speaking, the latter game is a middle game without queens, but in discussing Lasker's career we cannot omit this historic first meeting between two of the most phenomenal chess players the world has ever seen.

Game Extract 10   *White:* Dr E. Lasker   Tournament, St
                     Black: A. Rubinstein   Petersburg 1914
                                               Position after
                                               Black's 45th move

White has a slightly better position. His majority on the Kingside can advance more easily than Black's on the Queenside. Lasker converted this small advantage into a win in an instructive way.

| 46. K—Q3 | R—N3 | 48. P—B4 | K—Q2 |
| 47. P—KN3 | R—B3 | 49. R—K1 | R—B1 |

Worth considering was the simplification 49. ... P—N4; 50. B—K3, P × P; 51. B × P, B—B2. This would have given Black somewhat better chances to draw.

50. R—QR1   P—R4
Other possibilities: 50. ... R—B2; 51. R—R8, or 50. ... P—N4; 51. B—K3, or 50. ... K—B2; 51. P—KN4!

51. B—K3   P—N3   52. R—KB1
The final preparation for the advance of his majority.

52. ... K—Q3	**54. P × P P—B4**
53. P—N4 P × P	

Black also brings his majority into play.

55. P × Pch B × P	**57. P—B5 P × P**
56. B × Bch K × B	**58. P × P R—B3**

Despite the small amount of material remaining, White can win this ending.

59. R—B4

Already, Black is practically in zugzwang.

59. ...   P—N5

After 59. . . . P—Q5, Dr Tarrasch has given the following interesting win for White: 60. K—K4, R—Q3; 61. R—B3!, K—B5; 62. P—N3ch, K—N5; 63. R—Q3, K—B4; 64. K—K5, R—Q1; 65. P—B6, R—K1ch; 66. K—B5, K—Q4; 67. P—B7, R—B1; 68. K—B6, K—K5; 69. R—Q1, P—Q6; 70. K—K7, etc.

60. P—N3 R—B2	**61. P—B6 K—Q3**

The Black King must give way.

62. K—Q4 K—K3	**63. R—B2 K—Q3**

The Pawn ending after 63. . . . R × P; 64. R × Rch, K × R; 65. K × P is lost for Black.

64. R—QR2   R—B2

Again Black could not take the Pawn.

65. R—R6ch K—Q2	**66. R—N6**

Black resigns, since he loses both his Pawns.

Game Extract 11	*White:* Dr E. Lasker	Tournament, St
	Black: J. R. Capablanca	Petersburg 1914
		Position after
		Black's 28th move

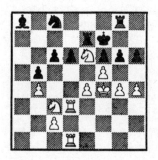

White has a preponderance in space and a strong Knight on K6. If he succeeds in penetrating with his Rooks, Black must lose. Moreover, Black's QP is weak. There followed:

29. R—N3   P—N4ch
Black hopes for 30. P × P, RP × Pch; 31. K—B3, R—R1, and Black now has the open file. The alternative, 29. ... P × P, would be answered by 30. NP × P, R × R; 31. K × R, R—K1; 32. K—N4!, and White has all kinds of possibilities, e.g. 32. ... R—N1ch; 33. K—R5, R—N7; 34. R—QR1, etc.

30. K—B3
To answer 30. ... P × P by 31. R—R3.

30. ...   N—N3
A courageous attempt to break the blockade. If now 31. R × P?, P × P; 32. R—R3, N—B5 and 33. ... N—K4ch gives Black strong counterplay.

31. P × P   RP × P   32. R—R3!
The open Rook file is much more important than Black's QP.

32. ...   R—Q2
Or 32. ... N—B5; 33. R—QR1.

33. K—N3
Anticipating a later P—K5 (move 35), White brings his King out of range of Black's QB.

33. ...   K—K1   35. P—K5!
34. R(1)—KR1   B—N2
A magnificent decision. White frees the K4 square for his QN.

35. ...   QP × P   37. N(6)—B5
36. N—K4   N—Q4
Wins the exchange, since the Black Rook cannot move on account of 38. N × B, R × N; 39. N—Q6ch.

37. ...   B—B1   40. R—R1   K—Q1
38. N × R   B × N   41. R—R8ch   B—B1
39. R—R7   R—B1   42. N—B5
Black resigns (42. ... N—B2; 43. R × Bch, K × R; 44. R × Nch, K × R; 45. N—K6ch, or 42. ... N—N3; 43. N—K6ch, K—K1; 44. R—N8).

6. LASKER'S ERRORS

Lasker made more errors than the other world champions. Hating quick draws, he played every game for the full point. His enterprising style led him from time to time along the edge of a precipice, and then accidents could happen. However, this occurred mainly in the first period of his career. For example, when Lasker was sitting across the board from promising young Rubinstein for the first time, he thoroughly under-rated him and was sharply punished.

Game 54   *White:* A. Rubinstein   Tournament, St Petersburg 1909
          Black: Dr E. Lasker   Queen's Gambit

1. P—Q4, P—Q4; 2. N—KB3, N—KB3; 3. P—B4, P—K3; 4. B—N5, P—B4 (enterprising, but not the best); **5. P × QP, KP × P; 6. N—B3, P × P** (theory gives 6. ... N—B3 as better); **7. KN × P, N—B3; 8. P—K3, B—K2** (Now Black runs into difficulties. Preferable was 8. ... B—QN5.); **9. B—N5, B—Q2; 10. B × KN, B × B; 11. N × P, B × N; 12. P × B, Q—N4; 13. B × N, B × B; 14. N—K3.**

    14. ...   0—0—0
After 14. ... B × P, White should not play 15. R—KN1 on account of 15. ... Q—R4ch; 16. Q—Q2, Q × Qch; 17. K × Q, B—K5; 18. R × P?, B—N3. Indeed, 14. ... B × P is better than the text, although not entirely satisfactory: 15. N × B!, Q × N; 16. Q—K2ch!, and 17. 0—0—0 with advantage for White.

    15. 0—0 KR—K1   16. R—B1!
Sets a fine trap, which is overlooked by Black.

    16. ...   R × N?
Lasker trapped! Preferable was 16. ... K—N1, after which White plays 17. R—B5, Q—B5; 18. P—Q5.

17. R × Bch
The refutation.

17. ... P × R   18. Q—B1! R × P
Lasker suggests as better: 18. ... R—K4; 19. Q × Pch, K—N1;
20. P × R, Q × P.

19. P × R   R—Q2
Black couldn't protect both his QBP and his KBP.

20. Q × Pch   K—Q1   21. R—B4
Threatens 22. Q—R8ch, K—K2; 23. R—K4ch.

21. ... P—B4
21. ... R—Q8ch; 22. K—B2, R—Q7ch; 23. K—K1 comes to
nothing for Black (23. ... R × NP, or 23. ... Q × P; 24. R—Q4ch).

22. Q—B5   Q—K2
Again, 22. ... R—Q8ch doesn't mean much: 23. K—B2, R—Q7ch;
24. K—K1, Q × P?; 25. Q—R5ch winning the Rook.

23. Q × Qch   K × Q   26. K—B3   R × QNP
24. R × P   R—Q8ch   27. R—QR5
25. K—B2   R—Q7ch
White, with a sound plus Pawn to the good, won after 27. ...
R—N2; 28. R—R6, K—B1; 29. P—K4, R—QB2; 30. P—KR4,
K—B2; 31. P—N4, K—B1; 32. K—B4, K—K2; 33. P—R5, P—R3;
34. K—B5, K—B2; 35. P—K5, R—N2; 36. R—Q6, K—K2;
37. R—R6, K—B2; 38. R—Q6, K—B1; 39. R—B6, K—B2;
40. P—R3, Black resigns (40. ... K—K2 or 40. ... K—B1;
41. K—N6). He is in zugzwang.

This game was apparently played by Lasker in the 'hurrah' style of
the previous century, though one should be aware that his opponent,
Rubinstein, who for ten years was a serious candidate for the world
title and never had a chance to play Lasker in a match, handled the
game, and especially the endgame, marvellously. Lasker himself
could not have played it better.

In Lasker's world championship match with Schlechter, it was
agreed that only ten games should be played. The first four ended
in draws. Schlechter was very difficult to beat and was nicknamed
'King of Draws'. Time and time again Lasker tried in vain to break
through Schlechter's solid line of defence. In the fifth game, in an
almost symmetrical position with only Rooks and Queens on the
board, he tried again. He walked his King from the Kingside to

the Queenside, apparently for no other reason than to complicate the game. After Black's 38th move the following position was reached.

Game Extract 12

White: C. Schlechter   Match, Berlin 1910
Black: Dr E. Lasker

Schlechter, perhaps bored by his opponent's stubbornness, sacrificed a pawn.

39. P—QR4

He was also certainly aware that the opening of one or two files on the Queenside could give some chances to White, especially in view of the vulnerability of the Black King. However, Lasker did not fear the consequences, as he had often played games with a 'naked King'.

39. ...	**Q × NP**	**41. R—N3**	**Q—R3**
40. P × P	**Q × NP**	**42. Q—Q4**	

It looks as though White's gain in space satisfactorily compensates for Black's material advantage of one Pawn.

42. ...   R—K1   43. R—N1

Threatens 44. R—QR1.

43. ...   R—K4   44. Q—N4

44. R—QR1 would now be answered by 44. ... R—R4. White hopes for 44. ... R—N4?; 45. Q—B4, and the White Queen penetrates via B7 or N8.

44. ...   Q—N4   45. Q—K1   Q—Q6

Things look rosy for Black, but the danger is not yet over. Instead of the text, 45. ... Q—R5 deserves consideration in order to occupy both open files: 46. R—N4, Q—R2 and 47. ... R—N4.

46. R—N4   P—QB4?
Much better is 46. . . . R—R4, threatening 47. . . . R—R6.

47. R—R4   P—B5   48. Q—QR1!
White sacrifices a second pawn to strengthen his attack.

48. . . .   Q × Pch   49. K—R2   R—N4
Black must play very carefully to parry the combined attack of the
Queen and Rook against his King. He now threatens 50. . . . Q—K4ch
with the exchange of Queens.

50. Q—R2   Q—K4ch   52. K—R2   P—Q4
51. K—N1   Q—K8ch   53. R—R8
The advance of the Black Pawns has made the position of the Black
King still more vulnerable. White threatens 54. Q—R7ch, R—N2;
55. Q—B5ch.

53. . . .   Q—N5   54. K—N2   Q—B4?
The decisive mistake. Even Lasker could not always withstand the
continuous pressure against his King in the open field. With 54. . . .
R—N2, Black could have defended himself, but it is very doubtful
whether more than a draw would have resulted.

55. Q—R6   R—N1
55. . . . R—N2 also loses: 56. Q—K6, R—N1; 57. Q—B7ch, etc.

56. R—R7ch   K—Q1   58. Q—R3
57. R × P   Q—N3
Black   resigns   (58. . . . Q—N5;   59. Q—R7,   or   58. . . . K—B1;
59. Q—B8ch).

Again, this was Lasker in his transition period. After a series of four
draws, he lost patience. Something had to happen in the fifth game.
   A certain similarity can be seen in Lasker's match with Capablanca.
After four colourless draws, Lasker took his chance. He first
sacrificed a Pawn, and later the exchange. But against Capablanca
at his best it was very risky to sacrifice, for in most cases one never
regained the sacrificed material.

Game 55   *White:* J. R. Capablanca   Fifth Match Game, Havana
            Black: Dr E. Lasker   1921
                                      Queen's Gambit, Orthodox
                                                      Variation

1. P—Q4, P—Q4; 2. N—KB3, N—KB3; 3. P—B4, P—K3;
4. B—N5, QN—Q2; 5. P—K3, B—K2; 6. N—B3, 0—0; 7. R—B1,

P—QN3 (7. . . . P—B3 is more solid, but Lasker is seeking adventure); **8. P × P, P × P; 9. Q—R4, P—B4** (Black sacrifices a Pawn, because 9. . . . B—N2; 10. B—R6 is not quite satisfactory on account of the weaknesses on Black's Queenside and Capablanca was a master of the attack against a weakened Queenside.); **10. Q—B6, R—N1; 11. N × P, B—N2** (Another possibility was 11. . . . N × N; 12. Q × N, B—N2, but then White maintains some advantage with 13. B × B, Q × B; 14. Q—N5, Q × Q; 15. N × Q, P × P; 16. R—Q1!); **12. N × Bch, Q × N; 13. Q—R4.**

Black has some counterplay for the Pawn, and he should now have played 13. . . . B × N; 14. P × B, P × P; 15. Q × P, N—K4. Instead, Lasker tries to complicate the game still more.

13. . . .   QR—B1?
This looks fine. Black wants to oppose on the QB file and then take advantage of White's postponement of castling. However, Capablanca is able to avert the danger with a few well-considered moves.

14. Q—R3
Pins the QBP.

14. . . .   Q—K3   16. B—R6!
15. B × N   Q × B
The end of Black's counterattack. If now 16. . . . P × P; 17. R × R, R × R; 18. 0—0!, White will maintain a sound plus Pawn (18. . . . B × B; 19. Q × B, R—B7; 20. Q—R4).

16. . . .   B × N
Black makes a virtue of necessity and sacrifices the exchange.

17. B × R   R × B   18. P × B   Q × P
The position is not yet easy for White, but the task of converting

the material advantage of the exchange can be safely entrusted to Capablanca, even under difficult circumstances and against such a skilful player as Lasker. There followed: **19. R—KN1, R—K1; 20. Q—Q3, P—N3; 21. K—B1, R—K5; 22. Q—Q1, Q—R6ch; 23. R—N2, N—B3; 24. K—N1, P×P; 25. R—B4!, P×P; 26. R×R, N×R** (26. ... P×Pch; 27. R×P, N×R would cost a piece after 28. Q—Q8ch, K—N2; 29. Q—Q4ch); **27. Q—Q8ch, K—N2; 28. Q—Q4ch, N—B3; 29. P×P** (Black has regained one Pawn, but now White has the initiative), **29. ... Q—K3; 30. R—KB2, P—KN4; 31. P—KR4, P×P; 32. Q×RP, N—N5; 33. Q—N5ch, K—B1; 34. R—B5, P—KR4; 35. Q—Q8ch, K—N2; 36. Q—N5ch, K—B1; 37. Q—Q8ch, K—N2; 38. Q—N5ch, K—B1; 39. P—N3, Q—Q3; 40. Q—B4, Q—Q8ch; 41. Q—B1, Q—Q2; 42. R×P, N×P; 43. Q—B3, Q—Q5; 44. Q—R8ch, K—K2; 45. Q—N7ch, K—B1?** (After 45. ... K—B3 the win would have required many more moves); **46. Q—N8ch,** Black resigns. He loses either his Knight (46. ... K—K2; 47. Q—K5ch), or his Queen (46. ... K—N2; 47. Q—R8ch).

In his period of glory Lasker also made mistakes, although they occurred very seldom and were of a totally different kind from the ones we have looked at. A characteristic example is the following game, which is really unique in chess literature.

Game 56   *White:* C. Torre   Tournament, Moscow 1925
            Black: Dr E. Lasker   Queen's Pawn Game

1. P—Q4, N—KB3; 2. N—KB3, P—K3; 3. B—N5 (unusual, but not bad), **3. ... P—B4; 4. P—K3, P×P; 5. P×P, B—K2; 6. QN—Q2, P—Q3; 7. P—B3, QN—Q2; 8. B—Q3, P—QN3; 9. N—B4, B—N2; 10. Q—K2, Q—B2** (both players develop without making things too difficult for each other); **11. 0—0, 0—0; 12. KR—K1, KR—K1; 13. QR—Q1, N—B1; 14. B—B1, N—Q4** (Lasker feels obliged to take some initiative); **15. N—N5, P—N4; 16. N—R3, P—N5; 17. P×P, N×P; 18. Q—R5** (Perhaps White is already looking for the following combination. Objectively better was 18. B—N1), **18. ... B×N** (White threatened 19. Q× BPch); **19. B×B, N×B; 20. R×N, Q—R4** (Not only attacking White's KR, but also threatening to win a piece by 21. ... P—KR3 or 21. ... P—B3.).

21. P—QN4!
White has the following combination in mind: 21. ... Q×P;

M

22. R—N1, Q—R4; 23. N—B4, Q—B2; 24. N × P, Q × N; 25. R × B, with counter chances.

21. ...   Q—KB4?
Black wishes to maintain his double threat (Q × R and P—KR3), but 21. . . . Q—Q4 would have been much better.

22. R—KN3
White apparently nods.

22. ...   P—KR3   23. N—B4!   Q—Q4?
Black falls into the trap, a rare event for Lasker. With 23. . . . P × B; 24. N × P, Q—N3; 25. Q × Q, N × Q; 26. N × B Black could probably have gained a draw.

24. N—K3   Q—N4?
In his winning mood, Black is blind to the danger. However, 24. . . . Q × QP; 25. B × P, N—N3; 26. B—N5, threatening 27. R—R3, would not save the game.

25. B—B6!!
This move deserves a diagram.

25. ...   Q × Q   27. R × P dis. ch   K—N1
26. R × Pch   K—R1
The rest is easy: **28. R—N7ch, K—R1; 29. R × B dis. ch, K—N1;**

30. R—N7ch, K—R1; 31. R—N5 dis. ch, K—R2; 32. R × Q, K—N3; 33. R—R3, K × B; 34. R × Pch, and White won.

7. COMPARING LASKER AND FISCHER

As has already been mentioned, such a comparison is almost impossible, because the specialities of the two chess giants are, for the most part, so different, and because Lasker's performances span such a long period of time.

In the opening, Fischer is certainly superior. Lasker did not study the openings, and he was perfectly satisfied if he held a reasonable position after the first phase of the game. This gave him the opportunity to start a real struggle.

In the middle game, Lasker emphasized the tactical element more than Fischer, although the latter, too, is prepared for tactical finesses. One might say that Lasker mostly played for tactical complications, while Fischer accepts them when they arise in the course of the game.

The ending, regardless of the type of position, is played to perfection by both players. We have seen in a number of games how Lasker and Fischer were able to convert the advantage of the exchange into a win, how a plus pawn was realized, and how the opponent was forced into zugzwang.

We reached the conclusion that there can be no clear preference for Capablanca or Fischer, nor for Alekhine or Fischer, and we have to make the same conclusion regarding Lasker and Fischer: both are great and, in their best periods (in which Fischer may still be), almost unbeatable.

We shall conclude this chapter with two of Fischer's games which, to a certain degree, are comparable to Lasker's. The first shows (again) Fischer's skill and his confidence in the endgame. The second shows Fischer's tactical capacity, both in attack and defence.

It is remarkable that these games were played in the very first phase of his career, when Fischer was only sixteen.

Game 57   *White:* R. Fischer   Tournament, Mar del Plata 1959
            Black: J. Bolbochan   Sicilian Defence

1. P—K4, P—QB4; 2. N—KB3, N—QB3; 3. P—Q4, P × P; 4. N × P, N—B3; 5. N—QB3, P—K3; 6. N(4)—N5, B—N5; 7. P—QR3, B × Nch; 8. N × B, P—Q4; 9. B—Q3 (Fischer chooses to play an ending that looks very drawish. The usual continuation is 9. P × P.), **9. ... P × P; 10. N × P, N × N; 11. B × N, Q × Qch; 12. K × Q.**

It is surprising that Fischer is contented with this position, which at first sight doesn't offer many chances. True, White has the two Bishops and the Pawn majority on the Queenside. However, the latter is of no account as long as the hostile King avoids castling Kingside.

12. ... B—Q2   13. B—K3 P—B4
It is understandable that Black advances his Kingside Pawns to emphasize his majority on this wing.

14. B—B3 P—K4   15. P—QN4
The logical continuation. White advances his majority.

15. ... 0—0—0   16. K—B1 N—Q5
Looks tempting, as White's pair of Bishops is now eliminated. On the other hand, Black's Pawn on Q5 allows White to move more freely, since the Queen file is closed.

17. B × N   P × B   19. K—Q2 B—N4
18. KR—K1 KR—K1
Thus Black prevents the siege of his isolated Pawn by the White King (K—Q3).

20. R × R   R × R   22. R—QB1 K—N1
21. P—QR4 B—B5
White threatened to play 23. P—B3.

23. P—B3 P × Pch   24. R × P B—B2
The Bishop has done its duty and can retire. In the meantime, White has brought together quite a number of small advantages: (1) the Black King is tied to the protection of his QNP, (2) White's King is centralized, (3) Black's Kingside Pawns may become weak, since his KBP is already advanced. This is especially true if the Rooks are exchanged.

25. P—R5   R—K2

25. ... P—QN3; 26. P—R6, can become very uncomfortable for Black.

26. R—K3   R—Q2ch

The exchange of Rooks would lead directly to a lost ending for Black (26. ... R × R; 27. K × R, P—KN4; 28. K—Q4).

27. R—Q3	**R—K2**	**29. R—KR8**	**P—KR3**
28. R—Q8ch	**K—B2**	**30. K—B3**	**P—R3**

Fixes the Queenside Pawns on the wrong colour, but 30. ... P—N3; 31. P—R6, would have been catastrophic.

31. K—Q4   B—K1

The sally 31. ... R—Q2ch; 32. K—K5, R—Q7 would accomplish nothing after 33. R—R7, etc.

32. R—KB8	**B—Q2**	**34. B—Q5**	**B—Q2**
33. P—R4	**B—B1**		

Black must wait and watch White strengthen his position move by move.

35. P—B4   P—KN3

After 35. ... B—B1; 36. R—B7, R × R; 37. B × R, K—Q3; 38. B—Q5, Black gets into zugzwang.

36. R—B6   B—K1   37. B—K6

Enables the White King to advance still further.

37. ...   B—B3   38. P—N3

38. R × NP, B × P; 39. R × P was also good, but White prefers to strangle his opponent.

38. ...   R—N2   39. K—K5   B—K1

White threatened to win offhand by 40. R—B7ch.

40. B—Q5	**P—R4**	**43. K—B6**	**R—R2**
41. R—N6	**K—B1**	**44. B—Q5**	**K—B1**
42. B—K6ch	**K—B2**	**45. R—K6**	

In the German book *Das Schachphanomen Robert Fischer*, the authors H. Kramer and S. H. Postma remark, 'With the patience of Lasker, Fischer pulls the net.' A further element of resemblance: Lasker and Fischer both have patience.

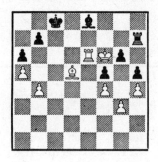

45. ...	K—Q1	48. B—N8	R—QB2
46. R—Q6ch	K—B2	49. B—K6ch	K—N1
47. R—N6	K—B1		

After 49. ... K—Q1, White also wins with 50. R—Q6.

50. R—Q6
Black resigns (50. ... K—R2; 51. R—Q8, B—N4; 52. K × NP, etc.).

Game 58   *White:* R. Fischer   Tournament, Zurich 1959
               Black: E. Bhend   Sicilian Defence

1. P—K4, P—QB4; 2. N—KB3, P—KN3; 3. P—Q4, P × P; 4. N × P, N—KB3; 5. N—QB3, B—N2? (a bad mistake costing two full tempi); **6. P—K5, N—N1; 7. B—KB4, N—QB3; 8. N × N, NP × N** (Black should have tried 8. ... QP × N, although the position after 9. Q × Qch, K × Q; 10. O—O—Och, K—K1 doesn't inspire much confidence.); **9. B—B4, P—B3** (An attempt to free the position.); **10. P—K6!** (White sacrifices a Pawn to strengthen his attack), **10. ... P × P** (10. ... P—Q4; 11. N × P, P × N; 12. Q × P, Q × Q; 13. B × Q loses material for Black, and 10. ... P—Q3; 11. Q—Q2 makes it practically impossible for him to bring his Knight into play); **11. Q—B3, Q—N3; 12. O—O, N—R3; 13. N—R4!** (intending to answer 13. ... Q—N2 with 14. N—B5, Q—N3; 15. N × P and wins), **13. ... Q—Q5** (Desperation. Black sacrifices the exchange to get some counterplay.); **14. B × N** (first eliminate a defender), **14. ... B × B** (14. ... Q × B would cost a piece after 15. P—QN3); **15. Q × QBPch, K—B2; 16. QR—K1** (A wise decision. After 16. Q × R, Q × B Black would have obtained counterchances. Now Black's KP(6) must fall.), **16. ... R—QN1; 17. B × Pch, K—N2; 18. B—Q5** (Looks fine, but the simple 18. B × B, KR × B; 19. R × Pch would have been crushing: 19. ... K—R1; 20. Q—K6, R—KB1; 21. R—Q7, etc.).

18. ... B—N4!

Opens a flight square for the wandering King. It is wonderful to see how Black, in this critical position, provides himself with counter-chances.

19. R—K4

Seemingly, this drives the Queen to a less active square.

19. ... Q—Q7

It appears later that the Queen can create counterplay from this square.

20. R × Pch   K—R3   21. R × QRP

Analyses after the game have shown that 21. P—KB4 would have been stronger here: 21. ... B × P; 22. Q × P, or 21. ... Q—Q5ch; 22. K—R1, B × P; 23. R—K4.

21. ... B—B4   22. P—QB4   QR—Q1

To answer 23. Q—B7 with 23. ... R—Q2.

23. N—B5

Now 24. Q—B7 is threatened again.

23. ... KR—K1!

Combines defence and attack. If 24. Q—B7, then 24. ... R—Q2!; 25. N × R, R—K8!, and Black wins. A diabolical trap.

24. N—K6!

Fischer, fully aware of the danger, closes the dangerous King file.

24. ... B × N   25. B × B   B—K6!

Again a surprise. White cannot take the Bishop, and Black threatens 26. ... Q × Pch and mate.

26. R—Q7

Repulses Black's attack. Black is now forced to simplify into a long ending.

26. ...	B × Pch	30. R × Pch!	K × R
27. R × B	Q—K8ch	31. Q—B7ch	K—R3
28. R—B1	Q—K6ch	32. Q × R	Q—K7
29. K—R1	R × B		

Or 32. ... Q—K8; 33. Q—Q3.

33. Q—Q1	Q × QNP	35. R × Q	
34. Q—B1ch	Q × Q		

The storm is over. White won after 35. ... R—K7; 36. P—QR3, R—R7; 37. P—B5, R × RP; 38. P—B6, R—R1; 39. P—B7, R—QB1; 40. K—N1, Black resigns.

CHAPTER IV

FISCHER AND THE LIVING
WORLD CHAMPIONS

1. FISCHER AND EUWE (+1, −1, =1)

I have played three games with the recent World Champion, but none of these games has any value for comparison, since at the time of the first two games (1956) Fischer was only a boy (although a promising one!), and with the last game (played in 1960) my world championship was already more than twenty years behind me.

In my opinion, there is no point in making an indirect comparison between Fischer and myself, as I did with Capablanca, Alekhine and Lasker. I am willing to concede that such a comparison would not turn out in my favour. Wisely perhaps, I have no ambition to claim one of the top places in chess history.

From my games with Fischer, one has already been given in Chapter 1 (Game 6). My win follows here.

Game 59 White: Dr M. Euwe   Exhibition Game, New York 1956
        Black: R. Fischer   Queen's Gambit, Manhattan
                                    Variation

1. P—Q4, N—KB3; 2. P—QB4, P—K3; 3. N—QB3, P—Q4; 4. P × P, P × P; 5. B—N5, B—QN5; 6. P—K3, P—KR3; 7. B—R4, P—B4; 8. B—Q3 (White need not fear the advance P—B5 as long as he has not played N—KB3, for in this case he can develop his Knight on K2 and eventually break the Black centre by P—B3 and P—K4), **8. ... N—B3; 9. N—K2, P × P** (Simplifies the game, but doesn't lead to complete equality, since White's minor pieces are better placed than Black's.); **10. P × P, 0—0; 11. 0—0, B—K3?** (Here the Bishop stands badly, as will soon be clear. Correct would have been 11. ... B—K2. See diagram overleaf.)

12. B—B2!
Preparing the mating attack by 13. Q—Q3 and 14 B × N.

12. ...   B—K2   13. N—B4!
Much stronger than the immediate 13. Q—Q3, which would be answered by 13. ... P—N3. The text practically prevents this defence.

(Position after Black's 11th move)

    13. ... Q—N3?

Now the catastrophe is complete. The only move, although far from attractive, was 13. ... P—KN4; 14. N × B, P × N; 15. B—KN3.

    14. B × N B × B   **15. Q—Q3**

Black cannot stop the penetration by the White Queen. (If 15. ... P—N3, then 16. N × NP.)

    15. ... KR—Q1   **16. QR—K1**

Threatens 17. N(4) × P, and Black cannot play 17. ... B × N on account of mate in two.

    16. ...   N—N5   **18. P—QR3!**
    17. Q—R7ch K—B1

Forces Black to give up the protection of his QP.

    18. ... N × B   **19. N(3) × P**

Attacks the Queen and threatens mate.

    19. ... R × N   **20. N × R**

Black resigns. He must lose his Queen and more.

2. FISCHER AND BOTVINNIK (+0, −0, =1)

Fischer and Botvinnik met only once, at Varna 1962. If Fischer had won one of the two Candidates Tournaments (Belgrade 1959 or Curacao 1962) during Botvinnik's championship, many more games between the two would have been played. However, Fischer was still too young at that time, and when he finally came out first, Botvinnik had already retired from chess.

We must be satisfied with that one game, which doesn't say much about the relative strength of the two world champions. The direct comparison fails, and an indirect comparison would not fit in with the design of this book as set out in the Introduction.

However, if such an indirect comparison had been made, I am

convinced that the conclusion would be that Botvinnik, too, should be counted as one of the best players in chess history.

The final phase of the game between Botvinnik and Fischer has already been discussed in Chapter 1, in the Game Extract 2. The beginning of this game follows here.

Game 60   *White:* M. Botvinnik   Olympiad, Varna 1962
             Black: R. Fischer   Grunfeld Defence

1. P—QB4, P—KN3; 2. P—Q4, N—KB3; 3. N—QB3, P—Q4; 4. N—B3, B—N2; 5. Q—N3, P×P; 6. Q×P, 0—0; 7. P—K4 (Botvinnik has a preference for a broad centre in this variation), **7. ... B—N5; 8. B—K3, KN—Q2** (Smyslov's manœuvre. The text opens the diagonal for the fianchettoed KB and brings the KN to the Queenside, where it can press against White's Q-wing.) **9. B—K2, N—QB3; 10. R—Q1, N—N3; 11. Q—B5, Q—Q3; 12. P—KR3** (After 12. Q × Q, BP × Q, Black's chances are certainly no worse than White's), **12. ... B × N; 13. P × B** (Not 13. B × B, on account of 13. ... Q × Q; 14. P × Q, N—B5), **13. ... KR—Q1** (After 13. ... Q × Q; 14. P × Q, B × Nch; 15. P × B, N—R5; 16. K—Q2, White wins as the Black Knight is cut off); **14. P—Q5** (According to Fischer, 14. P—K5 would have been better and sufficient for equality), **14. ... N—K4; 15. N—N5, Q—B3!; 16. P—B4, N(4)—Q2.**

17. P—K5?

A bad mistake. 17. Q × BP, Q × NP would probably not be good for White either, but with 17. Q—Q4 he could retire without damage. The text loses a Pawn in the simplest way. It is most remarkable that Botvinnik overlooked this, not only during the game, but also in his home analysis.

17. ...   Q × BP!

If White now makes the desperado move 18. Q × N, Black wins

after 18. .... Q—K5; 19. P—B3, Q—R5ch; 20. B—B2, Q—N5ch, etc.

18. B × Q   N × Q   19. N × BP   QR—B1

White has only temporarily regained his Pawn.

20. P—Q6!

The passed Pawn means some compensation for White.

20. ...   P × P   22. 0—0   N(3)—Q2
21. P × P   B × P

Botvinnik considers this move a mistake and recommends 22. .... N(4)—Q2. The difference is that White now controls his Q5 square, enabling him to prevent the important move 23. .... B—K4.

23. R—Q5   P—N3   24. B—B3

Both Botvinnik and Fischer agree that 24. B—B4 would have been better.

24. ...   N—K3   25. N × N?

Preferable was 25. B—K3, although Black has already surmounted the difficulties which arose after winning the Pawn.

25. ...   P × N   27. R—K3   P—K4
26. R—Q3   N—B4

Simplifies and leads to a favourable ending.

28. B × P

The only real chance for White was the sacrifice of the exchange: 28. R × P, B × R; 29. B × B.

28. ...   B × B   30. R—K7   R—Q2
29. R × B   R × P   31. R × R   N × R

Black has a healthy plus Pawn and should win. After **32. B—N4, R—B2; 33. R—K1, K—B2; 34. K—N2, N—B4; 35. R—K3, R—K2; 36. R—B3ch, K—N2; 37. R—B3, R—K5; 38. B—Q1, R—Q5; 39. B—B2, K—B3; 40, K—B3, K—N4; 41. K—N3,** we have reached the position discussed on pp. 50–51.

3.   FISCHER AND SMYSLOV (+3, −1, =5)

So far we have not discussed any of these games. Four were played before 1960 (results +1, −1, =2), when Smyslov was still among the top players—he won the world championship in 1957—and Fischer was learning. There can be no doubt therefore that Fischer's strength as a world champion exceeds Smylov's strength at his peak.

We discuss the four decisive games in chronological order.

Game 61 White: R. Fischer   Candidates Tournament, Bled-
        Black: V. Smyslov   Zagreb-Belgrade 1959
                                         Sicilian Defence

**1. P—K4, P—QB4; 2. N—KB3, P—K3; 3. P—Q4, P × P;
4. N × P, N—KB3; 5. N—QB3, P—Q3; 6. B—QB4, B—K2;
7. 0—0, P—QR3; 8. B—N3, P—QN4; 9. P—B4, 0—0** (After
9. ... P—N5; 10. N—R4, N × P; 11. P—B5! Black would run
into difficulties, e.g. 11. ... P—K4; 12. B—Q5); **10. P—B5** (Too
aggressive. According to theory 10. P—QR3 is preferable.), **10. ...
P—N5; 11. N(3)—K2, P—K4; 12. N—KB3, B—N2** (Now White
must lose a Pawn, for which he doesn't get sufficient compensation.);
13. N—N3, N × P; 14. N × N, B × N; 15. Q—K1, B × N (Black
doesn't wish to return the Pawn); **16. R × B, N—B3; 17. Q—K4**
(Another, probably more promising system of attack, was 17. P—B3,
P × P; 18. P × P, P—Q4; 19. Q—Q1, followed by 20. R—R3 and
21. Q—R5), **17. ... N—Q5; 18. R—R3, B—B3** (19. P—B6 was
threatened); **19. B—Q5, R—B1; 20. P—B3, P × P; 21. P × P,
N—N4; 22. B—Q2, R—B4; 23. K—R1, Q—Q2; 24. B—N3,
P—Q4; 25. Q—B3, N—Q3; 26. R—KB1** (26. B × P? loses a piece
after 26. ... P—K5!), **26. ... N—K5; 27. Q—R5** (at last the direct
attack, but it is already too late), **27. ... P—R3.**

28. B × P
A last try, but Black has the situation well in hand.

28. ... P × B   29. B—B2
29. Q × P doesn't lead anywhere either: 29. ... R(1)—B1; 30. B—
B2 (indirect attack on the Bishop), 30. ... B—N2; 31. Q—R7ch,
K—B1, etc.

**29. ... B—N4   31. B × N   P × B
30. P—B6 R—N1   32. R—N3**
The attack seems to revive.

32. ... Q—B4!   **33. K—N1 Q—N3**

The conclusive refutation of the attack.

The rest holds no further interest: **34. Q—K2, R—B3; 35. P—R4, R × KBP; 36. R × R, Q × R; 37. Q—R5, Q—B5; 38. K—R2, K—N2** (To liquidate into a won Rook ending.); **39. P × B, P × P; 40. Q × NPch, Q × Q; 41. R × Qch, K—B3; 42. R—R5, R—N8; 43. K—N3, R—KB8!** (Cuts off the White King from Black's passed Pawn.) **44. R—R4, K—B4; 45. R—R5ch, K—K3; 46. R—R6ch, P—B3; 47. R—R4, P—K6; 48. R—K4, P—B4,** White resigns.

Game 62   *White:* V. Smyslov   Candidates Tournament,
            Black: R. Fischer   Bled-Zagreb-Belgrade 1959
                                 Sicilian Defence, Najdorf Variation

1. P—K4, P—QB4; 2. N—KB3, P—Q3; 3. P—Q4, P × P; 4. N × P, N—KB3; 5. N—QB3, P—QR3; 6. B—KN5 (all according to theory), **6. ... P—K3; 7. P—B4, B—K2; 8. Q—B3, Q—B2; 9. 0—0—0, QN—Q2; 10. P—KN4, P—N4; 11. B × N, N × B; 12. P—N5, N—Q2; 13. B—R3** (13. P—QR3 is considered better), **13. ... P—N5** (A nice 'pendant' to the previous game, the difference being that Black, instead of winning a Pawn, obtains the intiative in the centre.); **14. QN—K2, B—N2; 15. K—N1?** (This move leads White into difficulties. Correct was 15. N—N3 at once, since, according to Fischer's judgment, the sacrifice 15. B × P, P × B; 16. N × P, Q—B5; 17. N × Pch, K—B1 gives White nothing.), **15. ... N—B4; 16. N—N3, P—Q4!** (With this move, Black attains a clear advantage.)

17. P—B5

Instead of accepting a passive position after 17. P—K5, P—N3, Smyslov tries to maintain the initiative with a Pawn sacrifice.

17. ... P × KP	19. N(4) × P P—N3!
18. Q—N4 P × P	

The refutation. After 19. ... 0—0 White would have obtained a winning attack by 20. N—R5, P—N3; 21. Q—N3!! (21. ... B—Q1; 22. R × B!).

20. N × B

After 20. N—R6 both 20. ... B—B1 and 20. ... Q—K4 are strong enough.

20. ... Q × N	23. R—B6 R—Q4
21. Q—B4 0—0	24. B—N4 N—Q2
22. R—Q6 QR—Q1	25. R—KB1 P—K6

Of course, Black cannot take the Rook: 25. ... N × R; 26. P × N and 27. Q—R6.

26. P—N3   R—Q7

Now Black threatens 27. ... N × R; 28. P × N, Q—B4!

27. B × N

White must simplify. The battle is decided.

There followed: 27. ... R × B; 28. R—K1, R—K1; 29. P—KR4, Q—B4; 30. Q—B4, Q × Q; 31. P × Q, R—Q5; 32. P—B5, R × P; 33. P—B6, B—B1; 34. R—Q6, R—QB5; 35. K—N2, K—N2; 36. K—N3, R—N5; 37. N—K2, R—K3; 38. R(1)—Q1 (Exchange of Rooks would make matters worse.), 38. ... R—N7; 39. N—B4, R × R; 40. R × R, R—Q7 (The rest is not worthwhile.); 41. R—Q3, R—B7; 42. R—Q4, P—K7; 43. N—Q3, B—B4; 44. P—B7, R—B6; 45. P—B8 = Q, B × Q; 46. R—K4, B—B4; 47. R × KP, B × N; 48. P × B, R × Pch; 49. K × P, R—Q4; 50. R—KN2, P—R3; 51. P × Pch, K × P; 52. P—R4, P—N4; 53. R—QB2, R—Q3; 54. K—B5, R—K3, White resigns.

The following game was played under very special circumstances. Fischer could not come to the Havana tournament, but he was still allowed to compete. He remained in New York and transmitted his moves by telephone.

Game 63   *White:* R. Fischer   Tournament, Havana 1965
             Black: V. Smyslov   Ruy Lopez, Steinitz Variation

1. P—K4, P—K4; 2. N—KB3, N—QB3; 3. B—N5, P—QR3; 4. B—R4, N—B3; 5. P—Q3 (An old variation which, however, is just as good as the modern continuation after 5. 0—0, B—K2; 6. R—K1), **5. ... P—Q3; 6. P—B3, B—K2; 7. QN—Q2, 0—0; 8. N—B1** (Steinitz also used to postpone castling and tried to attack

the hostile Kingside.), **8. ... P—QN4; 9. B—N3, P—Q4** (In view
of White's delay in castling, Black obviously tries to take the initiative in the centre. However, 9. ... N—R4 followed by 10. ...
P—B4, as usually played in the closed variation, would have been
preferable); **10. Q—K2, P × P** (Black should have maintained the
tension in the centre by 10. ... B—K3. He need not fear the loss of
a Pawn after 11. P × P?, N × P; 12. N × P, N × N; 13. Q × N,
because after 13. ... B—B3 Black can sacrifice on QB6 and gain a
material advantage); **11. P × P, B—K3** (Very original. Black
accepts isolated doubled Pawns in order to get control of the important squares Q4 and KB4. However, in the long run the weakness of
Black's KP will tell.); **12. B × B, P × B; 13. N—N3, Q—Q2;
14. 0—0, QR—Q1; 15. P—QR4, Q—Q6** (Smyslov believes it must
be more difficult for White to exploit the weakness of the King
Pawns without Queens on the board.); **16. Q × Q, R × Q; 17. P × P,
P × P; 18. R—R6, R—Q3; 19. K—R1** (to avoid the simplification
19. ... N—Q5), **19. ... N—Q2; 20. B—K3, R—Q1; 21. P—R3,
P—R3; 22. KR—R1, N(2)—N1; 23. R—R8, R—Q8ch; 24. K—R2,
R × R; 25. R × R, N—Q2** (Black should have played 25. ... P—N5
to increase his freedom of movement).

26. P—N4!
White prevents the advance of Black's QNP and gradually succeeds
in building up great pressure on the hostile position.

26. ...   K—B2   27. N—B1
This Knight must find a more active square.

27. ...	B—Q3	30. R—R6	N—QN1
28. P—N3	N—B3	31. R—R5	P—B3
29. N(1)—Q2	K—K2	32. K—N2	N(1)—Q2

One cannot see yet how White is going to win the ending, but
Fischer completes this masterpiece in a marvellous way.

33. K—B1   R—BQ1?

Fischer gives as Black's best continuation 33. ... N—K1; 34. N—N3, N—B2; 35. R—R7, R—QR1; 36. N—R5, N—N1; 37. R × R, N × R; 38. B—R7, K—Q2; 39. N—N7, and Black has chances to survive.

34. N—K1   N—K1   36. P—QB4   P × P
35. N—Q3   N—B2

Black is too late to exchange the Rooks, which would considerably increase his drawing chances, since 36. ... R—QR1? is refuted by 37. P—B5.

37. N × BP   N—N4

Now 37. ... R—QR1 would come too late: 38. R × R, N × R; 39. N—R5, N—N1; 40. B—R7, K—Q2; 41. N—B4, and White wins a Pawn.

38. R—R6   K—B3

It becomes clear what problems Black has in defending his King Pawns.

39. B—B1   B—N1   40. B—N2

What can be done against 41. P—B4?

40. ... P—B4

Despair.

41. N—N6!   N × N   42. R × N   P—B5

After 42. ... N—Q5, Fischer gives the following variation: 43. N × BP, B—R2; 44. N—Q7ch, K—N4; 45. P—R4ch, K—R4; 46. R—N7, R—B7; 47. R × B, R × B; 48. N × P, R × P; 49. R × P, etc.

43. N—B5   P—B6

The game was adjourned here, and Black resigned without resuming the game. The logical continuation would be: 44. B—B1, N—Q5; 45. N—Q7ch, K—K2; 46. N × B, N—N6; 47. R—N7ch, K—Q1; 48. R—Q7ch, K—K1; 49. R × P, etc.

Game 64   White: V. Smyslov   Interzonal Tournament, Palma de
　　　　　 Black: R. Fischer   Mallorca 1970
　　　　　　　　　　　　　　　　　　　　　　　　　　English Opening

1. P—QB4, P—KN3; 2. N—QB3, B—N2; 3. P—KN3, P—QB4; 4. B—N2, N—QB3; 5. P—N3, P—K3 (In a number of similar games Fischer has shown a preference for the development of his KN to K2.); **6. B—N2, KN—K2; 7. N—R4** (A radical move.

N

White eliminates Black's fianchettoed Bishop before completing his development.), **7. ... B × B; 8. N × B, 0—0; 9. P—K3** (White also wishes to develop his KN via K2. Better perhaps was 9. N—KB3 and 10. 0—0, or, in case Black plays 9. ... P—Q4, 10. P × P, P × P; 11. P—Q4), **9. ... P—Q4; 10. P × P, N × P; 11. N—K2, P—N3; 12. P—Q4?** (Leads to difficulties. Because of the text, White's QB3 square becomes weak and the diagonal KB1—QR6 is opened for Black. Moreover, White is behind in development. Castling Kingside was normal and satisfactory: 12. 0—0, B—R3; 13. P—Q3), **12. ... B—R3!; 13. P × P** (13. 0—0 would now cost a Pawn after 13. ... B × N and 14. ... P × P), **13. ... Q—B3!** (All Black's pieces are in action.); **14. N—B4** (After 14. Q—Q2, the answer 14. ... KR—Q1 would be very strong), **14. ... N—B6!.**

Black makes excellent use of the fact that White has not yet castled.

15. N × N
15. Q—B1, N × N; 16. K × N, QR—B1 seems no better for White, e.g. 17. P × P, N—R4, or 17. B × N, R × B; 18. P × P, P × P.

15. ...	**Q × Nch**		**18. P × B**	**Q—Q6ch**
16. K—B1	**KR—Q1**		**19. K—N1**	**QR—B1**
17. Q—B1	**B × Nch**		**20. P × P**	**P × P**

Black has ample compensation for the sacrificed Pawn.

21. Q—N2 N—R4   22. P—KR4
An interesting idea. White makes a virtue of necessity and tries to set up an attack via the KR file. However, this doesn't increase his drawing chances. True, after 22. B—B1, N × P Black would still have had possibilities, but with 22. Q × P, eliminating Black's last Queenside Pawn (22. ... N × P; 23. Q—N3), White would have made it extremely difficult for Black to play for a win.

22. ...   N × P   23. Q—B6
Consistent. Now 24. P—R5 is a real threat.

23. ...   Q—B4!
Excellent positional judgment. The ending is very favourable for Black: his Rooks are better placed, and Black's QNP becomes a real danger for White.

24. Q × Q   NP × Q   25. P—R5
With the double purpose of developing the KR via R4 and preparing P—R6, so tying at least one of the Black Rooks to the first rank.

25. ...   R—Q7   26. R—B1
Hoping to simplify the game by a concentrated attack against Black's Knight.

26. ...   R—B4!
Unpins the Knight. Not 26. ...   R × RP; 27. R—R4, P—N4; 28. B—B1, and the draw seems assured.

27. R—R4	**N—K4**	**30. P—R6**	**K—B1**
28. R × R	**P × R**	**31. R—R8ch**	**K—K2**
29. R—R4	**P—B5**	**32. R—QB8**	

White has no time to capture Black's RP by 32. R—KR8.

32. ...   R × RP
The first material success. White is lost.
There followed: **33. B—B1, R—B7; 34. K—N2, N—N5!; 35. K—N1, R × P; 36. B × P, R—B6; 37. K—N2, R × P; 38. R—KR8, N × P; 39. R × P, N—N5; 40. B—N5, R—N6; 41. B—B6, R—N7ch; 42. K—N1, N—K4; 43. B—R8, R—N1; 44. B—R1,** and White resigned after the adjournment.

4.   FISCHER AND TAL (−4, +2, =5)

Mikhail Tal is an enigma for the chess world.

In 1960, when he was only 24 years old, he beat Botvinnik very convincingly (+6, −2, =13), thus winning the World Championship. Everyone thought he would prove to be a super champion for years to come. However, he lost the revenge match against Botvinnik in 1961 in the same convincing way (+5, −10, =6).

Since then, his results have become poorly. Apparently his health was one of the great obstacles. In Curaçao 1962, when playing in the Candidate's Tournament, he had to enter hospital. After that, his career showed many ups and downs. Sometimes he obtained good results, although none that equalled his earlier successes, but from time to time he had very bad ones. Many of his failures can be explained by the serious handicap of ill health.

In comparing Robert Fischer with Mikhail Tal, the indirect comparison is very much in favour of Fischer, whose results and performances are undoubtedly superior. What about the direct comparison? Tal is in fact the only top ranking player who has a plus score against Fischer: should we therefore classify Tal among the highest ranking players in history, equal to Fischer, or, in view of their individual results, even above them?

The answer is no, because, just as when comparing Smyslov and Fischer, we must take into account the time when Tal and Fischer's games were played. All four of Fischer's losses occurred before 1960 and in one tournament, the Candidate's in 1959, when Fischer was 16 and Tal was at the top of his form, one year before his first match with Botvinnik. Fischer's wins were scored in Bled 1961, and in Curaçao 1962, when Tal's health was in bad shape. Since 1962, Fischer and Tal have not played a single game.

We must conclude that Tal does not belong among the top ranking players of chess history, although, during a short period of one or two years, he may have equalled Fischer's present strength.

On the other hand, when speaking of originality and genius instead of strength, Mikhail Tal must certainly be considered among the world's best, and he is only exceeded in this respect by Paul Morphy, the greatest chess star of all time.

We shall discuss four of the most interesting games between Tal and Fischer in chronological order.

Game 65	*White:* M. Tal	Candidate's Tournament,
	Black: R. Fischer	Bled-Zagreb-Belgrade 1959
		King's Indian Defence

1. P—Q4, N—KB3; 2. P—QB4, P—KN3; 3. N—QB3, B—N2; 4. P—K4, P—Q3; 5. B—K2, 0—0; 6. N—B3, P—K4; 7. P—Q5, QN—Q2; 8. B—N5, P—KR3; 9. B—R4, P—R3 (Before playing Q—K1, Black must prevent N—QN5.); **10. 0—0, Q—K1** (With this and the following moves, Black aims at eliminating White's QB.); **11. N—Q2, N—R2; 12. P—QN4, B—B3** (Funny is 12. ... P—KB4; 13. P×P, P×P?; 14. B—R5!); **13. B×B, N(2)×B** (Black has reached his goal, but it is doubtful whether this compensates for the lost tempi. White already has his Queenside action well under way.); **14. N—N3, Q—K2; 15. Q—Q2, K—R2; 16. Q—K3** (Now everything is ready for the advance P—B5.), **16. ... N—KN1; 17. P—B5, P—B4** (Both sides follow the required strategy: attack against the base of the hostile Pawn chain.); **18. KP×P, NP×P**

(If 18. ... R × P, then 19. B—Q3); **19. P—B4** (the logical continuation), **19. ... KP × P; 20. Q × P, P × P?** (It is not clear why Black doesn't choose the obvious continuation 20. ... N—K4, occupying the strong square and giving the QB a square for development. Perhaps he hoped to win a Pawn. However, it must be admitted that after 20. ... N—K4; 21. QR—K1 and 22. N—Q4, White's position is superior. With the text, Black goes down in a torrent of sacrifices.)

21. B—Q3!
Much stronger than 21. P × P, N × P; 22. QR—B1, which would probably lead to no more than the recapture of the sacrificed Pawn.

21. ...   P × P
Black could have offered more resistance by 21. ... Q—N2, after which White continues his attack with 22. B × Pch, K—R1; 23. N—K4.

22. QR—K1   Q—B3
Or 22. ... Q—Q3; 23. B × Pch, K—R1; 24. Q—Q4ch, Q—B3; 25. Q × P with advantage for White.

23. R—K6!
Perhaps Black was hoping for 23. B × Pch?, Q × B; 24. Q × Qch, R × Q; 25. R × R, P × N, and White has insufficient forces to carry on the attack.

23. ...   Q × N   24. B × Pch   R × B
Forced. After 24. ... K—N2 White wins: 25. R—N6ch, K—R1; 26. R × Pch, etc.

25. Q × Rch   K—R1
Or 25. ... K—N2; 26. R—N6ch, K—R1; 27. R—Nch!, etc.

26. R—B3!
A fine move. Black's Queen has only a few squares at its disposal—and not a single check!

26. ... Q—N7

26. ... Q—N2 would give White the extra tempo 27. R—N3 for his attack. After 27. ... Q—R2; 28. R—K8! wins (a charming Queen sacrifice).

27. R—K8

Threatens 28. R × Nch, K × R; 29. Q—B7ch, K—R1; 30. Q—K8ch and 31. R—B7ch.

27. ... QN—B3

The only move. Black returns the extra material and more.

28. Q × Nch   Q × Q
29. R × Q   K—N2
Black is completely tied up.

30. R(6)—B8   N—K2
31. N—R5

31. ...   P—KR4
32. P—KR4   R—N1

33. N—B4   P—N4
34. N—K5   Black resigns.

Game 66   White: R. Fischer   Candidate's Tournament,
            Black: M. Tal   Bled-Zagreb-Belgrade 1959
            Sicilian Defence, Fischer Variation

1. P—K4, P—QB4; 2. N—KB3, P—Q3; 3. P—Q4, P × P; 4. N × P, N—KB3; 5. N—QB3, P—QR3; 6. B—QB4 (favoured by Fischer), **6. ... P—K3; 7. B—N3, P—QN4; 8. P—B4, P—N5** (In a similar position in Game 61, Smyslov did not take the Pawn, but Tal is a real knight, without fear or reproach); **9. N—R4, N × P; 10. 0—0, P—N3?** (Directed against the advance of White's KBP, but it appears that the text merely provokes that advance. Correct would have been 10. ... B—N2.)

11. P—B5!   NP × P
If 11. ... KP × P, then 12. B—Q5, R—R2; 13. N × P, P × N; 14. Q—Q4!, attacking both Rooks.

12. N × BP   R—N1

After 12. ... P × N; 13. Q—Q5 (or 13. B—Q5), 13. ... R—R2;
14. Q—Q4 we have the same 'Rook fork'. However, 12. ... P—Q4
is better than the text.

13. B—Q5!

Again a wonderful move. After 13. ... P × B; 14. Q × P, White
recaptures the piece with a great advantage.

13. ...   R—R2   14. B × N

In his present form, Fischer would not have missed the chance of
pursuing the defeated enemy further, choosing the following variation, given by Kevitz: 14. B—K3, N—B4; 15. Q—R5, R—N3;
16. QR—K1.

14. ...   P × N   15. B × P   R—K2!

The only possibility of continuing the game.

16. B × B   Q × B   17. B—B4?

Fischer considers 17. P—B3 to be the only move to maintain the
advantage. Not good is 17. Q × P, R × Pch; 18. K × R, R—K7ch
and 19. ... B × Q.

17. ...   Q—B3

Threatens mate and attacks the White Knight.

18. Q—B3   Q × N

Once again, Tal dares everything.

19. B × P   Q—B3   21. K—R1   Q × B
20. B × N   Q—N3ch   22. Q—B6ch

Fischer demonstrates that 22. QR—K1 doesn't win, either, after
22. ... K—Q1!

22. ...   R—Q2   23. QR—K1ch   B—K2

23. ... K—Q1 fails against 24. R × P, B—K2; 25. R(7) × B, R × R;
26. R—Q1ch.

24. R × P   K × R   26. Q × R   Q—Q3
25. Q—K6ch   K—B1

The attack is beaten off. White has only drawing chances now.

The game continued: 27. Q—N7, R—N3; 28. P—B3, P—QR4;
29. Q—B8ch (With 29. P × P White could almost force a draw:
29. ... P × P; 30. P—QR3, or 29. ... Q × NP; 30. Q—B3ch,
K—N2; 31. Q—K2), 29. ... K—N2; 30. Q—B4, B—Q1; 31. P ×
P, P × P; 32. P—KN3? (preferable was 32. Q—K4), 32. ... Q—
B3ch; 33. R—K4, Q × Q; 34. R × Q, R—N3; 35. K—N2 (White's

only chance to draw is the elimination of Black's QNP. Of course,
35. P—QR3 right away is bad: 35. ... P—N6 and 36. ... B—K2
or 36. ... B—B3.), 35. ... K—B3; 36. K—B3, K—K4; 37. K—K3,
B—N4ch; 38. K—K2, K—Q4; 39. K—Q3, B—B3; 40. R—B2?
(Fischer recommends 40. P—N3 as the only possibility to save the
game.), 40. ... B—K4; 41. R—K2, R—KB3; 42. R—QB2, R—
B6ch; 43. K—K2, R—B2; 44. K—Q3, B—Q5; 45. P—QR3,
P—N6; 46. R—B8, B × P; 47. R—Q8ch, K—B3; 48. R—QN8,
R—B6ch; 49. K—B4, R—B6ch; 50. K—N4, B—R8; 51. P—QR4,
P—N7! White resigns.

An undeserved defeat for young Fischer.

Game 67 White: R. Fischer   Olympiad, Leipzig 1960
       Black: M. Tal   French Defence, Winawer Variation

**1. P—K4, P—K3; 2. P—Q4, P—Q4; 3. N—QB3, B—N5; 4. P—
K5, P—QB4; 5. P—QR3, B—R4; 6. P—QN4, P × QP** (or 6. ...
P × NP; 7. N—N5 threatening 8. N—Q6ch); **7. Q—N4, N—K2;
8. P × B** (perhaps 8. N—N5 is still better), **8. ... P × N; 9. Q × NP,
R—N1; 10. Q × P** (A rather wild start. Materially, both sides are
practically equal, since the White Pawn at QR5 doesn't count.
Positionally, White's game is preferable: his pieces have more possibilities, and his passed KRP may play a role.), **10. ... QN—B3;
11. N—B3, Q—B2** (11. ... Q × P is answered by 12. N—N5);
12. B—QN5, B—Q2 (After 12. ... R × P, Fischer gives 13. K—B1,
R—KN1; 14. R—KN1, R × Rch; 15. K × R, and Black's position
is hopeless.); **13. 0—0, 0—0—0; 14. B—N5?** (White should have
played 14. B × N to avoid the following spectacular combination.)

14. ...   N × KP!   15. N × N
After 15. B × Bch, R × B; 16. N × N, Q × N, Black's chances are
better on account of the threat 17. ... R—R1.

15. ...   B × B

The alternative, 15. ... Q × N; 16. B × N, R—R1; 17. KR—K1, probably leads to a draw.

16. N × P   B × R   18. N × KP
17. N × R   R × B

Practically forced for both sides.

18. ...   R × Pch!   19. K—R1!

The only move, because 19. K × B would lose after 19. ... R × RP!

19. ...   Q—K4

After 19. ... Q—B5; 20. Q × N, R—N1, White has the saving move 21. N—B4!, Q × N?; 22. Q—K6ch and 23. Q × R.

20. R × B   Q × N   21. K × R   Q—N5ch

Draw (perpetual check).

Game 68   *White:* R. Fischer   Tournament, Bled 1961
                 Black: M. Tal   Sicilian Defence,
                                            Taimanov Variation

1. P—K4, P—QB4; 2. N—KB3, N—QB3; 3. P—Q4, P × P; 4. N × P, P—K3; 5. N—QB3, Q—B2; 6. P—KN3, N—B3? (Black should have prevented 7. KN—N5 by 6. ... P—QR3); **7. KN—N5!. Q—N1** (or 7. ... Q—N3; 8. B—KB4, or 7. ... Q—R4; 8. B—Q2, Q—Q1; 9. B—KB4); **8. B—KB4!** (the importance of White's 6th move becomes clear), **8. ... N—K4** (Black has only a choice between two evils. After 8. ... P—K4; 9. B—N5, P—QR3; 10. B × N, White is better after both 10. ... P × B; 11. N—R3, P—N4; 12. N—Q5, and after 10. ... P × N; 11. B—N5.); **9. B—K2!, B—B4** (to prevent 10. Q—Q4); **10. B × N!, Q × B; 11. P—B4, Q—N1** (the only place for the Queen); **12. P—K5.**

12. ...   P—QR3

Forced. After 12. ... N—N1; 13. N—K4 Black would not break free again.

13. P × N   P × N   **15. N—K4   B—K2**
14. P × P   R—N1   **16. Q—Q4**

A terrible position for Black.

16. ...   R—R5

In Botvinnik's judgment, 16. ... Q—B2 would have been better.

17. N—B6ch   B × N   **19. 0—0—0   R × P**
18. Q × B   Q—B2   **20. K—N1   R—R3**

20. ... Q—R4 is refuted by 21. P—N3 and 22. B—R5.

21. B × P

The game is won anyway, but 21. B—R5, P—Q3; 22. KR—K1 would have been quicker.

21. ...   R—N3   **23. P × P!**
22. B—Q3   P—K4

A nice, although obvious, sacrifice of the Queen.

23. ...   R × Q   **26. B × R   Q × BP**
24. P × R   Q—B4   **27. KR—B1   Q × P**
25. B × P   Q—KN4   **28. B × Pch   K—Q1**

The rest holds no further interest. There followed: **29. B—K6, Q—R3; 30. B × P, B × B; 31. R—B7, Q × P; 32. QR × Bch, K—K1; 33. R(Q7)—K7ch, K—Q1; 34. R—Q7ch, K—B1; 35. R—B7ch, K—Q1; 36. R(KB7)—Q7ch, K—K1; 37. R—Q1, P—N4; 38. R—QN7, Q—R4; 39. P—KN4, Q—R6; 40. P—N5, Q—KB6; 41. R—K1ch, K—B1; 42. R × P, K—N2; 43. R—N6, Q—KN6; 44. R—Q1, Q—B2; 45. R(1)—Q6, Q—B1; 46. P—N3, K—R2; 47. R—QR6,** Black resigns.

5.   FISCHER AND PETROSIAN (+8, −9, =15)

Before 1960, the score was +0, −7, =3 in favour of Petrosian. Between 1960 and 1970 their record was +1, −1, =6. After 1970, Fischer outscored Petrosian with +7, −1, =6. These figures show that Fischer has gradually overtaken his rival. Petrosian has certainly declined in strength, but, bearing in mind that he was World Champion until 1969, the conclusion is that Fischer is a greater champion than Petrosian.

We have already discussed two games between Fischer and Petrosian (Game 7 and Game 33). We shall add three further only, among which is a superb win by Petrosian from their 1971 Candidate's Match.

First, a most remarkable game resulting in an ending with four Queens. In view of its length, we will only discuss the highlights.

Game 69   *White:* R. Fischer   Candidate's Tournament,
              Black: T. Petrosian   Bled-Zagreb-Belgrade 1959
                                      Caro-Kann Defence

1. P—K4, P—QB3; 2. N—QB3, P—Q4; 3. N—B3, B—N5; 4. P—KR3, B×N; 5. Q×B, N—B3; 6. P—Q3, P—K3; 7. P—KN3, B—N5; 8. B—Q2, P—Q5; 9. N—N1, B×Bch; 10. N×B, P—K4; 11. B—N2, P—B4; 12. O—O, N—B3; 13. Q—K2, Q—K2; 14. P—KB4, O—O—O; 15. P—R3, N—K1; 16. P—QN4, BP×P (more solid is 16. ... P—B3); **17. N—B4** (Fischer shows that 17. P×KP would have led to an advantage. One variation: 17. ... Q×P; 18. R×P, Q×P; 19. P—K5, Q—K6ch; 20. Q×Q, P×Q; 21. N—B4), **17. ... P—B3; 18. BP×P, BP×P; 19. P×P, N—B2; 20. N—R5, N—N4; 21. N×N, P×N; 22. R—B2, P—N3; 23. P—R4, K—N2; 24. P—R5, Q×P; 25. R—B7ch, K—N3; 26. Q—B2, P—R4; 27. P—B4, N—B6?** (Safer is 27. ... N—Q3); **28. R—KB1** (28. Q—B6 at once would have been much better), **28. ... P—R5; 29. Q—B6, Q—B4; 30. R×P** (30. Q—N7 would have forced a draw), **30. ... R(Q1)—KB1; 31. Q×NP, R×Rch; 32. B×R, R×R; 33. Q×R, P—R6; 34. P—R6, P—R7; 35. Q—N8, P—R8=Q; 36. P—R7.**

36. ... Q—Q3
Being short of time, Petrosian overlooked 36. ... N—K7ch; 37. K—N2, N×P!, after which White must take a draw: 38. Q—N8ch, K—R3; 39. Q—R8ch, Q—R2; 40. Q×Pch, etc.

37. P—R8 = Q   Q—R2   39. Q—KB8?
38. P—N4   K—B4
39. Q—R2 would have given White excellent winning chances.

39. ...   Q(2)—K2
White threatened 40. Q × Pch.

40. Q—R8   K—N5!   41. Q—KR2   K—N6!
It is peculiar to see how the Black King and Knight keep both
White Queens under control.

42. Q—QR1   Q—R6   44. Q—R6   Q—KB2
43. Q × Qch   K × Q   45. K—N2
If 45. Q × P, then 45. ... N—Q8.

45. ...   K—N6   46. Q—Q2
White must prevent 46. ... N—Q8.

46. ...   Q—KR2   48. Q—B2
47. K—N3?   Q × P!
48. P—N5 is better.

48. ...   Q—R8
Draw agreed. Black has some advantage in the final position.

Game 70   *White:* T. Petrosian   Second Match Game,
                   Black: R. Fischer   Buenos Aires 1971
                                                  Grunfeld Defence

**1. P—Q4, N—KB3; 2. P—QB4, P—KN3; 3. N—QB3, P—Q4;
4. B—B4, B—N2; 5. P—K3, P—B4** (The introduction to a gambit
continuation which gives chances to both sides.); **6. P × BP, Q—R4;
7. R—B1, N—K5; 8. P × P, N × N; 9. Q—Q2!** (By this fine move,
White can hold his own and gain some advantage.), **9. ... Q × RP;
10. P × N, Q—R4** (Black wins the Pawn back, but White has a
powerful majority in the centre.); **11. B—B4, N—Q2** (Black is in
no hurry to recapture the Pawn.); **12. N—K2, N—K4; 13. B—R2,
B—B4?** (This looks fine, because of the threat 14. ... N—Q6ch,
but it is probably the decisive mistake. Correct would have been
13. ... Q × P(4).); **14. B × N, B × B; 15. N—Q4!** (Black must
submit to the doubling of his KBP, unless he is willing to sacrifice
a Pawn.), **15. ... Q × P(4)** (15. ... B—Q2; 16. R—QN1, Q—B2;
17. P—B6! is favourable for White: 17. ... P × P; 18. P × P,
B × P?; 19. N × B, Q × N; 20. B—Q5, etc.) ;**16. N × B, P × N;
17. 0—0, Q—R4** (17. ... 0—0 would have been favourable for

White too: 18. Q—Q3, P—B5; 19. Q—B5, Q—Q3?; 20. B—N1);
18. Q—B2, P—B5; 19. P—B4!.

In combination with White's next move, a wonderful conception.

19. ...   P × P   20. P—B5!
White has complete confidence in the attack which will result from
the advancing Pawns, and is not over worried about the material
Black will gain in the next few moves.

20. ...   Q—Q7   22. QR—Q1 Q—K7
21. Q—R4ch   K—B1
Interesting would have been 22. ... P—K7; 23. R × Q, B × Pch;
24. K × B, P × R = Q; 25. P—Q6!, and White must win. One
variation: 25. ... R—KN1; 26. P × Pch, K—N2; 27. Q—Q4ch,
P—B3; 28. Q—N4ch, K—R1; 29. B × R, R × B; 30. R—Q8, etc.

23. P—Q6!
Forward again!

23. ...   Q—R4
23. ... B × Pch; 24. K × B, Q—R4ch; 25. K—N1, P—K7, would
have been still more complicated. White would then have won as
follows: 26. P × Pch, K—N2, (26. ... K × P; 27. KR—K1);
27. Q—Q4ch, P—B3; 28. R—Q3, P × R = Qch; 29. K × Q, Q—R8ch;
30. K—K2, Q—R4ch; 31. K—Q2, Q—R3ch; 32. K—Q1, Q—R4ch
(If 32. ... KR—K1, then 33. R—KR3, and if 32. ... Q—R8ch,
then 33. K—B2.); **33. R—B3!!** If Black now defends his KBP, he
loses his Queen (33. ... Q—N4; 34. R—N3, or 33. ... Q—R3;
34. R—N3ch).

24. P—B4   P—K7   26. R × Q
25. P × B   P × R = Q

It is remarkable that Black, although he is able to make White's advanced Pawn harmless, cannot stop the attack launched along the KB file.

26. ...   Q × KP
26. ... P × P is also answered by 27. R—KB1.

27. R—KB1   P—B3
If 27. ... P—K3, then 28. Q—Q7. 27. ... Q × BPch; 28. K—R1, P—B3 is met by 29. Q—N3, K—N2; 30. Q—B7ch, K—R3; 31. P × P. Finally, if 27. ... P—B4, then 28. Q—N3, P—K3; 29. Q × NP, Q × BPch; 30. K—R1, R—K1; 31. P—N4!, with the deadly threat 32. R × Pch.

28. Q—N3   K—N2   30. P × P   P—B4
29. Q—B7ch K—R3
30. ... K—N4 is refuted by 31. Q—N7ch.

31. R × P   Q—Q5ch   32. K—R1
Black resigns. A magnificent game!

Game 71   *White:* T. Petrosian   Sixth Match Game,
                   Black: R. Fischer   Buenos Aires 1971
                                                 Irregular Opening

1. N—KB3, P—QB4; 2. P—QN3, P—Q4; 3. B—N2, P—B3; 4. P—B4, P—Q5; 5. P—Q3, P—K4; 6. P—K3, N—K2; 7. B—K2, KN—B3; 8. QN—Q2, B—K2; 9. O—O, O—O (White has chosen a passive set-up, perhaps hoping that his opponent would overrate his own position and start an unfounded action.); **10. P—K4, P—QR3; 11. N—K1, P—QN4; 12. B—N4, B × B; 13. Q × B, Q—B1; 14. Q—K2, N—Q2; 15. N—B2, R—N1; 16. KR—B1, Q—K1; 17. B—R3, B—Q3; 18. N—K1, P—N3; 19. P × P?** (So far, White's moves were neither good nor bad, but the text is certainly a mistake,

since it soon gives Black the opportunity for a breakthrough on
QB5, which makes his QP a passed Pawn), 19. ... P×P; 20. B—
N2, N—N3; 21. N(1)—B3; R—R1; 22. P—QR3, Q—B2; 23. Q—
Q1, N—R4; 24. P—QR4 (This would be fine if Black's P—B5
could be prevented, but, on the contrary, this breakthrough is as it
were directly provoked.), 24. ... P×P; 25. P×P, P—B5!; 26. P×
P, N(3)×BP; 27. N×N, N×N; 28, Q—K2, N×B; 29. Q×N,
KR—N1; 30. Q—R2, B—N5; 31. Q×Qch, K×Q; 32. R—B7ch,
K—K3!

One of the points of this ending is that a White Rook cannot go
off plundering on the hostile Kingside, because Black's passed
Pawn will then become irresistible. For example, 33. R×P, B—B6;
34. R—B1, R×P, and after 35. ... R—R8; 36. R×R, B×R the
Black King will penetrate and support the victoriously advancing
Pawn.

33. P—N4	B—B6		36. P—R5	R—QR1
34. R—R2	R—QB1		37. P—R6	R—R2
35. R×R	R×R		38. K—B1	P—N4

Black cannot permit White to break up the Kingside by P—N5.

39. K—K2	K—Q3		41. N—N1	K—N4
40. K—Q3	K—B4		42. N—K2	

Note that the capture of White's RP, while permitting the exchange
of Rooks, would be of no use to Black: the Knight v. Bishop ending
is a draw, despite Black's plus Pawn on Q5.

42. ...	B—R4	43. R—N2ch

43. N—B1, R×P; 44. N—N3 would have made the win a little
more difficult, but not impossible: 44. ... R—R1; 45. R—R1,
R—R2; 46. R—R2, K—N5; 47. N—R1, R—QB2; 48. N—B2ch,
K—N6; 49. R×B, R—B6ch, etc.

43. ...	K×P	48. R—R2ch	K—N4
44. R—N1	R—QB2	49. R—N2ch	B—N5
45. R—N2	B—K8	50. R—R2	R—QB2
46. P—B3	K—R4	51. R—R1	R—QB1
47. R—B2	R—N2	52. R—R7?	

Makes things easier for Black. White should have waited until Black adopted the right plan, which is: (1) blocking the QB file with the King and Bishop, and (2) penetrating into the hostile position via the QR or QN files.

52. ...　B—R4

Prevents the retreat of the Rook.

53. R—Q7

If 53. R×P, then 53. ... B—N3 followed by 54. ... R—QR1 and 55. ... R—R6ch.

53. ...	B—N3	55. N—B1	K—R5
54. R—Q5ch	B—B4		

To prevent 56. N—N3.

56. R—Q7	B—N5	58. R—QN7	R—QR1
57. N—K2	K—N6	59. R×P	

Or 59. N—B1ch, K—N7; 60. N—K2, R—R6ch; 61. K—B4, P—Q6!; 62. R×Bch, K—B7, etc.

59. ...	R—R8	60. N×Pch	

In despair, but 60. N—N3 was just as useless: 60. ... R—R7; 61. N—B1, R—KB7, etc.

60. ...	P×N	61. K×P	R—Q8ch

Black won after: 62. K—K3, B—B4ch; 63. K—K2, R—KR8; 64. P—R4, K—B5; 65. P—R5, R—R7ch; 66. K—K1, K—Q6. White resigns.

This game shows that Fischer, just like his predecessors, has inexhaustible patience. We have mentioned this more than once. We hope the reader has shown the same patience when playing it over!

6. FISCHER AND SPASSKY (+7, −5, =13)

From 1960 until 1970, Spassky dominated (+3, −0, =2), but in their title match Fischer undoubtedly was the stronger player, winning by a score (not counting the Game which Spassky won by forfeit) of +7, −2, =11. We would conclude that Fischer out-stripped his rival around 1970.

Spassky was certainly the best player in the world for a time, but his reign was too short for him to be counted among the great players of chess history.

We have already discussed the 10th game of the Spassky–Fischer match on pp. 93–8 and parts of the 7th, 13th and 14th games on pp. 53–4 also. We add, in chronological order, two fine tournament wins by Spassky, and one convincing victory by Fischer in the match (6th game).

Game 72   *White:* B. Spassky   Tournament, Mar del Plata 1960
             Black: R. Fischer   King's Gambit

1. P—K4, P—K4; 2. P—KB4, P × P; 3. N—KB3, P—KN4 (Fischer later indicated 3. ... P—Q3 as the best move, in order to answer 4. P—Q4 with 4. ... P—KN4. The insertion of 3. ... P—Q3; 4. P—Q4 decreases the force of White's break through by P—KR4.); **4. P—KR4, P—N5; 5. N—K5, N—KB3; 6. P—Q4, P—Q3; 7. N—Q3, N × P; 8. B × P, B—N2** (After a wild start, the game moves into positional channels.); **9. N—B3** (Fischer condemns this move and recommends 9. P—B3), **9. ... N × N; 10. P × N, P—QB4; 11. B—K2, P × P; 12. 0—0** (both players continue the game in gambit 'style), **12. ... N—B3** (Black prefers to complete his development rather than protect his KNP by 12. ... P—KR4); **13. B × NP, 0—0; 14. B × B, R × B; 15. Q—N4, P—B4** (preferable is 15. ... K—R1); **16. Q—N3, P × P; 17. QR—K1** (17. B × P would give Black two tempi: 17. ... R—B3 and 18. ... R—N3), **17. ... K—R1; 18. K—R1, R—KN1; 19. B × P, B—B1!; 20. B—K5ch, N × B; 21. Q × Nch, R—N2; 22. R × P, Q × Pch** (Black still has his plus Pawn, and a good position); **23. K—N1, Q—N5?**

Black underrates White's attacking possibilities. He should have played for simplification by 23. ... Q—N6.

o

24. R—B2 B—K2   **26. Q—Q4! R—B1?**
25. R—K4 Q—N4

Black overlooks White's threat: 27. R—K5 winning a piece, because the Black Queen is forced to give up the protection of the Bishop. Correct would have been 26. ... B—B1. Black need not fear 27. N—K5, since he always has the parry 27. ... B—B4 at hand.

27. R—K5! R—Q1

Nothing helps: if 27. ... Q—R3, then 28. R × B, or 27. ... Q—R5; 28. Q × Q, etc.

28. Q—K4 Q—R5   **29. R—B4** Black resigns.

Just one moment of thoughtlessness! . . .

Game 73   *White:* B. Spassky   Olympiad, Siegen 1970
                   Black: R. Fischer   Grünfeld Defence

1. P—Q4, N—KB3; 2. P—QB4, P—KN3; 3. N—QB3, P—Q4; 4. P × P, N × P; 5. P—K4, N × N; 6. P × N, B—N2; 7. B—QB4, P—QB4; 8. N—K2, N—B3; 9. B—K3, 0—0 (the main line of this variation); **10. 0—0, Q—B2** (Theory continues by 10. ... P × P; 11. P × P, B—N5; 12. P—B3, N—R4; 13. B—Q3, B—K3; 14. P—Q5!? The outcome of this sacrifice of the exchange is uncertain.); **11. R—B1, R—Q1; 12. P—KR3, P—N3; 13. P—B4** (very enterprising), **13. ... P—K3; 14. Q—K1, N—R4; 15. B—Q3, P—B4** (Stops the attack, but only for a short time.); **16. P—N4!** (After 16. P—K5, P—B5 and 17. ... B—N2, Black's position is superior.), **16. ... P × KP; 17. B × P, B—N2; 18. N—N3, N—B5; 19. B × B, Q × B; 20. B—B2, Q—B3; 21. Q—K2** (an indirect protection for the QP), **21. ... P × P; 22. P × P, P—QN4** (now White's QP is 'en prise').

23. N—K4!
Spassky doesn't wish to restrict himself to defensive moves, such as
either Rook to Q1.

23. ...   B × P   24. N—N5   B × Bch
With 24. ... B—N3, Black could probably have drawn: 25. Q ×
Pch, Q × Q, etc.

25. R × B   R—Q3
25. ... R—K1 (Spassky) would have been a little better.

26. R—K1   Q—N3   27. N—K4!
A strong move, giving White a powerful initiative.

27. ...   R—Q5   28. N—B6ch   K—R1?
Preferable is 28. ... K—N2; 29. Q × P, Q × Q; 30. R × Q, which
might still lead to a draw.

29. Q × P
An exchange of Queens now would lead to a favourable ending for
White, who would already threaten R—K7 and mate. The point of
this move is that now the seemingly strong 29. ... R—Q8 fails
against 30. Q—B7, R × Rch; 31. K—N2, N—K6ch; 32. K—B3,
Q—B3ch; 33. K—N3, R—N8ch; 34. K—R4, R × Pch; 35. P × R,
Q—R8ch; 36. K—N5, R—QB1 (what else?); 37. Q—Q7, R—QN1
(37. ... R—B4ch; 38. P—B5); 38. Q—Q4, etc.

29. ...   R—Q3   30. Q—K4   R—KB1
30. ... R(1)—Q1 would have saved an important tempo.

31. P—N5   R—Q7   32. R(1)—KB1   Q—B2?
This definitely loses. But, after other moves White would still
maintain an advantage, e.g. 32. ... R × R; 33. R × R, Q—K6;
34. Q × Q, N × Q; 35. R—Q2, with a decisive preponderance.

33. R × R   N × R   34. Q—Q4
Threatens 35. N—K8 dis. ch.

34. ...   R—Q1   36. R—B2
35. N—Q5 dis. ch   K—N1
36. Q × N, Q—B4ch leads to nowhere for White.

36. ...   N—B5   37. R—K2
All White's pieces take part in the final attack. White threatens
38. R—K7.

37. ...   R—Q2   39. R—B8ch!
38. R—K8ch   K—B2
Black resigns (39. ... K × R; 40. Q—R8ch, K—B2; 41. N × Q, etc.).

Game 74 White: R. Fischer   Sixth Match Game, Reykjavik 1972
        Black: B. Spassky   Queen's Gambit, Tartakover
                                              Variation

**1. P—QB4, P—K3; 2. N—KB3, P—Q4; 3. P—Q4, N—KB3;
4. N—B3, B—K2; 5. B—N5** (With transposition of moves, we have
reached a position in the Orthodox Queen's Gambit.), **5. ... 0—0;
6. P—K3, P—KR3; 7. B—R4, P—QN3** (the Tartakover Variation);
**8. P×P N×P; 9. B×B, Q×B; 10. N×N, P×N; 11. R—B1,
B—K3** (Since the diagonal KR8—QR1 has been closed as a
consequence of the preceding exchange, there is no point in developing the Black QB on N2. Further, it should be noted that 11. ...
Q—N5ch; 12. Q—Q2, Q×Qch; 13. K×Q would lead to a favourable endgame for White.); **12. Q—R4, P—QB4; 13. Q—R3** (The
standard manœuvre in this variation: White pins and attacks
Black's QBP), **13. ... R—B1** (After 13. ... N—Q2, White would
play 14. B—N5, thus renewing the threat against Black's QBP);
14. B—N5, P—R3; 15. P×P, P×P (Fine recommends the Pawn
sacrifice 15. ... P—Q5; 16. N×P, B—Q4, protecting the QR and
thus attacking the Bishop. Black gets the initiative at the cost of a
Pawn.); **16. 0—0, R—R2** (Now Black threatens 17. ... P×B, but
both 16. ... Q—R2 and 16. ... Q—N2 would have been better);
17. B—K2, N—Q2; 18. N—Q4, Q—B1? (This move has been
severely criticized, and the general opinion is that 18. ... N—B3
would have been preferable. After 19. N—N3, Black then has the
choice between the retreat 19. ... N—Q2 and the advance 19. ...
P—B5. True, after 19. ... P—B5; 20. Q×Q, R×Q; 21. N—Q4
White's Knight is posted on a strong square, but, on the other hand,
Black can get considerable chances along the QN file.); **19. N×B!**
(in combination with White's next move, very strong), **19. ...
P×N; 20. P—K4!**

The most efficient way to attack the block of Black's centre
Pawns.

20. ... P—Q5?

Black had a difficult choice between moves which were all more or less favourable for White, but the text is certainly not the best choice. This can easily be seen from the continuation of the battle, which shows that after the text Black can no longer save the game. Instead of the text, three moves were to be considered: 20. ... P—B5; 20. ... N—B3 and 20. ... P × P. The last is preferred by Fine.

21. P—B4

White, who has a 4–3 majority on the Kingside, plays for a Kingside attack by advancing his Pawns on that wing.

21. ... Q—K2   22. P—K5

White prevents 22. ... P—K4, which would have decreased his attacking chances.

22. ... R—N1

Black hopes to get some counterchances along the QN file, but there is not much to be gained.

23. B—B4   K—R1   24. Q—R3   N—B1

24. ... R × P; 25. B × KP would certainly not be a good exchange for Black.

25. P—QN3   P—QR4

Still pursuing an idle goal. White's attack is developing much faster.

26. P—B5   P × P   27. R × P   N—R2

Black prevents 28. R—B7, which would be answered by 28. ... N—N4.

28. QR—B1   Q—Q1   30. P—KR4
29. Q—N3   R—K2

Now the sally of the Black Knight to N4 is prevented, and White can prepare the final attack with great ease.

There followed: 30. ... R(1)—N2; 31. P—K6 (Frees the KB6 square, but White can do this because an eventual N—B3 can be met by R × N!), 31. ... R(N2)—B2; 32. Q—K5, Q—K1; 33. P—R4, Q—Q1; 34. R(1)—B2, Q—K1; 35. R(2)—B3 (cat and mouse!), 35. ... Q—Q1; 36. B—Q3, Q—K1; 37. Q—K4! (Threatens mate in three: 38. R—B8ch, etc.), 37. ... N—B3; 38. R × N, P × R; 39. R × P, K—N1; 40. B—B4 (immobilizes Black's R at K2), 40. ... K—R1; 41. Q—B4, Black resigns.

CONCLUSION OR EPILOGUE

As expected, my research has not led to a clear answer to the question: 'Who is the greatest player of all time?'

In a way, this book could be considered as a collection of remarkable games by Lasker, Capablanca, Alekhine, and Fischer. In my opinion, these four world champions, together with Botvinnik, have played the greatest part in building the temple of Caïssa. As stated in the Introduction, because no comparison could be possible, I have left out of consideration the stimulating and brilliant performances of Paul Morphy and the pioneering theoretical work of Steinitz.

The five grandmasters mentioned are outstanding in all domains, but each of them has a special field of excellence: Capablanca—the endgame; Alekhine—the combination; Lasker—creativity; Botvinnik—the X-ray calculation; Fischer—the positional concept.

I have not done justice to Botvinnik's style in this work and I have explained why in the Introduction. There is only one of Botvinnik's games in this book, but a number of works, both in English and in other languages, are devoted to his performances.

It is impossible for me to favour one of the five great champions. This would mean placing a higher value on certain types of play than on others, and in my opinion all areas are equally important.